THE OPINIONS OF WILLIAM COBBETT

The Opinions of William Cobbett

Edited by

JAMES GRANDE,

JOHN STEVENSON

AND

RICHARD THOMAS

ASHGATE

Published by
Ashgate Publishing Limited
Wey Court East
Union Road
Farnham
Surrey, GU9 7PT
England

Ashgate Publishing Company
110 Cherry Street
Suite 3-1
Burlington, VT 05401-3818
USA

www.ashgate.com

British Library Cataloguing in Publication Data
A catalogue record for this book is available from the British Library

The Library of Congress has cataloged the printed edition as follows:
Cobbett, William, 1763–1835.
  [Works. Selections]
  The opinions of William Cobbett / edited by Richard Thomas, John Stevenson and James Grande.
     pages cm
  Includes bibliographical references and index.
  ISBN 978-1-4094-6432-7 (pbk) – ISBN 978-1-4094-6433-4 (ebook) –
  ISBN 978-1-4094-6434-1 (epub) 1. Cobbett, William, 1763-1835. 2. Great Britain – Politics and government – 1789-1820. 3. Politicians – Great Britain – Biography. 4. Journalists – Great Britain – Biography. I. Thomas, Richard H. II. Title.

  DA522.C5.A25 2013
  941.07'3092 – dc23
  [B]
                                                                    2013021100

ISBN 9781409464327 (pbk)
ISBN 9781409464334 (ebk – PDF)
ISBN 9781409464341 (ebk – ePUB)

Printed in the United Kingdom by Henry Ling Limited, at the Dorset Press, Dorchester, DT1 1HD

Contents

Foreword

'These are the things that people do not know,' Hilaire Belloc wrote in a poem. 'They do not know because they are not told.' Cobbett, the supreme journalist, believed that he had a duty to tell people – especially those who the politicians referred to as the 'lower orders' – all the things – especially the bad things they did not know.

Cobbett himself would have been regarded by many of his contemporaries as one of the lower orders. The son of a Surrey farmer, even after his death and after he had achieved so much and had so great an influence on events, his obituarists wrote condescendingly of him as a man who had come from nowhere and had made a name for himself without the benefit of a university education, or anything in the way of an education for that matter.

Yet it was Cobbett's great strength as a journalist that he was a self-taught man. Almost everything he said and wrote was the result of his personal experience. Whether he was telling people about corruption in parliament or instructing them in the right way to grow sweetcorn (something of an obsession) he had seen it all for himself, he had planted it with his own hands. He was not, like so many of the journalists he so despised, simply copying it all from a book.

'Never write about any matter that you do not well understand,' he advised his readers. He was convinced that he was capable of understanding things just as well as any politician educated at Eton and Oxford and as a result wrote endlessly, all his life, to explain to his readers what was being done in their name.

That may make him sound a bit of an old bore but it was Cobbett's genius always to be not only readable but amusing. There were others in his day calling for political reform but none of them had the wit and satirical spirit of Cobbett. This ensured him his huge readership even amongst those who could not read but who had Cobbett's *Political Register* read to them at special meetings in public houses.

It is fitting that 250 years after his birth a new collection of his writing should be published to remind readers of his extraordinary range and the continuing relevance of so much he has to say about history, politics, farming and the countryside.

Richard Ingrams

Preface and Acknowledgements

This book was produced as part of the commemoration of the 250th anniversary of William Cobbett's birth in 2013. It owes its origins to the initiative of the committee of the William Cobbett Society but sincere thanks are due to the support of Ashgate Publishing for allowing the project to be realised. We owe special thanks to Richard Ingrams for his generous offer to provide us with a Foreword.

This is not the first anthology of William Cobbett's writings, indeed Cobbett's works were being anthologised almost while he was still warm in the grave. Selections from *Porcupine's Works* and the *Political Register* were published in weekly parts by two of Cobbett's sons, John Morgan and James Paul, between 1835 and 1837, and published in six volumes by his daughter Anne in 1837. Almost a century later, in 1925, A.D.M. Hughes published a short selection of Cobbett's writings with some abridged assessments of him by other writers. Further selections were produced by G.D.H. and M.I. Cole in 1944, under wartime restrictions, and subsequently by John Derry. But it is now almost half a century since the last anthology of Cobbett's works and this commemoration appears in a different context from its predecessors. A less exclusive focus on British history in schools and universities means that many of the issues of the period in which Cobbett wrote are less familiar than they once were and no longer part of the common stock of knowledge. Cobbett was at one time a staple of the adult education and university extension classes in British economic and social history that the likes of G.D.H. Cole, his first serious biographer, and E.P. Thompson, the most widely-read writer on British popular history in the last 50 years, knew at first hand. However, in the intervening years, the visibility of Cobbett and the issues with which he wrestled has undoubtedly faded. This collection is an attempt to correct this tendency and in doing so the editors have provided a substantial general introduction, reflecting both traditional and recent scholarship on Cobbett and his times, as well as introductions and context to the extracts from Cobbett's writings. The extracts have been grouped to reflect some of the major themes which Cobbett addressed both as commentator and activist. To an extent they choose themselves, but Cobbett is represented here not solely as a campaigner for parliamentary reform, scourge of financiers and defender of the rural poor, but also as a transatlantic radical and part of a cultural and literary environment which has attracted an enormous amount of interest in its own right in recent years.

One aim of this volume is to bring Cobbett's unique blend of opinion and prejudice to audiences old and new. To do so we have drawn from the full range of his voluminous printed works and journalism and also from some of his less well known and extensive private correspondence, much of it still unpublished. Another is to encourage readers to return to Cobbett's own works for themselves. In the main we have referred these extracts back to the original source, but in the case where Cobbett's writings have modern and more accessible editions we have made reference to them. Where there have been several editions of his works, we have cited the most recent. We are grateful to the British Library for permission to quote from manuscripts in their possession and the Warden and Fellows of Nuffield College for permission to quote from the Cobbett papers held in the Cole Collection.

A final word of thanks must be made to Tom Gray of Ashgate for his consideration and assistance and a special one to Sandra Byford for her most efficient assistance in producing the manuscript.

J.G.   J.S.   R.T.

Introduction

William Cobbett was one of the most influential and singular English writers of the past three centuries. His talents as a journalist, political agitator, and commentator on the changing face of the country have earned him a place which remains unique both in the range of his subjects and the breadth of his admirers. Fresh from a career in the army where he had largely educated himself, he cut his journalistic teeth as the hammer of the radicals, the early supporters of the French Revolution, pursuing them with almost unrivalled venom and ferocity. Before long, however, his vehement prose found its targets in government corruption and its conduct of the Napoleonic Wars. For a period at least, his most potent vehicle, the *Political Register*, was read by high and low alike, his opinions reaching the village tavern, the cabins of men o'war and the drawing rooms of politicians. Such influence created powerful enemies drawing upon Cobbett's head prosecution, imprisonment and temporary exile as well as direct attacks in print and caricature. Nonetheless, Cobbett the 'Great Agitator' was credited by contemporaries with turning distressed labourers from riot and machine-breaking to the petitions and meetings which helped to bring about the Great Reform Act of 1832. But reform politics was only part of his remit. He inveighed against the poverty and degradation he believed had developed amongst the common labourers since the time of his youth and the taxes and corruption which he believed produced them; he defended the poor against grasping parsons, beguiling Methodists and 'Scotch feelosophers', while offering them advice on bettering their own lives through self-help and careful 'cottage economy'. His views and opinions ranged as widely as his readers, on everything from growing melons to choosing a wife, expressed with a vigour and style all his own. Undoubtedly Cobbett was a great bundle of opinions and prejudices, inevitably often contradicting himself, but always retaining the unmistakable stamp of the man. As his first serious biographer G.D.H. Cole remarked: 'Cobbett the Anti-Jacobin and Cobbett the Radical Reformer were definitely the same person. The opinions change, the attitudes remain at bottom the same.'[1]

Cobbett was also indefatigable. For over 30 years he produced his *Political Register* week in week out, whether in prison, in exile or at home. It has been estimated that during his long journalistic and literary career he published around 20 million words, contributing several thousand each week to the *Register* as well as producing a stream of pamphlets, essays and books on a very wide range of topics. An advertisement for his works near the end of his life, in

---

[1]   G.D.H. Cole (ed.), *Life and Adventures of Peter Porcupine* (London, 1927), p. 2.

1831, itemises 15 titles in print under four sub-heads: first, books for teaching languages, including Cobbett's English and French Grammars; second, books on 'Domestic Management and Duties', such as *Cobbett's Cottage Economy* and *Advice to Young Men*; third, books on 'Rural Affairs', which included *Cobbett's English Gardener* and *Cobbett's Woodlands;* and lastly, his works on the 'Management of National Affairs', *Paper Against Gold*, the *Rural Rides* and the *Poor Man's Friend.*[2] Even this fairly formidable list of works in print excluded a mass of earlier projects, set down or sold to others to meet debts and obligations, including Cobbett's *Parliamentary Register*, now known as *Hansard*, and his separate *Parliamentary History*. It excluded the voluminous writings of his first incarnation as Peter Porcupine in the United States in the 1790s and the work Cobbett himself regarded as his most successful publication after *Rural Rides*, his *History of the Protestant "Reformation" in England and Ireland*, first published in letter form in 1824–7. Undoubtedly vastly popular in its day, Cobbett claimed that *only* sales of the Bible outstripped those of his *History of the Protestant "Reformation"*. Although we may see Cobbett being tempted to hyperbole, one of his biographers, the late George Spater, puts the sales figures for this work within two years of publication at 700,000 copies. It is hardly surprising, therefore, that in Robert Altick's list of nineteenth-century 'best-sellers', Cobbett appears no less than five times.[3]

Moreover, besides his astonishingly wide and successful printed output, Cobbett maintained a voluminous correspondence with members of his family, his various literary assistants, and with political allies, friends and acquaintances, on both sides of the Atlantic and further afield. Only a fraction of Cobbett's correspondence has been published, yet much of it has the spontaneity, directness, verve and, it must be said, occasional brutality of his printed work. For example, his letters while imprisoned in Newgate in 1810 represent a fascinating and entirely characteristic cross-section of Cobbett's concerns – many of them intensely practical, concerning such matters as the settling of his troublesome financial affairs in the wake of his fine and imprisonment, the management in his absence of the affairs of his farm and property, including detailed instructions to his young son, William, about managing the farm, the obtaining of a steward, the regulation of his labourers and setting their tasks, the organisation of relays of the Cobbett household to come and live with him in Newgate to assist him in his literary work, as well as correspondence with his brother-in-law in Spain to obtain some Merino sheep.[4] Cobbett's letters, scattered across more than a score

---

[2]   Endpiece to *Cobbett's Two-Penny Trash or Politics for the Poor* (London, 1831), pp. 262–3.

[3]   See F.G.A.M. Aaarts, 'William Cobbett: Radical, Reactionary, and Poor Man's Grammarian'. Neophilolopus, LXX (1986), p. 606.

[4]   Nuffield College Library, Cole Collection, Cobbett Papers, Vol. XXIX, Letters 1806–12. See also J. Grande, 'William Cobbett's Correspondence, 1800–35', unpublished D.Phil. thesis (Oxford, 2011).

of libraries and depositories in both England and the United States, as well as even further afield, offer to add yet more hundreds of thousands of words to the Cobbett canon.

But to his contemporaries, however, and perhaps even now, Cobbett was seen above all as the greatest and potentially most effective political journalist of his day. Indeed, as Samuel Bamford suggested, Cobbett's most influential period came after the long wars with Revolutionary France when in 1816 and 1817 his cheap version of the *Political Register* was achieving a circulation of between 40,000 and 70,000 copies a week. At this time it was alleged that Cobbett was read by everyone, from government ministers to handloom weavers. Hazlitt was to sum up his influence most pithily when he called Cobbett a virtual 'Fourth Estate' in the politics of the country.[5] Leigh Hunt eulogised Cobbett's role in the creation of the popular press:

> The invention of printing itself scarcely did more for the diffusion of knowledge and the enlightening of the mind than has been effected by the Cheap Press of this Country. Thanks to Cobbett! The commencement of this twopenny register was an era in the annals of knowledge and politics which deserves eternal commemoration.[6]

Cobbett was thus portrayed as one of the great engines of improvement, a diffuser of useful knowledge, and a genuine friend to the poor by advising them to seek their remedies through education, the acquisition of political rights and the pursuit of reform. Put simply, Cobbett's message in the post-war years was to try to persuade the poor and distressed that it was through parliamentary reform that they could better their lot, that the real cause of their sufferings was corruption of government and elections, that their poverty and hardships stemmed from waste and misgovernment, amplified by Pitt's funding of the Napoleonic Wars. Throughout his political career he was to cling to what might be called the 'Country' platform, that the country required reform, not revolution, expressed in his remark:

> I know of no enemy to reform and of the happiness of the country, so great as that man who would persuade you that we possess *nothing good* and that all must be torn to pieces [...] We want great alteration, modification to suit the times and circumstances; but the great principles ought to be, and must be, the same, or else confusion will follow.[7]

[5] William Hazlitt, 'Character of Cobbett' in *The Complete Works of William Hazlitt*, ed. P.P Howe (21 vols, London, 1931), VIII, p. 50.

[6] Leigh Hunt, *White Hat*, 13 November 1819, quoted in W.H. Wickwar, *The Struggle for the Freedom of the Press, 1819–1832* (London, 1928), pp. 52–3.

[7] *Political Register*, 11 February 1816.

Cobbett's other great influence has been upon the historiography of the industrial revolution and as a commentator upon the changes being wrought in the pivotal years through which he lived, almost from the accession of George III to the accession of Queen Victoria, the classic period of the first industrial revolution as described by the Hammonds, Ashton and G.D.H. Cole. It was Cole who referred to Cobbett as the spokesman of the first generation of industrial workers 'torn from the land and flung into the factory'.[8] Right up to our own day, Cobbett's most famous work, his *Rural Rides*, has been seen as one of the classic contributions to the debate on the transformation of Britain from a rural, agricultural society to an urban and industrial one. If a single sentiment can be said to animate it, it is that the social conditions he saw about him in the rural counties in the 1820s represented a disastrous deterioration from those he had known in his youth. Cobbett's lament about a lost Golden Age for the labourers and yeomen of rural England provided one side of that powerful stream of criticism of the process of urbanisation and industrialisation of which the other lay in the exposure of conditions in the new environment through the 'Condition of England' novel and Parliamentary Blue Books.[9] Cobbett provided the sense of a lost rural idyll, an ideal of harmony and prosperity, already being undermined in the era after the Napoleonic Wars by a new world of commerce and social antagonism. This view has tended to shift appreciation of Cobbett towards the debate about the nature and consequences of the industrial and agricultural revolutions – a proponent of the 'world we have lost' and the celebration of a land lost and scarred, blighted forever by the rise of commerce and industry. Hence Cobbett figures prominently in the so-called 'Wiener thesis', British culture's apparent resistance to and devaluing of entrepreneurship and enterprise, and even attracted attention as a forerunner of ethical socialism.[10]

But Cobbett's intellectual pedigree did not lie in the world of Peel and Cobden, rather it belonged to the great maelstrom of events which burst over the Atlantic world from the 1770s. One of Cobbett's earliest memories was of attending the great hop-fair at Weyhill in the autumn of 1776 when news of the British capture of Long Island, carried by an Extraordinary Gazette, burst upon the assembled company, provoking lengthy and acrimonious debate. Cobbett and his father were among that part of the company which retired to an apartment where 'Washington's health, and success to the Americans, were repeatedly toasted'.[11] Cobbett joined the army after the loss of America; his

---

[8]   G.D.H. Cole, *The Life of William Cobbett* (3rd edn., London, 1947), p. 11.

[9]   See J. Stevenson, 'Social Aspects of the Industrial Revolution', in P. O'Brien and R. Quinault (eds), *The Industrial Revolution and British Society*, (Cambridge, 1993), pp. 229–32, 249–51.

[10]   See M.J. Wiener, *English Culture and the Decline of the Industrial Spirit, 1850–1980* (Cambridge, 1981).

[11]   Cole (ed.), *Life and Adventures*, p. 19.

formative years were spent as a soldier on Britain's imperial frontier in Canada; he received his discharge and returned to England two years after the fall of the Bastille. As with so many others of his generation, his 'mental furniture' was to be dominated by the turbulent intellectual climate of the French Revolution, the event that produced such a prodigious diaspora of mind and feeling. This was the generation for whom Hazlitt attempted to provide an epitaph:

> Kind feelings and generous actions there always have been, and there always will be, while the intercourse of mankind shall endure: but the hope, that such feelings and such actions might become universal, rose and set with the French revolution. That light seems to have been extinguished for ever in this respect. The French revolution was the only match that ever took place between philosophy and experience; and waking from the trance of theory to the sense of reality, we hear the words, *truth, reason, virtue, liberty*, with the same indifference or contempt, that the cynic who has married a jilt or a termagant, listens to the rhapsodies of lovers.[12]

Cobbett can be seen as a late entrant to this debate and one whose apparently maverick and multifarious concerns create problems as to where he should be placed. Cobbett has had a diverse range of admirers and commentators, a notable company which includes Karl Marx, Matthew Arnold, G.D.H. Cole, G.K. Chesterton, A.J.P. Taylor, Richard Hoggart, Raymond Williams, Michael Foot, Richard Ingrams, Asa Briggs, Edward Thompson and the late Lord Grimond. Although the majority of these figures belong to the left of centre, it is apparent that Cobbett cannot be claimed exclusively by either the Left or the Right. Cobbett's distinguished career as an advocate of parliamentary reform and a champion of the common people had been preceded in the 1790s by a decade of vehement pro-government propaganda as Peter Porcupine, when Cobbett had defended Pitt and the British Constitution, denounced Paine, Priestley and the radicals, and fiercely upheld the necessity of war with France. Moreover, Cobbett's liberal credentials have always had to contend with his fierce prejudices. His railings against a range of minorities, including Quakers, Methodists, Jews, Scots and intellectuals in general have raised difficulties for his biographers and commentators. Cobbett, hailed by A.H. Halsey as an 'ethical socialist', has also been seen by W.D. Rubinstein as an exponent of the 'dark side of populism'.[13]

It is clear from this why Cobbett might be ascribed the title of a 'one-man' Country Party, applying to the conditions of the late eighteenth and early

---

[12] *The Complete Works of William Hazlitt*, III, p. 156.

[13] W.D. Rubinstein, 'British Radicalism and the "Dark Side" of Populism', in *Elites and the Wealthy in Modern British Society* (Brighton, 1987), 339–73; see also K.W. Schweizer and J.W. Osborne, *Cobbett in his Times* (Leicester, 1990), 70–7.

nineteenth centuries the strictures of a Swift. The primary concern of the Country Party interest was the fear that the Court had acquired the means of corrupting the constitution. For Cobbett, those visible signs became evident during the 1800s after his return from America. Cobbett opposed the Peace of Amiens because he felt it allowed France to enjoy too many of her gains and displayed a supine weakness on the part of the government. Shocked, too, by what he perceived as the falling off of the living standards of the labourer, Cobbett became a parliamentary reformer when he considered standing at the Honiton Election of 1806. Cobbett retained the Country Party faith in the possibility of purifying the constitution. In 1809, he declared famously that 'I want to see no *innovation* in England. All I wish and all I strive for, is *The Constitution of England*, undefiled by corruption.'[14] Although Cobbett was eventually pushed along the road to a more extensive view of parliamentary reform, he always approached it from the view of one who saw the task as the restoration of something lost – a return to things as they were in the 'golden age' of his youth.

The other vital theme Cobbett inherited from the eighteenth century, and which is crucial to an understanding of his writings, is that of the 'Patriot', understood both as a genuine love of country and as an oppositionist stance. Cobbett's early career as a soldier left him with an innate sense of the place of England in the world. It is important to remember that Cobbett was an expatriate in North America on three separate occasions, as well as spending time in France. Cobbett's stance as a pro-government journalist based in America during the 1790s was steadfastly bellicose. Not only did he oppose peace with France but he prepared anti-invasion tracts and cooperated with William Windham in advocating a well-trained volunteer force to resist a French invasion. But Cobbett also sought to redress the ills of the country because he was a 'true Patriot' not some fair-weather loyalist or government toady. He may have been the kind of Patriot who *in extremis* might have cut off the head of his king to save his country, but we would be mistaking our man if we failed to recognise that he retained an attachment to the land and people of England, to its habits and customs, to its army and navy, to the monarchy and the traditional social order as he conceived they had once existed in the uncorrupted and bountiful times of his youth. It provided the mainspring of his conservatism *and* his radicalism.

Cobbett was also a man of his times, coming to consciousness at the time of the debates on the American Revolution, serving in Canada in the immediate aftermath of the loss of the colonies, and arriving back in England just as the French Revolution was about to detonate unprecedented political debate. He could not and did not escape the influences of the enlightenment and the republic of letters that it engendered. He became part of a transatlantic world of journalism, first as an anti-radical, later as a radical critic himself, and a victim

---

14   *Political Register*, 15 April 1809.

of oppression and exile. His feelings for America were complex, soured by some of his early experiences but admiring of much that he saw. France, fountainhead of enlightenment and revolution, was a failed destination, his intended sojourn thwarted by the growing radicalism of the French Revolution in 1792 and diverting him to America. His views on the French were by no means those of the simple-minded 'calf of John Bull' he styled himself. Not only did he teach Frenchmen English, but he composed a French grammar, could find praise for some of Napoleon's social and legal achievements and could sense the huge implications of what the French Revolution meant in terms of what he called 'an insurrection of talents and courage and industry against birth and rank'. He perceived in the transatlantic upheavals of the American and French Revolutions 'a change *in the mind of man* [...] such a *change* as will render their lives more happy and less humiliating'.[15]

Cobbett was thus no mere traditionalist. His instinctive 'Country Party' views were being articulated in a revolutionary atmosphere, elements of which clearly influenced him. His views on education echoed Rousseau whose opinions in almost every other respect he affected to despise. Children were to learn naturally, following where their interest took them; coercion, corporal punishment and rote learning had no part to play. He shared the humanitarian instincts of the early penal reformers, condemning flogging in the army and a 'bloody code' which hanged a woman for stealing a few potatoes from a cart during the post-war distress. He believed in progress, in the power of individuals to transform their own circumstances, as he had himself, by hard work, application and sober habits. Men of talent and ability should be allowed to rise unrestrained by social convention and mere privilege. In doing so Cobbett was articulating sentiments which would become familiar in the nineteenth century as mainstream 'Victorian values' of respectability and improvement. It was what made his 'Advice' books, grammars, and books on gardening best-sellers long after his death. But alongside the tone of Victorian earnestness, Cobbett carried forward from the eighteenth century the language of sensibility and feeling. Hard as it can be to believe with some of Cobbett's most aggressive, abusive and sardonic rhetoric ringing in our ears, his writing included his 'Advice to a Lover' and he self-consciously recorded his tender regard for his wife when having their first child, doing the housework and rushing home when thunder threatened because he knew it frightened her.

Above all Cobbett's outlook reflected his own rural background and a country which even at the time of his death was still far from fully industrialised and substantially rural. Born just after the middle of the eighteenth century he was at heart a countryman and had little liking for the new urban world, regarding London itself as 'the Wen', literally a swelling

---

15   *Political Register*, 9 November 1811.

or cyst on the body politic. It made it possible for him to consider that the country could subsist perfectly well without commerce and industry. Even amidst his busy journalistic life and political activism he was a farmer and horticulturalist, intensely passionate and knowledgeable about agriculture, plants and husbandry. His longing for a more harmonious social order was rooted in a rural world not an urban and industrial one. It places him in the context of Pugin's *Contrasts* and 'Young England', part of the reaction to the changing face of the country towards an increasingly commercial, industrial and utilitarian future. It renders comprehensible his extended and best-selling condemnation of the Protestant Reformation for its destruction of the monastic institutions which gave succour to the poor. The lands and wealth taken from the monasteries had been diverted by the monarchy for its own purposes, squandered on favourites and founding the fortunes of many of the nobles and gentry now foremost in abetting corruption and resisting reform. The deteriorating plight of the agricultural labourer in the bleak post-war years saw Cobbett driven to paroxysms of denunciations best encapsulated in *Rural Rides*. Similarly, attempts to reform the poor laws in the 1830s and finally enacted in the New Poor Law of 1834 he saw as designed to deprive the poor of their traditional rights of subsistence, yet one more assault on 'Old England'.

Cobbett's language of feeling and idealisation of rural England also reminds us that, in the terms of literary history, he belongs to the Romantic age. His denunciation of the 'dark Satanic mills' of the Industrial Revolution was as intense and instinctive as Blake's, and he railed against the sub-human factory conditions imposed by the 'the lords of the loom' and 'encouraged and assisted by this foolish government'.[16] His writing also has an autobiographical and elegiac tone that is surprisingly Wordsworthian. Cobbett's memories of his rural childhood became an important part of his self-mythology, while his later attachment to his farm at Botley, a few miles from Southampton, led James Gillray to caricature him as a 'Hampshire Hog'. His large-scale agricultural ambitions were repeatedly disrupted by imprisonment, exile and bankruptcy, and yet he continued farming until the end of his life. In 1800, the year Cobbett returned to England from America, Wordsworth wrote in the Preface to *Lyrical Ballads* about a new kind of poetry, based on subjects drawn from 'low and rustic life', and cast in 'the real language of men'. The attention to rural life in Cobbett's journalism mirrors this new impulse in poetry, while the emphasis on colloquial language – in both Cobbett and Wordsworth's writing – shows the influence of the revolutionary plain style of Thomas Paine.

Cobbett's connections to radical networks of writers and publishers began during his brief stay in London during the winter of 1791–2, before the

---

16   *Political Register*, 20 November 1824.

outbreak of war with France and at a time when the British response to the French Revolution was still being vigorously debated. His exposé of corruption in the army, *The Soldier's Friend* (1792), was published by James Ridgway, who was jailed the following year for publishing the second part of Paine's *Rights of Man*. When Cobbett was himself imprisoned in Newgate in 1810, his visitors included celebrated radicals such as William Godwin, the author of *Political Justice* and *Caleb Williams*, widower of Mary Wollstonecraft and father of Mary Shelley.[17] However, Cobbett would go on to combine the radical legacy of the 1790s with the emphasis on tradition, patriotism and the 'little platoon' of the family that is central to Edmund Burke's counter-revolutionary tour de force, *Reflections on the Revolution in France* (1790). Cobbett's experience of writing as a conservative and anti-Jacobin in the second half of the 1790s ensured that he was ideally placed to negotiate the competing arguments of the revolution controversy, and his later career can be read as an idiosyncratic attempt to combine Paine's common sense and democratic politics with Burke's organic and conservative vision of society.

The controversies of the 1790s lived on in Cobbett's journalism, and in the tumultuous years after Waterloo he was picked up enthusiastically by a new generation of readers, including John Keats, William Hazlitt and Percy Shelley: Shelley even insisted that the *Political Register* was sent out to him in Italy. Cobbett often expressed his disdain for contemporary literature, but he remained required reading for all the great writers of his day, and his opinions are inseparable from his strident, spontaneous and instantly recognisable style of prose. While his posthumous reputation has rested largely on the remarkable sequence of books he wrote between his mid-fifties and late sixties, including the *English Grammar*, *Cottage Economy*, *Advice to Young Men* and *Rural Rides*, his contemporaries knew him primarily as a journalist: first as the Tory, anti-Jacobin Peter Porcupine, and then as the increasingly radical editor of the *Political Register*. Cobbett wrote the vast majority of the newspaper himself, in leading articles that often ran to 10,000 words. Perhaps his most remarkable achievement was finding a mass audience for a publication which consisted of 32 columns of densely packed prose, without the illustrations and commercial advertising that modern newspapers rely on.

The basis of Cobbett's journalism was his clear and idiomatic use of English. In the *English Grammar*, he urged his student 'to bear in mind, that the *only* use of words is *to cause our meaning to be clearly understood*; and that the best words are those which are familiar to the ears of the greatest number of persons'. On composition, he advised:

---

[17]   *The Diary of William Godwin*, (eds) V. Myers, D. O'Shaughnessy and M. Philp (Oxford, 2010). http://godwindiary.bodleian.ox.ac.uk. See entries for 24 October, 29 October, 3 December and 18 December 1811.

The *order* of the matter will be, in almost all cases, that of your thoughts. Sit down *to write what you have thought*, and not *to think what you shall write*. Use the first words that occur to you, and never attempt to *alter a thought;* for, that which has come of itself into your mind is likely to pass into that of another more readily and with more effect than any thing which you can, by reflection, invent.[18]

The sheer scale of Cobbett's output and the evidence of surviving manuscripts suggests that this is an accurate description of his own method, and he rarely spent time re-writing first drafts. As Hazlitt writes, the pleasure of reading Cobbett is linked to the impression of immediacy and the clear flow of ideas: 'an argument does not stop to stagnate and muddle in his brain, but passes at once to his paper. His ideas are served up, like pancakes, hot and hot.'[19] However, his writing is not always as straightforward as he liked to claim, and recent accounts by Olivia Smith, Leonora Nattrass and Kevin Gilmartin have emphasised Cobbett's rhetorical sophistication and ability to adapt his style to different audiences.[20]

Cobbett's richly coloured prose puts a highly personal gloss on what, from the pen of a lesser writer, might have become dry or repetitive arguments. In a period before newspaper by-lines, Cobbett was the exception, signing his articles and delivering a vivid sense of his own character. His leading articles were often framed as open letters: a popular eighteenth-century form, which Cobbett used to directly address a specific politician or group of readers. *Rural Rides*, by far his most popular work today, first appeared as a weekly journal at the back of the *Register*, describing to his readers what he had seen on the road and reminding his political enemies that he had not forgotten them. As Edward Thompson writes, 'his relationship with his audience was peculiarly intimate [...] Cobbett's ideas can be seen less as a one-way propagandist flow than as the incandescence of an alternating current, between his readers and himself [...] Few writers can be found who were so much the "voice" of their own audience.'[21]

Cobbett is central to Thompson's seminal study *The Making of the English Working Class* (1963), which contains more references to Cobbett than to any other figure. Accounts of first reading the *Political Register* are a staple feature, even a rite of passage, in working-class autobiography up to the Chartist period, and its influence was perhaps most memorably described by the Lancashire weaver and radical Samuel Bamford:

---

[18]   *A Grammar of the English Language* (fourth edition, 1820), pp. 71–2, 182.

[19]   *The Complete Works of William Hazlitt*, VIII, p. 57.

[20]   See O. Smith, *The Politics of Language, 1791–1819*, (Oxford, 1984), L. Nattrass, *William Cobbett: The Politics of Style* (Cambridge, 1995) and K. Gilmartin, *Print Politics: The Press and Radical Opposition in Early Nineteenth-Century England* (Cambridge, 1996).

[21]   E.P. Thompson, *The Making of the English Working Class* (London, 1961; first pub. 1963), pp. 833–4.

At this time the writings of William Cobbett suddenly became of great authority; they were read on nearly every cottage hearth in the manufacturing districts of South Lancashire, in those of Leicester, Derby, and Nottingham; also in many of the Scottish manufacturing towns. Their influence was speedily visible. He directed his readers to the true cause of their sufferings—misgovernment; and to its proper corrective— parliamentary reform.[22]

Bamford is here remembering the period of mass meetings and unrest that followed the end of the Napoleonic Wars, but parliamentary reform was not achieved until the Great Reform Act of 1832, a full 15 years later. Having been one of the leaders of the reform movement for almost three decades, and never one for false modesty, Cobbett declared that he deserved much of the credit for this constitutional landmark. Fittingly, he was returned to the reformed parliament as an MP for the newly created constituency of Oldham and he planned, but never completed, an autobiography, under the title, 'The Progress of a Ploughboy to a Seat in Parliament, as exemplified in the History of the Life of WILLIAM COBBETT, Member for OLDHAM'.[23] In reality, the 1832 Reform Act had arrived too late for Cobbett to have a successful parliamentary career: he was now almost 70, suffering from increasingly poor health and largely estranged from his family. However, he continued his battles in parliament, using this new platform to express his determined opposition to the New Poor Law.

In the years after his death in 1835, Cobbett's influence seemed to be quickly eclipsed, with new titles such as the *News of the World* pioneering a more salacious and commercially driven form of journalism. Further industrialisation and new political theories made his opinions seem increasingly anachronistic. In 1853, Karl Marx gave the equivocal verdict that Cobbett was 'the creator of old English Radicalism' and a writer who 'has not been surpassed', but ultimately a primitive radical, who 'saw the effects, [but] did not understand the causes, the new social agencies at work'.[24] However, this did not prevent readers returning to his work. In his early career as a parliamentary reporter, Charles Dickens had transcribed Cobbett's speeches from the Reporters' Gallery of the House of Commons, and James T. Fields remembered how, in later life, 'there were certain books of which Dickens liked to talk during his walks. Among the especial favourite were the writings of Cobbett, De Quincey, the lectures of Moral Philosophy of Sydney Smith, and Carlyle's *French Revolution*.'[25] Both Cobbett's style and subject matter lend themselves to such outdoor conversations: the poet Edward Thomas

---

22   Samuel Bamford, *Passages in the Life of a Radical* (London, 1844), p. 7.

23   *Political Register*, 15 February 1834.

24   Karl Marx, letter to the *New York Daily Tribune*, 22 July 1853.

25   James T. Fields, 'Some Memories of Charles Dickens', in *The Mystery of Edwin Drood, and Some Uncollected Pieces* (Boston, 1870), p. 4.

– like Dickens, a formidable walker – described the rhythms of Cobbett's prose as 'a bodily thing. His sentences do not precisely suggest the swing of an arm of a leg, but they have something in common with it. His style is perhaps the nearest to speech that has really survived.'[26] *Rural Rides* became a forerunner of such twentieth-century 'Condition of England' travelogues as George Orwell's *The Road to Wigan Pier* and J.B. Priestley's *English Journey*, which both contain a distinctively Cobbettian mix of personal anecdote, reportage and polemic, couched in a colloquial style.

Cobbett's influence can now be seen in many different directions. He is an important figure in radical historiography and E.P. Thompson's 'heroic age of popular radicalism' (1816–20), while the pro-Federalist, anti-Jacobin chapter of Cobbett's career in the 1790s has been given novelistic treatment by William Safire, a former speechwriter for Richard Nixon. Raymond Williams has used Cobbett as a case study in changing representations of country and city life in English culture, while Linda Colley argues that Cobbett's influence survives in the British press: 'his brilliant, pithy, bellicose writing transformed British political journalism, and has left a mark even today. His true successor may be the violent, undeferential, hugely popular and not unimportant *Sun* newspaper.'[27]

Cobbett belonged to no one age. He was never a theorist or the progenitor of an 'ism'. As Cole wrote 'He went by what he saw, or felt, around him, reacting directly to his environment and making his generalisations to fit the practical causes he espoused.'[28] We might wish to say that with Cobbett the Country Party met with the Man of Feeling and produced a version of Self-Help; certainly Cobbett's identity and self-image were composed of a complex set of ideas and sentiments for which, of course, we do have a word – 'Cobbettian'. His works are more easily available than ever and, in many cases, can be easily and cheaply downloaded on the internet. However, with 20 million words, it can be difficult to know where to start. The following chapters give a guide to some of the main themes in Cobbett's writing, and present a selection of some of his most memorable passages of prose.

---

[26]   Edward Thomas, introduction to Everyman edition of *Rural Rides*, 2 vols (London, 1912), vol. 1, p. ix.

[27]   L. Colley, 'I am the Watchman', *London Review of Books*, 20 November 2003.

[28]   Cole (ed.), *Life and Adventures*, p. 5.

Chapter 1
Cobbett's Early Life and Progress

Cobbett saw his humble origins and self-education as a both a platform for his own views and an example to others. He had been almost entirely self-educated, had gone on to do extraordinary things and was unafraid of using his own exemplary life to show what could be achieved without the privileges of high birth or a classical education. The first few extracts below vividly convey Cobbett's memories of growing up in Farnham, where he was 'bred at the plough-tail', and then joining the army. These memories assumed talismanic significance in Cobbett's myth of his own progress.

Cobbett believed that his own success was due to his adherence to a few basic principles: early rising, exercise, sobriety, frugality and industry. This, rather puritanical, set of principles was re-iterated throughout his writings. In the second half of his career he wrote a series of educational guides on a wide range of subjects. He advertised this series as 'The Cobbett Library', with the frank admission:

> When I am asked what books a young man or young woman ought to read, I always answer, Let him or her read *all* the books that I have written. This does, it will doubtless be said, *smell of the shop*. No matter. It is what I recommend; and experience has taught me that it is my duty to give the recommendation.[1]

This wide-ranging collection was part of a contemporary trend towards collections of cheap books, designed to satisfy a growing appetite for self-education among the middle and working classes. However, the diverse set of books in 'The Cobbett Library' are all, to varying degrees, autobiographical. Cobbett liked to use his own life as an example of the argument he wished to convey: in the words of his fellow journalist William Hazlitt,

> His egotism is delightful, for there is no affectation in it. He does not talk of himself for lack of something to write about, but because some circumstance that has happened to himself is the best possible illustration of the subject, and he is not the man to shrink from giving the best possible illustration of the subject from a squeamish delicacy.[2]

---

[1] Endpiece to Cobbett's *Two-Penny Trash or Politics for the Poor* (London, 1831), pp. 262–3.

[2] Hazlitt, 'Character of Cobbett' in *The Complete Works of William Hazlitt*, ed. P.P Howe (21 vols, London, 1931), VIII, pp. 52–3.

In 1829, Cobbett published *Advice to Young Men, and (Incidentally) to Young Women*, a conduct book which was first issued in 14 monthly, sixpenny parts. His emphasis on self-improvement later appealed to Victorian readers, and his influence can be seen in works such as Samuel Smiles's *Self Help; with Illustrations of Character, Conduct and Perseverance* (1859). One recent study of nineteenth-century book history and reading practices describes a copy of *Advice to Young Men* bearing the simple, anonymous, inscription: 'This volume was one of the Factors in my success in life.'[3]

*

Cobbett was intensely proud of his humble ancestry which rooted him in the soil of 'Old England'. Throughout his life he used his origins both to point to his own life as an examplar of progress and self-improvement but also as a basis from which to launch his criticism of government and its actions. It gave him a basis as a traditionalist to criticise innovation, as a countryman to be wary of commerce, cities, and, later, industry, and as a former 'plough boy' to take the side of the common man against the rich and the powerful. Even in his account of his forbears and earliest years he could not resist gibes at those he had come to despise in later life whether radical 'sans culottes' or impractical 'philosophers'.

> To be descended from an illustrious family certainly reflects honour on any man, in spite of the sans-culotte principles of the present day. This is, however, an honour that I have no pretension to. All that I can boast of in my birth, is, that I was born in Old England; the country from whence came the men who explored and settled North America; the country of Penn, and of all those to whom this country is indebted.
>
> With respect to my ancestors, I shall go no further back than my grandfather, and for this plain reason, that I never heard talk of any prior to him. He was a day-labourer; and I have heard my father say, that he worked for one farmer from the day of his marriage to that of his death, upwards of forty years. He died before I was born, but I have often slept beneath the same roof that had sheltered him, and where his widow dwelt for several years after his death. It was a little thatched cottage, with a garden before the door. It had but two windows; a damson tree shaded one, and a clump of filberts the other. Here I and my brother went every Christmas and Whitsuntide to spend a week or two, and torment the poor old woman with our noise and dilapidations. She used to give us milk and bread for breakfast, an apple pudding for our dinner, and a piece of bread and cheese for supper. Her fire was made of turf, cut from the

---

[3] W. St Clair, *The Reading Nation in the Romantic Period* (Cambridge, 2004), p. 276.

neighbouring heath, and her evening light was a rush dipped in grease. [...]

Every one will, I hope, have the goodness to believe, that my grandfather was no philosopher. Indeed he was not. He never made a lightning-rod, nor bottled up a single quart of sun-shine, in the whole course of his life. He was no almanack-maker, not quack, nor chimney-doctor, nor soap-boiler, nor ambassador, nor printer's devil: neither was he a deist, and all his children were born in wedlock. The legacies he left, were, his scythe, his reap-hook, and his flail; he bequeathed no old and irrecoverable debts to an hospital: he never *cheated the poor during his life*, nor *mocked them in his death*. He has, it is true, been suffered to sleep quietly beneath the green sord; but, if his descendants cannot point to his statue over the door of a library, they have not the mortification to hear him daily accused of having been a whore-master, a hypocrite, and an infidel.

My father, when I was born, was a farmer. The reader will easily believe, from the poverty of his parents, that he had received no very brilliant education: he was, however, learned, for a man in his rank of life. When a little boy, he drove plough for two pence a-day; and these his earnings, were appropriated to the expenses of an evening school. What a village school-master could be expected to teach, he had learnt; and had, besides, considerably improved himself, in several branches of the mathematics. He understood land-surveying well, and was often chosen to draw the plans of disputed territory: in short, he had the reputation of possessing experience and understanding, which never fails, in England, to give a man in a country place, some little weight with his neighbours. He was honest, industrious, and frugal; it was not, therefore, wonderful, that he should be situated in a good farm, and happy in a wife of his own rank, like him, beloved and respected.

So much for my ancestors, from whom, if I derived no honour, I derive no shame.

[*The Life and Adventures of Peter Porcupine*, pp. 17–20, in G.D.H. Cole (ed.) *Life and Adventures of Peter Porcupine with other records of his early career in England and America* (London, 1927).]

*

Cobbett was also proud of the inheritance of hard physical work which he had acquired from his farming background and that he had not received much in the way of formal education.

A father like ours, it will be readily supposed, did not suffer us to eat the bread of idleness. I do not remember the time, when I did not earn my living. My first occupation was, driving the small birds from the turnip-seed, and the rooks from the peas. When I first trudged a-field, with my wooden bottle and my satchel swung over my shoulders, I was hardly able to climb the gates and stiles; and, at the close of the day, to reach home, was a task of infinite difficulty. My next employment was weeding wheat, and leading a single horse at harrowing barley. Hoeing peas followed, and hence, I arrived at the honour of joining the reapers in harvest, driving the team, and holding plough. We were all of us strong and laborious, and my father used to boast, that he had four boys, the eldest of whom was but fifteen years old, who did as much work as any three men in the parish of Farnham. Honest pride, and happy days!

I have some faint recollection of going to school to an old woman, who, I believe, did not succeed in learning me my letters. In the winter evenings, my father learnt us all to read and write, and gave us a pretty tolerable knowledge of arithmetic. Grammar he did not perfectly understand himself, and therefore his endeavours to learn us that, necessarily failed; for, though he thought he understood it, and though he made us get the rules by heart, we learnt nothing at all of the principles.

[*The Life and Adventures of Peter Porcupine*, pp. 20–1, in G.D.H. Cole (ed.) *Life and Adventures*.]

*

Revisiting a childhood haunt, Cobbett believed that the combination of hard work, country pursuits and the simple enjoyments of childhood games had given him the best kind of education possible. Self-consciously or not, he was at one with some of the leading thinkers of the day in his view that a 'natural' upbringing gave him superiority over those conventionally educated.

In quitting Tilford we came on to the land belonging to Waverly Abbey, and then, instead of going on to the town of Farnham, veered away to the left towards *Wrecklesham*, in order to cross the Farnham and Alton turnpike-road, and to come on by the side of *Crondall* to *Odiham*. We went a little out of the way to go to a place called the *Bourne*, which lies in the heath at about a mile from Farnham. It is a winding narrow valley, down which, during the wet season of the year, there runs a stream beginning at the *Holt Forest*, and emptying itself into the *Wey* just below Moor-Park, which was the seat of *Sir William Temple*, when *Swift* was residing with him.[4] We went to this Bourne in order that I might show

---

[4]   Jonathan Swift, one of Cobbett's literary heroes, received part of his education while living with the statesman and author William Temple (1628–99) and acting as his secretary.

my son the spot where I received the rudiments of my education. There is a little hop-garden in which I used to work when from eight to ten years old; from which I have scores of times run to follow the hounds, leaving the hoe to do the best that it could to destroy the weeds; but the most interesting thing was a *sand-hill*, which goes from a part of the heath down to the rivulet. As a due mixture of pleasure with toil, I, with two brothers, used occasionally to *desport* ourselves, as the lawyers call it, at this sand-hill. Our diversion was this: we used to go to the top of the hill, which was steeper than the roof of a house; one used to draw his arms out of the sleeves of his smock-frock, and lay himself down with his arms by his sides; and then the others, one at head and the other at feet, sent him rolling down the hill like a barrel or a log of wood. By the time he got to the bottom, his hair, eyes, ears, nose and mouth, were all full of this loose sand; then the others took their turn, and at every roll, there was a monstrous spell of laughter. I have often told my sons of this while they were very little, and I now took one of them to see the spot. But, that was not all. This was the spot where I was receiving my *education;* and this was the sort of education; and I am perfectly satisfied that if I had not received such an education, or something very much like it; that, if I had been brought up a milksop, with a nursery-maid everlastingly at my heels; I should have been at this day as great a fool, as inefficient a mortal, as any of those frivolous idiots that are turned out from Winchester and Westminster School, or from any of those dens of dunces called Colleges and Universities. It is impossible to say how much I owe to that sand-hill; and I went to return it my thanks for the ability which it probably gave me to be one of the greatest terrors, to one of the greatest and most powerful bodies of knaves and fools, that ever were permitted to afflict this or any other country.

[*Rural Rides*, ed. I. Dyck (London, 2001), pp. 11–12 (27 September 1822).]

*

After one attempt at running away to sea, prompted by his sight of the fleet riding at anchor at Portsmouth, Cobbett did finally break free and made his way to London where he was fortunate enough to be befriended and given work as a clerk. Although he hated the work, it was a decisive step away from his rural upbringing and a career outside agriculture. But his desire for freedom and adventure could not tolerate for long an existence as an office drudge and drove him once again to seek to enlist in the armed forces. Joining, as he thought, the Marines, he found himself in fact in a regular line regiment which now gave him the opportunity to exercise his talent for hard work and develop his rudimentary learning.

No part of my life has been totally unattended with pleasure, except the eight or nine months I passed in Gray's Inn. The office (for so the dungeon where I wrote was called) was so dark, that, on cloudy days, we were obliged to burn candle. I worked like a galley-slave from five in the morning till eight or nine at night, and sometimes all night long. How many quarrels have I assisted to foment and perpetuate between those poor innocent fellows, John Doe and Richard Doe! How many times (God forgive me!) have I sent them to assault each other with guns, swords, staves and pitchforks, and then brought them to answer for their misdeeds before our Sovereign Lord the King seated in His Court of Westminster! When I think of the *saids* and *soforths*, and the counts of tautology that I scribbled over; when I think of those sheets of seventy-two words, and those lines two inches apart, my brain turns. Gracious heaven! if I am doomed to be wretched, bury me beneath Iceland snows, and let me feed on blubber; stretch me under the burning line, and deny me thy propitious dews; nay, if it be thy will, suffocate me with the infected and pestilential air of a democratic club-room; but save me from the desk of an attorney! [...]

I never quitted this gloomy recess except on Sundays, when I usually took a walk to St. James's Park, to feast my eyes with the sight of the trees, the grass, and the water. In one of these walks I happened to cast my eye on an advertisement, inviting all loyal young men, who had a mind to gain riches and glory, to repair to a certain rendezvous, where they might enter into His Majesty's marine service, and have the peculiar happiness and honour of being enrolled in the Chatham Division. I was not ignorant enough to be the dupe of this morsel of military bombast; but a change was what I wanted: besides, I knew that marines went to sea, and my desire to be on that element had rather increased than diminished by my being penned up in London. In short, I resolved to join this glorious corps; and, to avoid all possibility of being discovered by my friends, I went down to Chatham and enlisted, into the marines as I thought, but the next morning I found myself before a Captain of a marching regiment. There was no retreating: I had taken a shilling to drink his Majesty's health, and his further bounty was ready for my reception. [...]

I enlisted early in 1784, and, as peace had then taken place, no great haste was made to send recruits off to their regiments. I remained upwards of a year at Chatham, during which time I was employed in learning my exercise, and taking my tour in the duty of the garrison. My leisure time, which was a very considerable portion of the twenty-four hours, was spent, not in the dissipations common to such a way of life, but in reading and study. In the course of this year I learnt more than I had ever done before. I subscribed to a circulating library at Brompton, the greatest part of the books in which I read more than once over. The library was not very considerable, it is true, nor in my reading was I directed by any degree of taste or choice. Novels, plays, history, poetry, all were read, and nearly all with equal avidity.

[*The Life and Adventures of Peter Porcupine*, pp. 30–3, in G.D.H. Cole (ed.) *Life and Adventures.*]

*

As well as devouring all the books he could get hold of, Cobbett also used his time in the army to teach himself grammar. This was an experience that he often returned to in his later writings.

I learned grammar when I was a private soldier on the pay of sixpence a day. The edge of my berth, or that of the guard-bed, was my seat to study in; my knapsack was my book-case; a bit of board, lying on my lap, was my writing-table; and the task did not demand any thing like a year of my life. I had no money to purchase candle or oil; in winter time it was rarely that I could get any evening-light but that of *the fire*, and only my *turn* even of that. And if I, under such circumstances, and without parent or friend to advise or encourage me, accomplished this undertaking, what excuse can there be for *any youth*, however poor, however pressed with business, or however circumstanced as to room or other conveniences? To buy a pen or a sheet of paper I was compelled to forego some portion of food, though in a state of half-starvation; I had no moment of time that I could call my own; and I had to read and to write amidst the talking, laughing, singing, whistling and brawling of at least half a score of the most thoughtless of men, and that, too, in the hours of their freedom from all controul. Think not lightly of the *farthing* that I had to give, now and then, for ink, pen, or paper! That farthing was, alas! a *great sum* to me! I was as tall as I am now; I had great health and great exercise. The whole of the money, not expended for us at market, was *two pence a week* for each man. I remember, and well I may! that upon one occasion I, after all absolutely necessary expenses, had, on a Friday, made shift to have a half-penny in reserve, which I had destined for the purchase of a *red-herring* in the morning; but, when I pulled off my clothes at night, so hungry then as to be hardly able to endure life, I found that I had *lost my half-penny*! I buried my head under the miserable sheet and rug, and cried like a child! And, again I say, if I, under circumstances like these, could encounter and overcome this task, is there, can there be, in the whole world, a youth to find an excuse for the non-performance? What youth, who shall read this, will not be ashamed to say, that he is not able to find time and opportunity for this most essential of all the branches of book-learning?

[*Advice to Young Men* (London, 1829), para. 44.]

*

His army career also showed how 'in early life' he had 'contracted the blessed habit of husbanding well my time'.

To this, more than to any other thing, I owed my very extraordinary promotion in the army. I was *always ready:* if I had to mount guard at *ten*, I was ready at *nine:* never did any man, or any thing, wait one moment for me. Being, at an age *under twenty years*, raised from Corporal to Sergeant Major *at once*, over the head of thirty sergeants, I naturally should have been on object of envy and hatred; but this habit of early rising and rigid adherence to the precepts which I have given you, really subdued these passions; because every one felt, that what I did he had never done, and never could do. Before my promotion, a clerk was wanted to make out the morning report of the regiment. I rendered the clerk unnecessary; and, long before any other man was dressed for the parade, my work for the morning was all done, and I myself was on the parade, walking, in fine weather, for an hour perhaps. My custom was this: to get up, in summer, at day-light, and in winter at four o'clock; shave, dress, even to the putting of my sword-belt over my shoulder, and having my sword lying on the table before me, ready to hang by my side. Then I ate a bit of cheese, or pork, and bread. Then I prepared my report, which was filled up as fast as the companies brought me in the materials. After this I had an hour or two to read, before the time came for any duty out of doors, unless, when the regiment or part of it went out to exercise in the morning. When this was the case, and the matter was left to me, I always had it on the ground in such time as that the bayonets glistened in the *rising sun*, a sight which gave me delight, of which I often think, but which I should in vain endeavour to describe. If the *officers* were to go out, eight or ten o'clock was the hour, sweating the men in the heat of the day, breaking in upon the time for cooking their dinner, putting all things out of order and all men out of humour. When I was commander, the men had a long day of leisure before them: they could ramble into the town or into the woods; go to get raspberries, to catch birds, to catch fish, or to pursue any other recreation, and such of them as chose, and were qualified, to work at their trades. So that here, arising solely from the early habits of one very young man, were pleasant and happy days given to hundreds.

Money is said to be *power*, which is, in some cases, true; and the same may be said of *knowledge;* but superior *sobriety*, *industry* and *activity*, are a still more certain source of power; for without these, *knowledge* is of little use; and, as to the power which *money* gives, it is that of *brute force*, it is the power of the bludgeon and the bayonet, and of the bribed press, tongue and pen.

[*Advice to Young Men* (London, 1829), paras 39–40.]

*

When Cobbett returned to England in 1800, having achieved fame as 'Peter Porcupine', he reflected on how far he had come from his ordinary rural childhood. This passage is taken from Cobbett's journal of his second spell in the United States (1817–19), which followed the suspension of Habeas Corpus in Britain.

When I returned to England, in 1800, after an absence from the country parts of it, of sixteen years, the trees, the hedges, even the parks and woods, seemed so *small!* It made me laugh to hear little gutters, that I could jump over, called *Rivers!* The Thames was but a "*Creek!*" But, when, in about a month after my arrival in London, I went to *Farnham*, the place of my birth, what was my surprise! Every thing was become so pitifully *small!* I had to cross, in my post-chaise, the long and dreary heath of Bagshot. Then, at the end of it, to mount a hill, called Hungry Hill; and from that hill I knew that I should look down into the beautiful and fertile vale of Farnham. My heart fluttered with impatience, mixed with a sort of fear, to see all the scenes of my childhood; for I had learnt before, the death of my father and mother. There is a hill, not far from the town, called *Crooksbury Hill*, which rises up out of a flat, in the form of a *cone*, and is planted with Scotch fir trees. Here I used to take the eggs and young ones of crows and magpies. This hill was a famous object in the neighbourhood. It served as the superlative degree of height. "*As high as Crooksbury Hill*" meant, with us, the utmost degree of height. Therefore, the first object that my eyes sought was this hill. *I could not believe my eyes!* Literally speaking, I for a moment, thought the famous hill removed, and a little heap put in its stead; for I had seen in New Brunswick, a single rock, or hill of solid rock, ten times as big, and four or five times as high! The post-boy, going down hill, and not a bad road, whisked me, in a few minutes to the Bush Inn, from the garden of which I could see the prodigious *sand hill*, where I had begun my gardening works. What a *nothing!* But now came rushing into my mind, all at once, my pretty little garden, my little blue smock-frock, my little nailed shoes, my pretty pigeons that I used to feed out of my hands, the last kind words and tears of my gentle and tender-hearted and affectionate mother! I hastened back into the room. If I had looked a moment longer, I should have dropped. When I came to reflect, *what a change!* I looked down at my dress. What a change! What scenes I had gone through! How altered my state! I had dined the day before at a Secretary of State's[5] in company with Mr. *Pitt*, and had been waited upon by men in gaudy liveries! I had had nobody to assist me in the world. No teachers of any sort. Nobody to shelter me from the consequence of bad, and no one to counsel me to good, behaviour. I felt proud. The distinctions of rank, birth, and wealth, all became nothing in my eyes; and from that moment (less than a month after my arrival in England) I resolved never to bend before them.

[*A Year's Residence in the United States of America* (London, 1819), 15 January 1818.]

*

In *Advice to Young Men*, Cobbett looked back over his own progress to show how he had achieved his success. His remarkable career was not 'only' the result of genius, he argued, but of industry, perseverance and 'extraordinary exertion'.

To communicate to others the knowledge that I possess has always been my taste and my delight; and few, who know any thing of my progress through life, will be disposed to question my fitness for the task. Talk of rocks and breakers and quagmires and quick-sands, who has ever escaped from amidst so many as I have! Thrown (by my own will indeed) on the wide world at a very early age, not more than eleven or twelve years, without money to support, without friends to advise, and without book-learning to assist, me; passing a few years dependent solely on my own hard labour for my subsistence; then becoming a common soldier and leading a military life, chiefly in foreign parts, for eight years; quitting that life after really, for me, high promotion, and with, for me, a large sum of money; marrying at an early age, going at once to France to acquire the French language, thence to America; passing eight years there, becoming bookseller and author, and taking a prominent part in all the important discussions of the interesting period from 1793 to 1799, during which there was, in that country, a continual struggle carried on between the English and the French parties; conducting myself, in the ever active part which I took in that struggle in such a way as to call forth marks of unequivocal approbation from the government at home; returning

---

[5]   William Windham (1750–1810), politician, disciple of Edmund Burke, secretary at war in Pitt's Cabinet (1794–1801) and Cobbett's patron and close ally after his return to England.

to England in 1800, resuming my labours here, suffering, during these twenty-nine years, two years of imprisonment, heavy fines, three years self-banishment to the other side of the Atlantic, and a total breaking of fortune so as to be left without a bed to lie on, and, during these twenty-nine years of troubles and of punishments, writing and publishing, every week of my life, whether in exile or not, eleven weeks only excepted, a periodical paper, containing more or less of matter worthy of public attention; writing and publishing, during *the same twenty-nine years*, a grammar of the French and another of the English language, a work on the Economy of the Cottage, a work on Forest Trees and Woodlands, a work on Gardening, an account of America, a book of Sermons, a work on the Corn-plant, a History of the Protestant Reformation; all books of great and continued sale, and the *last* unquestionably the book of greatest circulation in the whole world, the Bible only excepted; having, during *these same twenty-nine years*, of troubles and embarrassments without number, introduced into England the manufacture of Straw-plat; also several valuable trees; having introduced, during *the same twenty-nine years*, the cultivation of the Corn-Plant, so manifestly valuable as a source of food; having, during the same period, always (whether in exile or not) sustained a shop of some size, in London; having, during the whole of the same period, never employed less, on an average, than ten persons, in some capacity or other, exclusive of printers, book-binders and others, connected with papers and books; and having, during these twenty-nine years of troubles, embarrassments, prisons, fines and banishments, bred up a family of seven children to man's and woman's state.

If such a man be not, after he has survived and accomplished all this, qualified to give Advice to Young Men, no man can be qualified for that task. There may have been natural *genius:* but genius *alone;* not all the genius in the world, could, without *something more*, have conducted me through these perils.

[*Advice to Young Men* (London, 1829), paras 4–5.]

*

Cobbett concluded his *English Grammar*, written as a series of letters to James Cobbett, with some general advice to his son. He evidently felt that he could not improve on it, and re-printed these final lines a decade later as the conclusion to *Advice to Young Men*.

I am now, my dear son, arrived at the last paragraph of my treatise, and I hope, that, when you arrive at it, you will understand grammar sufficiently to enable you to write without committing frequent and glaring errors. I shall now leave you, for about four months, to read and write English: to practise what you have now been taught. At the end of those four months, I shall have prepared a Grammar to teach you the *French Language*, which language I hope to hear you speak, and to see you write, well, at the end of one year from this time. With English and French on your tongue and in your pen, you have a resource, not only greatly valuable in itself, but a resource that you can be deprived of by none of those changes and chances which deprive men of pecuniary possessions, and which, in some cases, make the purse-proud man of yesterday a crawling sycophant to-day. Health, without which life is not worth having, you will hardly fail to secure by early rising, exercise, sobriety, and abstemiousness as to food. Happiness, or misery, is in the *mind*. It is the mind that lives; and the length of life ought to be measured by the number and importance of our ideas; and not by the number of our days. Never, therefore, esteem men merely on account of their riches or their station. Respect goodness, find it where you will. Honour talent wherever you behold it unassociated with vice; but, honour it most when accompanied with exertion, and especially when exerted in the cause of truth and justice; but, above all, when it steps forward to protect defenceless innocence against the attacks of powerful guilt.

[*A Grammar of the English Language* (New York, 1818), pp. 183–4.]

Chapter 2

Corruption

'Corruption' was central to Cobbett's criticism of the political, economic and social world in which he found himself. In many respects he was deeply conservative in the sense of believing that if only things had remained undisturbed and unchanged, then the country would be in a much better condition than it found itself. Time and time again he avowed that he only wished to return the country to the happier condition it was in at the time of his birth. His stance was one with a long history – the so-called 'Country Party' opposition who saw the evils of the country as emanating from the 'court', the 'evil councillors' or ministers, who misgoverned the country in their own interest and brought ruin upon it. Cobbett had read Swift, who as a Tory writer almost a hundred years earlier had inveighed against what he saw as the ruinous mismanagement of the War of Spanish Succession by the government of the day. Cobbett followed in that tradition. As a man of the 'country' in a literal sense and one, as he so frequently reminded readers, who had risen from the humblest origins entirely by his own efforts, he felt in an unrivalled position to represent the interests of the true people of England in the face of the incompetence and malpractice of the politicians, their alleged 'betters'.

Cobbett first gave vent to these feelings when he found himself better able to interpret orders and organise affairs in the army as a self-taught sergeant major than his supposed superiors, the officers. He uncovered and assembled evidence of widespread corruption and sought to bring it to the attention of authority, though he was ultimately frustrated in the attempt. Even as a vehemently pro-government writer in the 1790s, he refused to become a mere government hack, steadfastly maintaining his independence when he returned to England in 1800 as the first phase of the war with Revolutionary France was coming to an exhausted close. Increasingly, however, when war was resumed he believed that vast new opportunities for corruption had developed, notably in the funding associated with the Revolutionary and Napoleonic Wars. He condemned the rise of a race of 'merchants and manufacturers, and bankers and loan-jobbers and contractors' whose only interest was their own good and not that of the country at large. He warned Pitt in 1804 when he resumed the reins of government and renewed war against France: 'We must be great again or we must be nothing; and greatness is not to be reacquired by implicitly yielding to the councils of merchants, manufacturers, and bankers.'[1] Soon, however, he lost any faith that Pitt would take notice of his warnings and argued with increasing vehemence

---

[1]   *Political Register*, 18 February 1804.

that the moneyed interest or 'Pitt system' was corrupting and usurping the whole social order. The traditional hierarchy was being over-turned and the growing wealth spreading out to the squires, farmers and parsons was undermining the traditional relationship between men and masters, in turn destroying the spirit and security of the labourer.

When he turned his attention to remedying these abuses through the electoral system he found it too riddled with corruption. Initially outraged by the bribing and treating of electors, he increasingly widened his demands for reform to ensure a parliament uncorrupted by bribery and improper influence. His diagnosis of the country's ills therefore rested heavily upon the blame he placed upon those in power who, in their various ways, had subverted an otherwise sound and healthy country, by corrupting its political institutions, its finances and its social relations.

*

Cobbett's experience in the army as a sergeant-major brought him face-to-face with embezzlement and the failure of the officers to do anything about it. For Cobbett, the issue was one of general principle as well as damaging to the army. His anger grew directly out of his sense that he was at least the equal of those who were supposed to be his superiors.

> The object of my quitting the army, to which I was, perhaps, more attached than any man that ever lived in the world; was, to bring certain officers to justice for having, in various ways, *wronged both the public and the soldier*. With this object in view, I went strait to London, the moment I had obtained my liberty and secured my *personal safety*, which, as you will readily conceive, would not have been the case if I had not first got my discharge. [...] I enlisted at Chatham in 1784; I joined the regiment, in Nova Scotia, in 1785; I was almost immediately made a Corporal; in a few months afterwards I was made a Serjeant; and, at the end of about a year and a half, I was made the Serjeant Major.—While I was a corporal I was made *clerk* to the regiment. In a very short time, the whole of the business, in that way, fell into my hands; and, at the end of about a year, neither adjutant, pay-master, or quarter-master, could move an inch without my assistance. The *military* part of the regiment's affairs fell under my care in like manner. About this time, the new *discipline*, as it was called; that is to say, the mode of handling the musket, and of marching, &c. called "*Dundas's System*," was sent out to us, in little books, which were to be studied by the officers of each regiment, and the rules of which were to be immediately conformed to.—Though any old woman might have written such a book; though it was excessively foolish, from beginning to end; still, it was to be complied with; it ordered and commanded a *total change*,

and this change was to be completed before the next annual review took place.—To make this change was left to me, who was not then twenty years of age, while not a single officer in the regiment paid the least attention to the matter; so, that when the time came for the annual review, I, then a *corporal*, had to give lectures of instruction to the officers themselves, the colonel not excepted; and, for several of them, if not for all of them, I had to make out, upon large cards, which they bought for the purpose, little plans of the position of the regiment, together with lists of the words of command, which they had to give in the field.—Is it any wonder, that we experience *defeats*? There was I, at the review, upon the flank of the Grenadier Company, with my worsted shoulder-knot, and my great, high, coarse, hairy cap; confounded in the ranks amongst other men, while those who were commanding me to move my hands or my feet, thus or thus, were, in fact, uttering words, which I had taught them; and were, in every thing excepting mere authority, my inferiors; and ought to have been commanded by me.—It was impossible for reflections of this sort not to intrude themselves; and, as I advanced in experience, I felt less and less respect for those, whom I was compelled to obey. One suffers injustice from men, of great endowments of mind, with much less of heart-burning than from men, whom one cannot help despising; and, if my officers had been men of manifest superiority of mind, I should, perhaps, not have so soon conceived the project of bringing them, or some of them, at least, to shame and punishment for the diverse flagrant breaches of the law, committed by them, and for their manifold, their endless, wrongs against the soldiers and against the public.

[*The Court Martial*, pp. 127–9, in G.D.H. Cole (ed.) *Life and Adventures*.]

*

Cobbett therefore took it upon himself at great personal risk at least of demotion or possibly a flogging to challenge the long-established corrupt practices within the army and gather evidence to bring the offenders to justice.

This project was conceived so early as the year 1787, when an affair happened, that first gave me a full insight into regimental justice. It was shortly this: that the Quarter Master, who had the issuing of the men's provisions to them, *kept about a fourth part of it to himself.* This, the old serjeants told me, had been the case *for many years*; and, they were quite astonished and terrified at the idea of my complaining of it. This I did, however; but, the reception I met with convinced me, that I must never make another complaint, 'till I got safe to England, and safe out of the reach of that most curious of courts, a *Court Martial.*—From this time forward, I began to collect materials for an exposure, upon my return to England. I had ample opportunities for this, being the keeper of all the books, of every sort, in the regiment, and knowing the whole of its affairs better than any other man. But, the winter previous to our return to England, I thought it necessary to make extracts from books, lest the books themselves should be destroyed. And, here begins the history of the famous *Court Martial*. In order to be able to *prove* that these extracts were correct, it was necessary that I should have a *witness* as to their being *true copies*. This was a very ticklish point. One foolish step here, would have sent me down to the ranks with a pair of bloody shoulders. Yet, it was necessary to have the witness. I hesitated many months. At one time, I had given the thing up. I dreamt twenty times, I dare say, of my papers being discovered, and of my being tried and flogged half to death. At last, however, some fresh act of injustice towards us made me set all danger at defiance. I opened my project to a corporal, whose name was *William Bestland*, who wrote in the office under me, who was a very honest fellow, who was very much bound to me, for my goodness to him, and who was, with the sole exception of myself, the only sober man in the *whole regiment*.—To work we went, and during a long winter, while the rest were boozing and snoring, we gutted no small part of the regimental books, rolls, and other documents. Our way was this: to take a copy, sign it with our names, and clap the regimental seal to it, so that we might be able to swear to it, when produced in court.—All these papers were put into a little box, which I myself had made for the purpose. When we came to Portsmouth, there was a talk of searching all the boxes, &c. which gave us great alarm; and induced us to take out all the papers, put them in a bag, and trust them to a custom-house officer, who conveyed them on shore, to his own house, whence I removed them in a few days after.

[*The Court Martial*, pp. 129–31, in G.D.H. Cole (ed.) *Life and Adventures*.]

*

On his return to London, he pursued the matter relentlessly, petitioning the King and obtaining an interview at the War Office with the Secretary at War, Sir Charles Yonge. Frustrated by the delay and the prospect of the Court Martial being held in Portsmouth where he believed it unlikely he would get justice, he wrote to the Prime Minister, William Pitt, and for the first time gave vent to his general distrust of the 'public robbers'.

Plainly seeing what was going forward, I, on the 7th of March, made, *in a letter to Mr. Pitt*, a representation of the whole case, giving him a history of the obstacles I had met with, which letter concluded thus: "I have now, Sir, done all a man can do in such a case. I have proceeded regularly, and, I may add, respectfully, from first to last: if I am allowed to serve my country by prosecuting men, who have injured it, I shall do it; if I am thwarted and pressed down by those, whose office it is to assist and support me, I cannot do it: in either case, I shall be satisfied with having done my duty, and shall leave the world to make a comparison between me and the men whom I have accused."—This letter (which, by-the-by, the public robbers have not published) had the effect of changing the place of the Court-martial, which was now to be held in London.

[*The Court Martial*, p. 133, in G.D.H. Cole (ed.) *Life and Adventures*.]

*

Even with the transfer of the investigation back to London, Cobbett became concerned that the regimental books upon which his charges depended would be tampered with and any witnesses put in danger of punishment. Moreover, he became convinced that he would himself be charged with sedition, if not worse. Fearing the consequences for him and for others of what was likely to be an unsuccessful attempt to bring his superiors to book he decided not to appear, in effect giving up the chance of exposing his superiors' corruption. Not for the last time, Cobbett felt himself the victim of persecution and injustice in attempting to correct abuse.

[...] as to my other great ground of complaint, the leaving of the *regimental books unsecured*, it had no effect at all; and, it will be recollected, that, without those books, there could be, as to most of the weighty charges, no proof produced [...]

Without these written documents nothing of importance could be proved, unless the non-commissioned officers and men of the regiment should happen to get the better of their dread of the lash; and, even then, they could only speak from memory. All, therefore, depended upon those written documents, as to the principal charges. Therefore, as the Court-martial was to assemble on the 24th of March, I went down to Portsmouth on the 20th, in order to know for certain what was become of the books; and, I found, as, indeed, I suspected was the case, that they had *never been secured at all*; that they had been left in the hands of the accused from the 14th of January to the very hour of trial; and that, in short, my request, as to this point, the positive condition as to this most important matter, had been totally disregarded.—There remained then, nothing to rest upon with *safety* but our extracts, confirmed by the evidence of *Bestland*, the corporal, who had signed them along with me; and this I had solemnly

engaged with him not to have recourse to, unless he was first out of the
army; that is to say, out of the reach of the vindictive and bloody lash. He
was a very little fellow: not more than about five feet high; and had been
set down to be discharged when he went to England; but, there was a
suspicion of his connection with me, and, therefore, they resolved to keep
him. It would have been cruel, and even perfidious, to have brought him
forward under such circumstances; and, as there was no chance of doing
anything without him, I resolved not to appear at the Court-martial,
unless the *discharge* of Bestland was first granted. Accordingly, on the
20th of March, I wrote, from Fratton, a village near Portsmouth, to the
Judge Advocate, stating over again all the obstacles that had been thrown
in my way, complaining particularly that the books and documents had
been left in possession of the accused, contrary to my urgent request
and to the positive assurances of the Secretary at War, and concluded
by demanding the discharge of a man, whom I should name, as the only
condition upon which I would attend the Court-martial. I requested him
to send me an answer by the next day at night, at my former lodging; and
told him, that, unless such answer was received, he and those to whom my
repeated applications had been made, might do what they pleased with
their Court-martial; for, that I confidently trusted, that a few days would
place me beyond the scope of their power.—No answer came, and, as I
had learned, in the meanwhile, that there was a design to prosecute me
for *sedition*, that was an additional motive to be quick in my movements.
As I was going down to Portsmouth, I met several of the serjeants coming
up, together with the music-master; and, as they had none of them been
in America, I wondered what they could be going to London for; but,
upon my return, I was told by a *Capt. Lane*, who had been in the regiment,
that they had been brought up to swear, that, at an entertainment given
to them by me before my departure from the regiment, I had drunk "*the
destruction of the House of Brunswick.*" This was false; but, I knew that
that was no reason why it should not be *sworn* by such persons and in
such a case. I had talked pretty freely, upon the occasion alluded to; but
I had neither said, nor thought anything against the king, and, as to the
House of Brunswick, I hardly knew what it meant. My head was filled with
the corruptions and the baseness in the army. I knew nothing at all about
politics. Nor would any threat of this sort have induced me to get out
of the way for a moment; though it certainly would, if I had known my
danger; for glorious "Jacobinical" times were just then beginning. Of this,
however, I knew nothing at all. I did not know what *the Suspension of the
Habeas Corpus Act* meant. When you have a mind to do a thing, every
trifle is an additional motive. Lane, who had enlisted me, and who had
always shown great kindness towards me, told me they would send me

to Botany Bay; and, I now verily believe, that, if I had remained, I should have furnished a pretty good example to those, who wished to correct military abuses. I did not, however, leave England from this motive. I could not obtain a chance of success, without exposing the back of my poor faithful friend Bestland, which, had I not pledged myself not to do, I would not have done. It was useless to appear, unless I could have tolerable fair play; and, besides, it seemed better to leave the whole set to do as they pleased, than to be made a mortified witness of what it was quite evident they had resolved to do.

[*The Court Martial*, pp. 134–8, in G.D.H. Cole (ed.) *Life and Adventures.*]

*

'Independence' was the great eighteenth century watchword for those who wished to criticise government corruption. After he quit the army, Cobbett embarked on a career as a teacher, bookseller and journalist in North America. It brought him into the maelstrom of controversy and partisanship over the French Revolution in which he carved a reputation as a vehemently patriotic supporter of the British government and bitter opponent of its enemies both foreign and domestic. Faced with the charge that he was in the pay of the British government, Cobbett always maintained that his motivation was entirely genuine and independent.

I have every reason to believe, that the British Consul was far from approving of some, at least, of my publications. I happened to be in a bookseller's shop, unseen by him, when he had the goodness to say, that I was a "*wild fellow.*" On which I shall only observe, that when the King bestows on me about five hundred pounds sterling a-year, perhaps, I may become a *tame fellow*, and hear my master, my countrymen, my friends, and my parents, belied and execrated, without saying one single word in their defence.

Had the Minister of Great Britain employed me to write, can it be supposed that he would not furnish me with the means of living well, without becoming the retailer of my own works? Can it be supposed, that he would have suffered me ever to appear on the scene? It must be a very poor king that he serves, if he could not afford me more than I can get by keeping a book-shop. An ambassador from a king of the gypsies, could not have acted a meaner part. What! Where was all the "gold of Pitt"?

[*The Life and Adventures of Peter Porcupine*, pp. 55, in G.D.H. Cole (ed.) *Life and Adventures.*]

*

Cobbett explained exactly what 'corruption' meant in practice, in this case pecuniary inducements were offered to writers like him to make them government supporters. He was offered a lucrative portion of the dividend from one of the loans being taken out by Pitt's government, but determined to set up his newspaper free of government influence and independent or, as he put it, 'self-dependent'.

> It was the custom in those glorious times of Pitt and Paper, to give to the literary partisans of the Government what were called 'slices' of a loan. For instance, Moses was the loan-monger; and, as the *scrip*, as it used to be called, was always directly at a premium, a bargain was always made with the loan-monger that he should admit certain favourites of the Government to have certain portions of scrip, at the same price that he gave for it; I was offered such portion of scrip,[2] which, as I was told, would put a hundred pounds or two into my pocket at once. I was frightened at the idea of becoming responsible for the immense sum, upon which this would be the profit. But I soon found that the scrip was never even to be shown to me, and that I had merely to pocket the amount of the premium. I positively refused to have anything to do with the matter, for which I got heartily laughed at. But this was of great utility to me; it opened my eyes with regard to the nature of these transactions; it set me to work to understand all about the debt and the funds and the scrip and the stock and everything belonging to it. At every step I found the thing more and more black, and more and more execrable, and it soon brought my mind to a conclusion, that the system was what the accursed thing was in the camp of the Israelites,[3] and that the nation never could be happy again until it was got rid of; in which opinion I have remained from that day to this.
>
> I set out as a sort of self-dependent politician. My opinions were my own. I dashed at all prejudices. I scorned to follow anybody in matter of opinion. Before my time, every writer of talent enlisted himself under the banners of one party, or one minister, or other. I stood free from all such connections; and, therefore, though admired by many, I was looked upon with an evil eye by all. All had been used to see men of no rank glad to receive the approbation of men of rank. All had been used to see talent crouch to power. All were, therefore, offended at my presumption, as they

---

2   Shares from which Cobbett would receive dividends.

3   In the Book of Joshua, the 'accursed thing' was loot taken from Jericho by the Israelite Achan for himself and hidden in the camp of the Israelites against the command of Yahweh for which he was stoned to death.

deemed it. My great success as a writer; the great admiration which my writings frequently excited; the effect on the public mind which they frequently produced: these were much more than sufficient to draw down on me the mortal hatred of the 'race that write'.

My undertaking was my own; it was begun without the aid, without the advice, and even without the knowledge of any person, either directly or indirectly connected with the Ministry. 'The Porcupine' never was in America, nor was it ever in England, the blind instrument of party. [...]

I had no intention to range myself in a systematic opposition to His Majesty's Ministers, or to their measures. The first object was to contribute my mite toward the support of the authority of that Sovereign, whom God had commanded me to honour and obey. The uniform intention of my writings was, and is, to counteract the effects of the enemies of monarchy in general, and of the monarchy of England in particular, under whatever guise those enemies have appeared; to check the spirit and oppose the progress of levelling innovation, whether proceeding from clubs of Jacobins, companies of traders, synagogues of saints, or boards of government; to cherish an adherence to long-tried principles, an affection for ancient families and ancient establishments.

[*The Autobiography of William Cobbett*, ed. William Reitzel (London, 1933), pp. 85–8.]

*

In July 1805 Cobbett launched a bitter attack on the Prime Minister, William Pitt the Younger, who had resumed office in 1804, for using pensions paid for by the taxpayer to 'buy' support in Parliament. His attack was all the fiercer and his sense of betrayal all the greater because of Pitt's adoption of the mantle of reformer in his early career, professing himself dedicated to economy in government and eschewing any use of government patronage in the interests of the Crown and the government of the day. With heavy irony he rebuked the 'heaven-born' Pitt with the protestations of economy he had made at the outset of his career and his practice in office, reinforced by the evidence presented to Parliament of pensions and grants to individuals by the government after his resumption of the position of Prime Minister.

THE HEAVEN-BORN MINISTER.—Actions ought always to be estimated with due reference to the professions, or the generally ascribed motives or character of the person from whom they proceed. A lavish expenditure of public money, and especially when evidently made for purposes of private ambition, or any other purpose disconnected from, if not opposed to, the good of the nation, must, in any minister, call for the censure of all loyal and public-spirited men, in whatever rank of life they may be placed; when, therefore, we see such an expenditure falling from the hands of one, who [...] acquired his power over the public purse by the most solemn promises to guard it with vigilance and fidelity; when in such a person we meet with a waste of the public treasure surpassing all former example, it is certainly just that our indignation should be greater against him than against a person from whom we had never heard any profession of purity.—The facts brought to light by the zeal and integrity of the Earl of St. Vincent and the Commissioners of Naval Inquiry have, indeed, produced a general feeling of indignation, accompanied with that astonishment, which was naturally excited by the discovery of a system of peculation so extensive under the administration of WILLIAM PITT, a name which many of us had hitherto credulously regarded as a sort of charm or spell sufficiently potent to protect us against all the demons of corruption. The greater part of us, who have the misfortune to have arrived at a state of manhood in these days so disgraceful to our country, must well remember the circumstances under which Mr. Pitt rose to the prime ministry of England. We remember, that, when he, for the first time, opened his lips in parliament, in the year 1781, it was for the purpose of severely censuring the conduct of all those, who appeared to him to be, or, whom he chose to consider, adverse to a plan for diminishing the influence and the expenses of the crown; and, that he then insisted, that it was the duty of the House of Commons to guard the properties of the people with even more care than their liberties or their lives [...] We remember, that, in his second parliamentary speech, in the same year, he complained, that there only remained to the parliament the odious power of taxing the people, and of making them pay for the minister's wild schemes and lavish corruption [...] we remember [...] the description, with which he prefaced his proposition for the making of such a reform in the Commons House of Parliament as should, in future, give to the people the means of checking the influence of the crown by preventing the public money from being lavished upon the creatures, the dependents [sic], the tools, of the minister of the day. We remember, that it was by conduct like this; by professions like these, that he obtained the good will and applause of great numbers of the honest and disinterested part of the people; and that, to this cause, more than to any other, he owed that support, which afterwards placed him, and, for so many years secured him, at the head of His Majesty's councils. We remember, that, when, in 1784, a contest arose between him and the party of which Mr. Fox was at the head, he owed his success to the opinion which the people were induced to entertain of his superior purity, of his abhorrence of all jobbing and clandestine influence of every sort, and of his resolution to adhere, in defiance of all obstacles, to a system of economy the most rigid that could be devised by the mind of man. [...] We remember, that, when, in 1785, he became minister himself, he publicly declared his resolution, never to neglect any means that might tend even in the most minute particular, to prevent abuses, or to promote economy, in the expenditure of the public money. [...] All this we now remember. [...] We found, that, at the end of his long administration; at the end of eighteen years, during which he had had the absolute command of our purses, and, politically speaking, of our persons, we found our condition much worse, in every respect much worse, than when we blindly yielded ourselves up to his sway [...] we have but a very imperfect view of the transactions [...] which have taken place, since Mr. Pitt's return to the Treasury, in May, 1804, and which transactions can be duly estimated only by a careful perusal of the whole account respecting the pensions granted by the crown, and the additions made to salaries of public offices, which account was ordered to be printed by the House of Commons [...] the vehement advocate of economy, *has mortgaged our property and our labour*, in this one year, for the purpose of gratifying his adherents, and, thereby, of *preserving his power*. [...] Another observation for the reader to make, is, that the heaven-born minister and his colleagues began their operations the moment they resumed the reins of power.

[*Political Register*, 27 July 1805.]

*

With the immediate threat of invasion in 1803–5 over, Cobbett believed that the greatest threat the country faced was the unprecedented lengths to which the government had gone to finance the war effort. Its effect was to create a whole network of corruption for which the people paid with their taxes, what he henceforth called the 'Pitt system'.

The system of upstarts; of low-bred, low-minded sycophants usurping the stations designed by nature, by reason, by the Constitution, and by the interests of the people, to men of high birth, eminent talents, or great national services; the system by which the ancient Aristocracy and the Church have been undermined; by which the ancient gentry of the kingdom have been almost extinguished, their means of support having been transferred, by the hand of the taxgatherer, to contractors, jobbers and Jews; the system by which but too many of the higher orders have been rendered the servile dependants of the minister of the day, and by which the lower, their generous spirit first broken down, have been moulded into a mass of parish fed paupers.

[*Political Register*, 20 April 1805.]

*

Cobbett's first English newspaper, *The Porcupine*, founded in October 1800, failed to achieve the expected circulation and it was sold by Cobbett in November 1801. Cobbett blamed this in part on his refusal to allow himself to sink to the level of the corrupt practices that he witnessed in the generality of the press, writing later: 'I could not sell *paragraphs*. I could not throw out hints against a man or a woman's reputation in order to bring the party forward to pay me for silence.'[4] Refusing to indulge in 'vending lies by the line and inch' he also found his expected sales to America and the West Indies frustrated by the Secretary of the Post Office who expected payment for forwarding newspapers to the Colonies. Cobbett took this as another species of corruption invoking the still novel concept of 'the Liberty of the Press' in his complaint to Lord Auckland, the Postmaster-General about the corruption of his lower officials.[5]

> But, my Lord, it is not the injury, that my interests have sustained, and do yet sustain, from the regulations of the post-offices and the conduct of its inferior officers, that would justify my having taken up so much of your Lordship's time; it is the more serious injury, which I am convinced will arise, therefrom, to the cause of truth, of real liberty, and of unfeigned loyalty, that has urged me to take up the pen on this occasion. From what I have stated, it is evident, that the Secretary of the General Post-Office and his subalterns possess an influence over the press, which no man, or set of men, ever ought to possess. We may talk about *the liberty of the press,* my Lord, but, while the Secretary has the power, in virtue of his exclusive privilege of franking, to give one news-paper, or other periodical publication, a preference over another, in America and the West Indies; while this privilege almost enables him entirely to exclude, from those extensive and populous countries, any paper, or other periodical publication, which he happens to dislike; while his power of exacting the full postage for packets (from America or elsewhere), or of remitting that postage, at his will, places every news-paper at his mercy, in a very important branch of its foreign concerns, and while the discretion, invested in him, of giving, or witholding [sic], as his interest or prejudice may dictate, the advertising custom of the General Post-Office, creates, as it ever must do, a strong temptation, in every news-printer, to truckle to his will; while the Clerks of the Roads, by carrying on the business of news-men, have it in their power to add to the sale of one news-paper, and to diminish that of another, at the same time that the public purse supports them in a very unfair rivalship against the news-men

---

4   See 'Cobbett's New Year's Gift to Old George Rose', *Political Register*, 4 January 1817.

5   For an account of *The Porcupine* and its fortunes see M.L. Pearl, *William Cobbett: a Bibliographical Account of His Life and Times* (Oxford, 1953), pp. 53–4.

of London and Westminster; while the Clerks in the foreign letter-office assume the sole proprietorship of the news that arrives by the Hamburgh mails, which news they compel the news-printers to purchase, which they sell on terms that they themselves most insolently dictate, and that they can vary towards different persons, at their pleasure; while some people in the post-office (no matter who) are permitted to publish a news-paper without a stamp, to print it in, and issue it from, buildings appropriated to the public use, and to circulate it, through the medium of the Penny-Post, postage-free, at the same time that all other news-printers are compelled to pay a heavy stamp-duty, to print and publish their papers in buildings provided at their own expense, and to allow a considerable per-centage for the circulating of them; while these things are, my Lord, we may talk about the *liberty of the press,* we may say we possess it, we may boast of it as the birthright of Englishmen; but it will exist no where, except in the imaginations of those who are unacquainted with the facts, which I have here had the honour of submitting to your Lordship.

[William Cobbett to Lord Auckland, Pall Mall, 15 June 1801, British Library Add. MSS. 34,455, ff. 403–5.]

*

Just as he maintained independence as a journalist and writer, Cobbett was at pains to demonstrate that he was not to be bought off by office. He was at pains to point out both at the time and subsequently that when his friend and ally William Windham took office in the 'Ministry of all the Talents', formed in early 1806 following the death of Pitt, he refused any favours or to compromise his right to criticise government.

When the *Whigs,* as they were called, came into power, and when Mr. Windham came to fill the high office of Secretary of State for the War and Colonial Departments, every one thought, that *my turn* to get rich was come. I was importuned by many persons *to take care of myself,* as they called it. But as soon as I found from him that he actually *was in place,* I told him, "now Sir, to make all smooth with regard to me, I beg you to be assured that it is my resolution to have no place, and not to touch one single farthing of the public money, in any shape whatever;" and justice to his memory demands that I should say, that he, upon that occasion, told me, that I never should forfeit any part of his esteem by opposing the ministry; "no", said he, "not even by any censure that you may think it your duty to pass upon my own conduct."

[*Political Register,* 4 January 1817.]

*

When in 1809, against a background of military reverses in the war against Napoleon, a scandal broke about the mistress of the Duke of York, the commander-in-chief of the army, selling army commissions, Cobbett was in little doubt that corruption threatened the very security of the nation.

> Yet, I think, it is as clear as the noon-day sun, that, if this nation is not to be conquered; if this government is not to be overthrown; if England is not to share the fate of Holland and Italy, as I trust she is not, she will owe her salvation to those, who have set about, and shall set about, and shall effect, the rooting out, while there is yet time, those corruptions, and all those abominations, which, more than the armies of Napoleon, have contributed to the fall of the old governments upon the continent of Europe.

> [*Political Register*, 18 March 1809.]

*

By the time Cobbett wrote his famous address 'To the Journeymen and Labourers' in 1816, urging the common people to obtain redress for their grievances through a reform of parliament, corruption lay at the heart of his diagnosis of what was wrong with country. The poverty and misery of the people was caused by the high taxes necessary to support the 'Pitt system' and the lavish expenditure required by governments to buy support and maintain themselves in power. Cobbett noted the more favourable position of labourers in America which had much lower taxes, a direct result of a more economical system of government. Citing the cost of a single 'placeman or pensioner' to the country at large, he argued that the resources of an intrinsically rich country and the labour of the ordinary journeymen and labourers were being exploited to support a corrupt establishment which only parliamentary reform could put right. The improvement of the condition of the people required support for parliamentary reform.

> The times in which we live are full of peril. The nation, as described by the very creatures of the government, is fast advancing to that period when an important change must take place. It is the lot of mankind, that some shall labour with their limbs and others with their minds; and, on all occasions more especially on an occasion like the present, it is the duty of the latter to come to the assistance of the former. We are equally interested in the peace and happiness of our common country. It is of the utmost importance, that in the seeking to obtain those objects, our endeavours should be uniform, and tend all to the same point. Such an uniformity

cannot exist without an uniformity of sentiment as to public matters, and to produce this later uniformity amongst you is the object of this address.

As to the *cause* of our present miseries, it is the *enormous amount of the taxes*, which the government compels us to pay for the support of its army, its placemen, its pensioners, &c. and for the payment of the interest of its debt. That this is the *real* cause has been a thousand times proved; and, it is now so acknowledged by the creatures of the government themselves. *Two hundred and five* of the Correspondents of the Board of Agriculture ascribe the ruin of the country to *taxation*. Numerous writers, formerly the friends of the Pitt System, now declare, that taxation has been the cause of our distress. Indeed, when we compare our present state to the state of the country previous to the war against France, we must see that our present misery is owing to no other cause. The taxes then annually raised amounted to about 15 millions: they amounted last year to 70 millions. The nation was then happy: it is now miserable.

['To the Journeymen and Labourers of England, Wales, Scotland, and Ireland', *Political Register*, 2 November 1816.]

Chapter 3
Patriotism and Nationalism

Cobbett was an avowed patriot. As a self-styled 'calf of John Bull' it was a concept fundamental to almost all his writings on politics and the general state of the nation. He recorded how as a youth his patriotic feelings were aroused by the sight of the fleet at anchor, convincing him that he should seek a career as a sailor. His account of how this sight affected him implies that he had been brought up on tales of past naval victories and, as he later implied, the feats of British arms over the centuries. Frustrated in his desire to join the navy, the army claimed him and he made his career as a soldier on the 'imperial frontier' in Canada, where the infant United States was an ever-present threat to British possessions. Released from the army, Cobbett's first sojourn in the United States from 1792 found his patriotism sharpened in the aftermath of the French Revolution. Setting himself up as the defender of 'Old England' he positively invited opposition and revelled in the opportunities it gave him to extol its virtues and pour scorn upon its enemies both at home and abroad.

His return to England as someone who had championed the war policy of Pitt's government through thick and thin put him at odds with the growing war-weariness of the country and the readiness of the government to seek a respite. One of the few people to publicly oppose the short-lived Peace of Amiens, he found himself on the receiving end of popular disfavour. Welcoming the return of hostilities in 1803 he authored a rallying-cry against a French invasion distributed by the government the length and breadth of the country. But Cobbett was at pains to distinguish his patriotism from the craven 'loyalism' of the hangers-on of government and the financiers and office-holders who he saw as making a profit from the war. Disillusioned with the conduct of the war and enraged by its, to him, ruinously expensive and corrupt financing, he increasingly identified his form of patriotism with calls for an efficient conduct of the war and the need for reform.

Cobbett's patriotic feelings did not necessarily lead him to a narrow-minded xenophobia. He inveighed against the barbarities of the French Jacobins and the cruelties the Napoleonic armies imposed on conquered territories, but was ready to praise in the warmest terms the French people he had met in 1792 and even to admit that some of Napoleon's reforms had been beneficial to the people of France. He had taught English to Frenchmen who had fled the revolution and composed a French Grammar. Hostility towards the Scots was a feature of the early years of the reign of George III when complaints against carpet-bagging Scots, not least the unpopular Prime Minister, the Earl of Bute, were commonplace. Cobbett would have taken them in as a boy, but later softened them as he saw them as fellow subjects oppressed by a corrupt government. Most remarkable of all he never showed the anti-Catholicism which had often characterised English patriotism in the past. It made him ready to include the Irish as fellow countrymen. Cobbett often used the words English and British indiscriminately, seemingly subsuming everyone, Irish, Scots and Welsh into his idea of 'Old England', as he wrote: 'I have never been able, for single moment, to look upon Ireland or Scotland, other than as parts of my native country. I have never been able for one single moment, to view an Irishman as other than my own countryman.'[1]

*

Cobbett claimed his patriotic instincts were first stimulated in seeing the British fleet at anchor in Portsmouth, stirring him to prove himself worthy of his forbears.

> Towards the autumn of 1782, I went to visit a relation who lived in the neighbourhood of Portsmouth. From the top of Portsdown, I, for the first time, beheld the sea, and no sooner did I behold it, than I wished to be a sailor. I could never account for this sudden impulse, nor can I now. Almost all English boys feel the same inclination: it would seem that, like young ducks, instinct leads them to rush on the bosom of the water.
>
> But it was not the sea alone that I saw: the grand fleet was riding at anchor at Spithead. I had heard of the wooden walls of Old England: I had formed my ideas of a ship, and of a fleet; but, what I now beheld, so far surpassed what I had ever been able to form a conception of, that I stood lost between astonishment and admiration. I had heard talk of the glorious deeds of our admirals and sailors, of the defeat of the Spanish Armada, and of all those memorable combats, that good and true Englishmen never fail to relate to their children about a hundred times a year. The brave Rodney's victories over our natural enemies, the French and Spaniards, had long been the theme of our praise, and the burden of our songs. The sight of the fleet brought all these into my mind; in confused order, it is true, but with irresistible force. My heart was inflated with national pride. The sailors were my countrymen; the fleet belonged to my country, and surely I had my part in it, and in all its honours; yet, these honours I had not earned; I took to myself a sort of reproach, for possessing what I had no right to, and resolved to have a just claim by sharing in the hardships and dangers.

[*The Life and Adventures of Peter Porcupine*, pp. 24–5, in G.D.H. Cole (ed.) *Life and Adventures*.]

---

[1]   *Political Register*, 11 March 1834.

*

Cobbett demonstrated his patriotism during his residence in America when his showing of a print celebrating the British naval victory over the French on the 1 June 1794 aroused strong opposition amongst many Americans. Cobbett chided them for their attitude.

> The next charge is, I have "the *astonishing effrontery* to expose for sale, certain prints, indicative of the prowess of the British, and the disgrace of the French." Here the hang-in-chains writer alludes to a print, entitled, "Earl Howe's Decisive Victory over the French Fleet, on the first of June, 1794." This print has had a vast concourse of admirers. I had but two of them, one was sold instantly, and I have had more than five hundred applications for the other. What is very singular, is, that one-third part of those who have wished to purchase this print were French Republicans. The print is not sold, nor shall it be. I will keep it in my window, as long as any violence is talked of, and when that ceases, I will have it put in a gilt frame, and hung up in a conspicuous part of my house.
>
> This offensive print is no more than a true representation of the action of the famous *first of June*, and if it be "indicative of the disgrace of our allies," it is no fault of mine. If defeat is disgrace, they were certainly most shockingly disgraced on that day. But, I thought it had long ago agreed on, that, though the fleet got a drubbing, and a pretty decent one too, the victory was, *in fact*, on the side of the French. I am sure Barrere told the French people so; and I am sure most of our Newspapers told the people of America the same story. How many believed them, I will not pretend to say; but if it was a victory, *in fact*, I am treating people with a representation of it, that's all, and am by no means exposing what is "indicative of British prowess."
>
> When William Penn was tracing out his beloved city of Philadelphia; if any one had told him, that the time would come, when a man should be threatened with murder, for offering for sale, in one of the streets, a print "indicative of British prowess," I must question, if the good man, though a Quaker, would not have said that it was a d—ned lie. Poor old fellow! he little dreamed what was to happen at the close of the "enlightened eighteenth century."
>
> I could turn back to American publications, in which the prowess of Britons is the pleasing theme; in which the French are called, what I never called them, "poor effeminate poltroons." I could bring my readers back to the time, when they set the savages on to scalp the people of these States, and when the people of these States solicited the King of Great Britain to march an army against them. Had the American Revolution entirely changed the dispositions, affections, and even nature of the two rival nations? Did

Great Britain lose every spark of courage, generosity, and virtue, when she lost America? That event certainly could not metamorphose the then inhabitants of the Island, nor could it have any great effect on their children, or at least I presume so. The people of the United States have solemnly declared, in their declaration of Independence, that the British nation are by nature, *just* and *magnanimous*; and will they now swallow their words at the command of the hirelings of the devastators of France?

To return to the print "indicative of British prowess;" have I not as good a right to exhibit proof of this prowess at my window, as the Democrats have to exhibit the proofs of theirs on the front of the church opposite it? The half-destroyed bust of George II. remains as a monument of their valour, and why should I not be permitted to expose a print to perpetuate the valour of Earl Howe and his gallant fleet? These two pieces are, besides, necessary as the explanation of each other; for when a stranger asks, why the bust of the old king was so unmercifully mangled, the person he addresses himself to, shows him the naval victory of Lord Howe. "There, Sir," says he, "is the fatal cause." If the impertinent querist goes on, and asks, how George of Scotland, who died upwards of thirty years ago (and whose bust remained untouched during the whole of the American war) could deserve this rough treatment on account of the drubbing given to the French fleet in 1794, we cut him short at once, by telling him, that he is a rank aristocrat, and totally unfit to live in a land of freedom.

[*The Scarecrow*, pp. 76–80, in G.D.H. Cole (ed.) *Life and Adventures*.]

*

In September 1800 in a prospectus for a new daily newspaper, *The Porcupine*, Cobbett attested his passionate commitment to Britain's war with France and extolled the benefits of the British monarchy to the nation.

THE PORCUPINE will, of course, embrace all the usual topics of a Newspaper: Parliamentary and Law Reports, Court, City, and Country News, &c.–An early and correct account of those foreign events, which may be considered as *news* is a thing so much in the beaten track, and so indispensably necessary, that any specific promise on that head would be superfluous; but it may not be amiss to mention, that, to faithful translations from foreign journals, I shall endeavour to add such a commentary as will prevent my paper from being (what too many others are) a mere vehicle for those articles, which are fabricated on the Continents of Europe and America, for the sole purpose of deceiving the too credulous people of this kingdom. The intrigues of the French, the servile, the insidious, the insinuating French, shall be an object of my constant attention. Whether at war or at peace with us, they still dread the power, envy the happiness, and thirst for the ruin of England. Collectively and individually, the whole and every one of them hate us. Had they the means, they would exterminate us to the last man; they would snatch the crutch from our parents, the cradle from our children, and our happy country itself would they sink beneath those waves, on which they now flee from the thunder of our cannon. When we shall sheath the sword it is for our Sovereign to say; but, while we retain one drop of true British blood in our veins, we never shall shake hands with this perfidious and sanguinary race, much less shall we make a compromise with their monkey-like manners and tiger-like principles. [...]

The subjects of a British King, like the sons of every provident and tender father, never know his value till they feel the want of his protection. In the days of youth and of ignorance, I was led to believe, that comfort, freedom, and virtue, were exclusively the lot of Republicans. A very short trial convinced me of my error, admonished me to repent of my folly, and urged me to compensate for the injustice of the opinions I have conceived. During an eight years absence from my country, I was not an unconcerned spectator of her perils, nor did I listen, in silence, to the slanders of her enemies. Though divided from England by the ocean, though her gay fields were hidden, perhaps for ever, from my view, still her happiness and her glory were the objects of my constant solicitude; I rejoiced at her victories, and mourned at her defeats; her friends were my friends, and her foes were my foes. Once more returned; once more under the safeguard of that Sovereign, who watched over me in my infancy, and the want of whose protecting arm I have so long had occasion to lament, I feel an irresistible desire to communicate to my countrymen the fruit of my experience; to show them the injurious and degrading consequences of discontentment, disloyalty, and innovation; to convince them, that they are the freest, as well as happiest, of the human race; and, above all, to warn them against the arts of those ambitious and perfidious demagogues, who would willingly reduce them to a level with the cheated slaves, in the bearing of whose yoke I have had the mortification to share.

[*Prospectus of a New Daily Paper to be entitled The Porcupine By William Cobbett*, (London, 1800).]

*

Cobbett's continued commitment to the war with France at the same time as the government sought to make peace and the country was becoming war-weary put him at odds with the crowds which joyfully greeted the French representative and prepared to celebrate the signing of peace preliminaries. He railed against the mob's behaviour.

Pall Mall, 10 October 1801.

Sir,

   With that sort of dread, which seizes on a man when he has heard, or thinks he has heard, a supernatural voice predicting his approaching end, I sit down to inform you, that the guns are now firing for the peace, and that half an hour ago, a very numerous crowd, *drew the Aide de Camp of Bonaparte in triumph through Pall Mall!*[2] [...] The modest sansculotte bore all this with great complacency, as you may easily suppose; whether the *peace-makers* saw it with unconcern I know not, but I know that it has sunk my heart within me, and I look forward to a revolution with as great certainty as I do to Christmas or New Year's day. This is the first time an English mob ever became the cattle of a *Frenchman;* and, they are willing to be such now, not because the[y] love the Frenchman as such, but because he is one of those who have killed kings and queens and noblemen, and have destroyed rank and property. This indication of the temper and sentiments of the lower orders is a most awful consideration. Whether it will make any impression on the peacemakers I do not know. You must remember, Sir, that previous to the revolutions in Switzerland and elsewhere, we always heard of *some French messenger of peace being received with caresses by the people*; the next post or two brought us an account of partial discontents, tumults, insurrections, murders and revolutions always closed the history. God preserve us from the like, but I am afraid our abominations are to be punished in this way.

[William Cobbett to William Windham, British Library Add. MSS. 37,853, f. 14.]

*

His refusal to illuminate his windows in celebration of the peace preliminaries led to the anticipated attack upon his house, but left his views on the war unchanged.

For the Government to illuminate, is, in fact, to *force* every private person to follow its example, or, to expose him to the insults and violences of the mob. Do I say, then, that Government is *never* to exhibit this mark of joy and applause? No. There are certain events, at which every *good* and *loyal* subject must *necessarily* rejoice; such, for instance, as the return of the Birth Day

---

2   General Lauriston.

of the King, a signal victory over the enemy, or the like, in the celebrating of which the Ministry may, with great propriety, take the lead. But, I do conceive, my Lord, that it is not very proper, nor very seemly, for *Ministers* to force (either directly or indirectly), or even to invite, the public to applaud, and exult at, *any,* measure of *the Cabinet*, more especially a measure, the only apology that can be offered for which, is, *dire necessity*.–There are many considerations, which may induce a man to *submit* quietly, and in silence, to national calamity and disgrace: but nothing short of the most odious and detestable tyranny can make him join in *rejoicing* at either. This species of tyranny, my Lord, I have had to resist.

From the scenes of violence and outrage, which had taken place on the preceding Wednesday night, in some parts of the town, not far from Pall-Mall, I had reason to expect, that, on the arrival of the Ratification of the Preliminaries, my dwelling-house here, as well as my Printing-Office in Southampton-street, would be attacked; because my sentiments respecting those Preliminaries were publicly known, and because it could not be imagined that I should belie by any manifestation of joy at night, the principles and sentiments, which I had promulgated in the morning. Impressed, my Lord, with this belief, and still more deeply impressed with the ideas, which I had imbibed in my childhood, that an Englishman's house was his castle, and that every subject of His MAJESTY possessed the right of exercising his unbiassed judgement, so long as he paid implicit obedience to the laws of the realm, I made application to the Bow-street Magistrates for legal protection. At their desire I went to their office, and was very politely received by the Magistrates then sitting, Mr. BOND and Sir WILLIAM PARSONS, to whom I related the grounds of my apprehensions, and from whom I received a promise of all *practicable* protection.

It happened, my Lord, precisely as I had expected, about eight o'clock in the evening, my dwelling-house was attacked, by an innumerable mob, all my windows were broken, and when this was done, which occupied about an hour, the villains were preparing to break into my shop, and had actually made one of the shutters give way. Fearing that the cannibals might murder myself and my children, I now ordered my windows to be lighted; but even this, my Lord, did not satisfy this unlawful and ferocious rabble, who, ever and anon howled out that I was the publisher of the PORCUPINE. The attack continued at intervals, till past one o'clock on the Sunday morning. During the whole of this time, not a constable, nor peace officer of any description, made his appearance; nor was the smallest interruption given to the proceedings of this ignorant and brutal mob, who were thus celebrating the Peace. [...]

"*You stand alone*," say some persons. This is not true to the extent which is meant to be conveyed by the words. I do, indeed, stand almost alone with respect to the demolition of my house; but, had no fear of the mob existed in London and Westminster, that house would have been amongst the vast majority. The *Public Offices* gave an invitation to a general manifestation of joy, and the rabble *enforced* it. When I began my opposition to French principles and French influence in America, even my countrymen called on me to desist, telling me that I "stood *alone*;'" but I stood long enough to find myself in the majority. I stood long enough to hear *ça ira* exchanged for *God save the King*. I stood long enough to see the people of Philadelphia, who had threatened to murder me because I openly exhibited, at my window, a picture of Lord HOWE's victory over the French; I stood long enough to see these very people make a public celebration of Lord NELSON's victory of the Nile. Nay, my Lord, I stood long enough to see the time, when I was the only writer in the country, who dared to stand forward on behalf of a body of injured and unfortunate *Frenchmen*, who finally owed to me, and to me alone, their deliverance from ruin, and, perhaps, from death.

But, my Lord, with shame and grief I confess, that the Americans were not so far gone in baseness as Englishmen now are. Amidst all their Republican follies, they still retained some little sense of national honour. Their government did, indeed, repeatedly debase itself at the feet of the insolent tyrants of France; but, there was always a considerable portion of the people, who put in their unequivocal protest against this debasement; and, never did even the vilest of the rabble dare to become the beasts of the *sans-culotte* agents. We have seen the Americans make Peace with France; since that we have seen the French Envoy arrive amongst them; but, we have heard of no public demonstrations of joy on the occasion, much less have we heard of any scene, such as that which was exhibited in London, on the 10th of October. They received him, as it was proper to receive the agent of an insidious and malignant foe, with whom they found it necessary to live in peace; without insult, indeed, but with coldness and reserve. They knew the value of Peace as well as we: they knew they had neither fleet nor army to carry on War; they yielded too far to the enemy; they, too, may be justly accused of cowardice; but they have not, like us, proclaimed that cowardice to the world, through every channel that sound or sense can supply.

However, my Lord, England, humble and base as she is become, is still my country; and, though I can neither retrieve her character nor prevent her destruction, it is my duty to stand by her side, and partake in her fate. I feel some consolation, too, in reflecting, that, if my children should out-live the storm, and see better days, they will remember, with pride, that their father never bowed the knee to the regicides of France.

[*Letters to the Right Honourable Lord Hawkesbury, and to the Right Honourable Henry Addington, on the Peace with Bonaparte, to which is added, an Appendix,* Letter III, 16 October 1801, pp. 15–18, 23–5.]

*

In spite of his rough handling by the mob Cobbett retained faith in the basic loyalty of the people and their attachment to a sense of national honour which he shared.

And, as to the other great public virtue, patriotism, which, when it exists in its proper degree, is a principle of the mind as strong and as uniform in its effects, as a love of kindred or of life itself; whence does it arise? Not from the desire to get a contract or a job, like that of the patriotism of Sir Brook's committees; not from anxiety for the funds like that of the patriotism of Lloyd's and the bank: not from an affection for the earth, the mere dirt, for the dirt is still dirt, whatever be its geographical description. In the minds of the great and the rich, the principle of patriotism may be strengthened by consideration of individual interest; but, amongst the common people, the fighting part of the community, the prospect seldom extends beyond food and raiment; food and raiment, indeed, of a coarser or finer sort; but, after all, food and raiment are every thing that any soil, under any government, can possibly give them. It is true, that every man has an instinctive attachment to the spot where he first drew his breath; but, his country may be conquered without at all interrupting the indulgence of this grovelling feeling; and, as to mere appellation, in that respect, even Rome herself has lost nothing. No, Sir; in none of these has the virtue of patriotism its foundation, but in that anxious desire, which every man of sound sense and honest nature has, to see preserved untarnished the reputation of that country which he is obliged to own, whose name he can never shake off, from whose calamities he may possibly flee, but in all whose disgraces he must inevitably share. What, for instance, induced me, when so far distant from my country, voluntarily to devote myself to her cause? Her commerce? I neither knew nor cared anything about it. Her funds? I was so happy as hardly to understand the meaning of the word. Her lands? I could, alas! lay claim to nothing but the graves of my parents.–What, then, was the stimulus? What was I proud of? It was the name and fame of England. Her laws, her liberties, her justice, her might; all the qualities and circumstances that had given her renown in the world, but above all her deeds in arms, her military glory.

[*Political Register*, 27 October 1804.]

*

The renewal of war with France in 1803 gave Cobbett the opportunity for violent denunciation of the French regime, a graphic depiction of the consequences of an invasion, and a patriotic rallying-cry in *Important Considerations for the People of this Kingdom*. First printed in the *Political Register* in July 1803, unattributed, it was reprinted the same month and distributed by the government, headed with the Royal Coat of Arms, to the officiating minister of every parish in England and Wales for display and distribution. Cobbett, who was concerned to maintain his independence, only disclosed his authorship of his 'fight them on the beaches' polemic six year later.

> The same generals, the same commissaries, the same officers, the same soldiers, the very same rapacious and sanguinary host, that now hold Holland and Switzerland in chains, that desolated Egypt, Italy, and Germany, are, at this moment, preparing to make England, Ireland, and Scotland, the scenes of their atrocities. For some time past, they have had little opportunity to plunder: peace, for a while, suspended their devastations, and now, like gaunt and hungry wolves, they are looking towards the rich pastures of Britain: already we hear their threatening howl; and if, like sheep, we stand bleating for mercy, neither our innocence nor our timidity will save us from being torn to pieces and devoured. The robberies, the barbarities, the brutalities they have committed in other countries, though, at the thought of them, the heart sinks and the blood runs cold, will be mere trifles to what they will commit here, if we suffer them to triumph over us. The Swiss and the Suabians were never objects of their envy; they were never the rivals of Frenchmen, either on the land or on the sea; they had never disconcerted or checked their ambitious projects, never humbled their pride, never defeated either their armies or their fleets. We have been and we have done all this: they have long entertained against us a hatred engendered by the mixture of envy and of fear; and they are now about to make a great and desperate effort to gratify this furious, this unquenchable, this deadly hatred. What then, can we expect at their hands? What but torments, even surpassing those which they have inflicted on other nations. They remained but three months in Germany; here they would remain for ever; there, their extortions and atrocities were, for want of time, confined to a part of the people; here they would be universal: no sort, no part, no particle of property would remain

unseized; no man, woman or child would escape violence of some kind or other. Such of our manufactories as are moveable, they would transport to France, together with the most ingenious of the manufacturers, whose wives and children would be left to starve. Our ships would follow the same course, with all the commerce and commercial means of the kingdom. Having stripped us of every thing, even to the stoutest of our sons, and the most beautiful of our daughters, over all that remained they would establish and exercise a tyranny, such as the world never before witnessed. All the estates, all the farms, all the mines, all the land and the houses, all the shops and magazines, all the remaining manufactories, and all the workshops, of every kind and description, from the greatest to the smallest; all these they would bring over Frenchmen to possess; making us their servants and their labourers. To prevent us from uniting and rising against them, they would crowd every town and village with their brutal soldiers, who would devour all the best part of the produce of the earth, leaving us not half a sufficiency of bread. They would, besides, introduce their own bloody laws, with additional severities: they would divide us into separate classes; hem us up in districts; cut off all communication between friends and relations, parents and children, which latter they would breed up in their own blasphemous principles; they would affix badges upon us, mark us in the cheek, shave our heads, split our ears, or clothe us in the habit of slaves!–And, shall we submit to misery and degradation like this, rather than encounter the expenses of war; rather than meet the honourable dangers of military combat; rather than make a generous use of the means which Providence has so bounteously placed in our hands? The sun, in his whole course round the globe, shines not on a spot so blessed as this great, and now united Kingdom; gay and productive fields and gardens, lofty and extensive woods, innumerable flocks and herds, rich and inexhaustible mines, a mild and wholesome climate, giving health, activity, and vigour to fourteen millions of people; and shall we, who are thus favoured and endowed; shall we, who are abundantly supplied with iron and steel, powder and lead; shall we, who have a fleet superior to the maritime force of all the world, and who are able to bring two millions of fighting men into the field; shall we yield up this dear and happy land, together with all the liberties and honours, to preserve which our fathers so often dyed the land and the sea with their blood; shall we, thus, at once dishonour their graves, and stamp disgrace and infamy on the brows of our children; and shall we, too, make this base and dastardly surrender to an enemy, whom, within these twelve years, our countrymen have defeated in every quarter of the world? No; we are not so miserably fallen; we cannot, in so short a space of time have become so detestably degenerate: we have the strength and the will to repel the hostility, to chastise the insolence of the foe. Mighty, indeed, must be our efforts, but mighty also is the need. Singly engaged against the tyrants of the earth, Britain now attracts the eyes and the hearts of mankind; groaning nations look to her for deliverance; justice, liberty, and religion are inscribed on her banners; her success will be hailed with the shouts of the universe, while tears of admiration and gratitude will bedew the heads of her sons, who fall in the glorious contest.

[*Political Register*, 30 July 1803.]

*

Increasingly critical of the conduct of the war and the venality and corruption of successive governments, Cobbett was enraged that the loyalty and patriotism of the people was being taken for granted. He took great exception to a speech towards the end of the war by George Canning, MP for Liverpool and later Foreign Secretary and Prime Minister, who claimed the people should resist the French irrespective of conditions at home.

We are told, that it is an "*instinctive* patriotism," a "*devotion to native soil*, which is the foundation of *national independence*." We will, by and by, inquire what is meant by these two last words, the use of which is so common, and the meaning of which is so very vague; but, at present, let us suppose that the Speaker means, that the effect of this "*instinctive* patriotism," this "*devotion to native soil*," is the exertion of a people to keep an enemy out of their country. In other words, that there requires nothing but this love of their native soil to make men fight against an invader; that this feeling, "this genuine feeling of the heart," is quite sufficient without any other consideration. But, not to speak of the *fact* again yet, how does this agree with the Speaker's observation, that men fight for the *homes* in which they have dwelt; for their *wives and children*, and other objects? They fight, he says, against an invader, because these objects, so dear to them, should not be *exposed to violence*. In short, they hazard their lives in repelling invasion, because they fear that the invader will take away *their property and make them miserable;* and, not because they fear he will insult or dishonour the dirt upon which they walk, or the place where they happen to have been born, and upon which particular spot not one out of five hundred is living.— What becomes, then, of his doctrine of "*instinctive* patriotism," if it be for houses, goods, chattels, churches, wives and children, that men repel invasion? These are under the safe-guard of laws, that is to say, *political institutions*, without which there can be no property, or ownership, in anything.—What becomes, then, of his degrading doctrine; what becomes of his assertion, that a mere cattle-like attachment to the earth, is of itself sufficient to make men fight against an invading enemy? [...] we see "many nations" actuated, in this question of invasion, not by any "*instinctive*" feeling about the *soil;* but by motives of self-interest; by considerations connected with their property and political institutions; we see them, in short, making *calculations*, putting the good against the evil likely to arise to them from the invasion of their country; and deciding in favour of the former. We see "*whole nations; many nations,*" acting thus; Mr. Canning himself exhibits them to us as thus acting; and yet, with the statement of this fact, this notorious fact, upon his lips, he, from his innate love of cattle-like feeling in the people, he tells his hearers, that a twenty years' war had decided this great question, has put reforming philosophy to shame, and has clearly proved, that "*a devotion to native soil*" alone is the foundation of national independence, and that is quite sufficient for the purpose of keeping out or driving out an invader, without the aid of any motive connected with political institutions.

[*Political Register*, 5 February 1814.]

*

But Cobbett was no xenophobe. Whatever his strictures on the French Jacobins he had a kind regard for the common people of France based on his short-lived visit in 1792.

I arrived in France in March, 1792, and continued there till the beginning of September following, the six happiest months of my life. I should be the most ungrateful monster that ever existed, were I to speak ill of the French people in general. I went to that country full of all those prejudices, that Englishmen suck in with their mother's milk, against the French and against their religion: a few weeks convinced me that I had been deceived with respect to both. I met everywhere with civility, and even hospitality, in a degree that I never had been accustomed to. I found the people, among whom I lived, excepting those who were already blasted with the principles of the accursed revolution, honest, pious, and kind to excess.

People may say what they please about the misery of the French peasantry, under the old government; I have conversed with thousands of them, not ten among whom did not regret the change. I have not room here to go into an inquiry into the causes that have led these people to become the passive instruments, the slaves of a set of tyrants such as the world never saw before, but I venture to predict, that, sooner or later, they will return to that form of government under which they were happy and under which alone they can ever be so again.

[*The Life and Adventures of Peter Porcupine*, pp. 39–40, in G.D.H. Cole (ed.) *Life and Adventures*.]

*

Similarly, Cobbett refused to share in the common prejudices against the Irish or their religion. Though visiting Ireland late in his life he was fulsome in his recognition of their sufferings at the hands of the English.

I never have been able, for one single moment, to view an Irishman other than as my own countryman; and, I could appeal to the acts of my whole life, in proof of my practice having been consonant with my principle in this respect. Therefore, I have always considered the wrongs done to Ireland (and they are beyond all number, and beyond all calculations as to magnitude); I have always considered these wrongs as participated in by myself. [...]

They have been a miserable people, and, perhaps, more or less so from the time of the assumption of the sovereignty of England over Ireland. Certainly from the time of the Reformation, as it is falsely called, from the time that "old BESS" sent over her Protestant parsons; from that time there has been great suffering on the part of the people of Ireland, and from a very obvious cause; but, what does this prove as to the native character of the Irish people? For three hundred years it has been a Catholic people, tyrannized over by a Protestant hierarchy; and unprovided, observe, with any of that relief for the indigent, which the Roman Catholic church so amply provided for them. It is notorious; it is recorded in the most authentic documents, that rebellion after rebellion was excited for the express purpose of forming pretences for confiscation. It is notorious that JAMES the First seized upon whole counties, as his property, unless the owners and possessors of the soil could produce the original grants from the crown; and that his Attorney-General ousted them by ejectments in behalf of the King, as sovereign lord of all the land. And, because a people became miserable under such Government as this; under such at once savage, cool, and hypocritical tyranny as this, having what they deemed a damnable heresy imposed upon them at the same time, as the sole condition of their preserving their property; is it surprising that, under treatment like this, a people should become miserable and almost barbarous?

[*Political Register*, 17 May 1834.]

Chapter 4
Parliamentary Reform

Cobbett was to become renowned in the early nineteenth century as one of the leading advocates of parliamentary reform, namely an overhaul of the system of political representation, voting rights and the conduct of elections. Starting from a conservative position in which he thought little or no change was necessary, he gradually extended his view of the extent of what was required. He remained, however, always a reformer rather than a revolutionary, concentrating his efforts on making the House of Commons reflect the needs of the country as Cobbett viewed them. In the run-up to the first major breakthrough of the parliamentary reformers in the 'Great' Reform Act of 1832, Cobbett was one of the major voices of the popular wing of the reform movement, a movement which stretched from the corridors of Parliament to the fields, workshops and factories of a rapidly changing country. He became through his *Political Register* and other writings not only a major critic of government corruption and its mishandling of affairs but also the voice of the artisans, labourers and workmen who remained largely unheard under the existing arrangements. When Cobbett began his journalistic career, the electoral system was both archaic and wholly unrepresentative in a modern, democratic sense. Only a tiny percentage of the population, less than five per cent, possessed the vote, there were no women voters at all, and voting qualifications varied wildly, resting upon a hotch-potch of customary arrangements. The distribution of seats bore no relation to that of the current population, with many growing commercial and industrial centres, such as Manchester and Birmingham, completely unrepresented, and once important places which had dwindled into insignificance or even disappeared altogether still sent members to parliament. Many constituencies, especially the English towns or 'boroughs' and many Scottish seats, were effectively under the control of local landowners who could often 'nominate' who the members were. Many seats were filled without a contest and some remained uncontested for decades during the eighteenth century. The small size or even non-existence of many borough electorates produced a parliament dominated by members elected by a totally unrepresentative fraction of the population. In 1776 it was estimated that of the 558 members, 224 were produced from a *total* electorate of only 5,723 persons. This combination led critics to claim that the majority of seats in the House of Commons were under the influence of the government of the day or a small group of large landowners, many of them sitting in the House of Lords. It was common for the government to be able to virtually appoint MPs they favoured to some of the seats it controlled, while many seats were effectively in the gift of powerful landed families. Indeed, according to a modern authority, Professor John Cannon, there were as many as over 250 borough seats under some degree of influence.[1] Moreover when elections occurred they were often noted for their violence and intimidation, a consequence of voting taking place in the open, usually over several days or weeks, in which 'treating' with money, drink and accommodation was an accepted part of electioneering. In effect politics was a rich man's game, electioneering was expensive and in any event a property qualification debarred all but the well-to-do from becoming MPs, who also had to be able to support themselves without any formal salary while members.

Criticism of the electoral system had developed in the mid-eighteenth century against the loss of 'independence' of the House of Commons, particularly in periods of political contention. Fears after the accession of George III in 1760 of the monarchy utilising a corrupt system to dominate the House of Commons and destroy its independence led to demands for reform of various aspects of the system. Much the most comprehensive were the proposals put forward by Major John Cartwright in the 1770s, for manhood suffrage, annually elected parliaments, equally-sized constituencies, secret ballot, no property qualification for MPs and payment of MPs. This was to remain the 'radical' programme of parliamentary reform well into the nineteenth century. For many potential reformers these proposals were far too radical and various more modest proposals to reclaim the independence of the House of Commons were suggested. British failures in the American War of Independence led to a powerful call, taken up by the Prime Minister of the day, William Pitt the Younger, to remove seats from some of the smaller boroughs and redistribute them to the larger towns and the counties, where there were larger numbers of voters. Others ventured proposals for parliaments to be elected every three years, 'Triennial Parliaments', instead of the existing seven, and widening the franchise in varying degrees.

With the ending of the American War, pressure for reform fell away and Pitt was unable to obtain a majority even for modest proposals in 1785, after which he put the subject aside. There was a revival of interest in parliamentary reform with the outbreak of the French Revolution in 1789. As well as a renewal of modest proposals to reduce oligarchic control of seats, the radical writings of Thomas Paine, notably his *Rights of Man*, published in two parts in 1791–2, popularised the idea of a radical overhaul of parliament, effectively creating a republican regime and abolishing the House of Lords, and the introduction of universal suffrage, at least for men. Popular reform societies sprang up in response in places such as London, Sheffield and Manchester, drawing artisans and labourers into organised political agitation for the first time. But the excesses of the French revolutionaries, including the execution of the French King and Queen, the coming of war with France in 1793 and growing alarm at the spread of radical ideas, provoked a conservative reaction of which Cobbett was initially

---

[1]   J. Cannon, *Parliamentary Reform, 1640–1832* (Cambridge, 1973), p. 50, n. 1.

a part. In the event many pro-reformers were disillusioned by what they saw happening when reform was attempted across the Channel, but the government saw to it that radicals were persecuted, the laws of treason extended, and public meetings put under restriction in what became known by opponents as Pitt's 'Reign of Terror'. Although mild in comparison to what was happening under the Jacobins in France during the 1790s, the repression effectively suppressed the reformers and the popular reform movement had virtually ceased to exist or been driven underground by the end of the decade.

Initially, Cobbett was as vehement an opponent of parliamentary reform as he was later to be its advocate. His initial opposition was part and parcel of his patriotic defence of the traditional status quo against its foreign enemies and domestic critics like the dissenters, Dr Joseph Priestley and Dr Richard Price, and the supporter of American Independence, Thomas Paine, all of whom to Cobbett appeared little short of traitors to 'Old England'. Indeed he set out his strong opposition to reform in a pamphlet condemning Priestley on his emigration to the United States in 1794. Cobbett remained an anti-reformer well into the second phase of the Napoleonic Wars, although increasingly disillusioned with the conduct of government and the onerous cost of the war to ordinary people. As late as 1806 his opinion was that parliamentary reform would not correct the corrupt 'Pitt system' which he saw as the cause of the high taxes which brought misery and poverty to the common people. That year, however, he considered standing for the seat of Honiton and declared himself an enemy to votes changing hands for money, pledging himself to an anti-bribery stance. He allied this to a determination, if elected, to remain 'independent' and not join the ranks of so many other MPs as subject to 'influence', from government or opposition. Under the pressure of continuing war and evidence of military incompetence and corruption, reform ideas saw a revival from 1807 in which Cobbett found himself forced to consider more radical measures of parliamentary reform. Where he had once believed that the elimination of bribery at election would cure *all* the nation's ills by ensuring an independent House of Commons, he now argued that end could only be obtained by introducing manhood suffrage and 'Annual Parliaments'. Thus in 1816 Cobbett solemnly urged the Luddites, the machine-breakers reacting to the post-war distress, that it was not machinery that was the cause of their misfortunes but a corrupt parliament for which remedy was not breaking machines but annually elected parliaments.

Cobbett remained steadfastly to his view that parliamentary reform was the key to the bettering of the condition of the people. It was the essential prerequisite of curing the funding system, eliminating corruption, and lowering taxes which he was convinced was the cause of the pauperisation of the labourers. Cobbett remained a committed advocate of parliamentary reform during the long haul through the post-war period from 1815 when the government was unwilling to grant any degree of reform and the Whig opposition earned Cobbett's undying scorn for failing to make a clearer stand in its support. As government persecution of reformers grew, treating them as potential revolutionaries, his view of what was required had widened. By 1830 his 'Plan of Parliamentary Reform addressed to the Young Men of England' advocated the radical programme set out by Cartwright back in the 1770s and adopted by the popular political societies in the 1790s in the wake of the French Revolution. But Cobbett still continued to stress his adherence to the old-fashioned but to him essential virtue of 'independence' and 'no-bribery', stressing these elements when he campaigned successfully for election for Oldham in 1832 after the passing of the Great Reform Act. He was at pains to stress in a series of lectures in 1831 that what he wanted to do as an MP was to reduce the burden of sinecures, pensions, tithes, and to bring about a reduction in the general expense of government by a disposal of assets. He accepted the 1832 Reform Act as what it was, a half measure, hoping for the rest of the radical programme to be implemented in due course. He would not live to see the next reform Act, which would not occur until over 30 years after his death, in 1867.

*

In 1794, writing in America, Cobbett set out his opposition to parliamentary reform in his blistering attack on the English dissenter, scientist and reform supporter, Dr Joseph Priestley. Based in Birmingham and a member of the famous Lunar Society which included men such as the manufacturer Matthew Boulton and the inventor James Watt, Priestley had been an early supporter of the French Revolution and its principles. He saw in the French espousal of full political and religious liberty in the early days of the Revolution something which Britain should emulate while he and his fellow dissenters still suffered from legal disabilities which prevented them from playing a full part in the civil life of the nation. Unless dissenters were prepared to attend Anglican services or subscribe to the 39 Articles of the Church of England, they could not, in theory, take positions such as member of parliament or justice of the peace. A campaign to remove these disabilities had been mounted from the late 1780s, but had failed to obtain a parliamentary majority. The campaign had however exacerbated ill-feeling between Anglicans and Dissenters in places such as Birmingham even before the French Revolution broke out in 1789. Priestley's support for the French as the crisis there deepened led to violence in July 1791. An attempt by Priestley and his liberal-minded friends to hold a dinner to celebrate the second anniversary of the fall of the Bastille in July 1791 provoked violent 'Church and King' rioting in which Priestley's house and laboratory were wrecked, along with the premises of other reformers. Priestley fled Birmingham and eventually the country, seeking refuge in America in 1794 as the government moved actively against reformers. His emigration to America was met with scorn by Cobbett, who took the opportunity to condemn reform of any kind as intrinsically dangerous. Cobbett's *Observations* was initially published in Philadelphia in 1794 then re-printed in London, and enlarged the following year. It began Cobbett's print war against the pro-French 'democrats' both in America and at home in England.

The Doctor, and his fellow-labourers, who have lately emigrated to Botany Bay, have been continually bawling out: "A reform of Parliament." The same visionary delusion seems to have pervaded all reformers in all ages. They do not consider what *can* be done, but what they think ought to be done. They have no calculating principle to direct them to discover whether a reform will cost them more than it is worth or not. They do not set down to count the cost, but, the object being as they think desirable, the means are totally disregarded. If the reformers in France had sat down to count the cost, I do not believe they were villains enough to have pursued their plan as they did. To save a tenth part of their income, they have given the whole, or rather it has been taken from them. To preserve the life of a person, now and then perhaps unjustly condemned, they have drenched the country with the blood of the innocent. Even the Bastile, that terrible monument of tyranny which has been painted in such frightful colours, contained but *two* state prisoners when it was forced by the mob; and the reformers to deliver these two prisoners, and to guard others from a like fate, have erected Bastiles in every town and in every street. Before the Revolution there were only *two* state prisoners, there are now above *two hundred thousand*. Do these people calculate? Certainly not: They will not take man as they find him, and govern him upon principles established by experience; they will have him to be "a faultless monster that the world ne'er saw,"[2] and wish to govern him according to a system that never was, or can be brought into practice. The waking dreams would be of no more consequence than those of the night, were they not generally pursued with any unjustifiable degree of obstinacy and intrigue, and even villainy; and did they not, being always adapted to flatter and inflame the lower orders of the people, often baffle every effort of legal power. Thus it happened in England in the reign of Charles the First; and thus has it happened in France. Some trifling innovation always paves the way to the subversion of a government. The axe, in the forest, humbly besought a little piece of wood to make it a handle: the forest, consisting of so many stately trees, could not, without manifest cruelty, refuse the "humble" request; but, the handle once granted, the before-contemptible

---

[2] 'There's no such thing in Nature, and you'll draw/ A faultless Monster which the world ne're saw', John Sheffield, 1ˢᵗ Duke of Buckinghamshire, *An Essay Upon Poetry* (1682), ll. 234–5.

tool began to lay about it with so much violence, that in a little time not a tree nor even shrub was standing. That a parliamentary reform was the handle by which the English revolutionists intended to effect the destruction of the constitution, need not be insisted on: at least if we believe their own repeated declarations. Paine, and some others, clearly expressed themselves on this head: the Doctor was more cautious while in England, but, safely arrived in his "asylum," he has been a little more undisguised. He says, the troubles in Europe are the natural offspring of the "*forms of government*" that exist there; and that the abuses spring from the "*artificial distinctions in society.*" [...]

It is clear that a parliamentary reform was not the object: an after-game was intended; which the vigilance of government, and the natural good sense of the people, happily prevented; and the Doctor, disappointed and chagrined, is come here to discharge his heart of the venom it has been long collecting against his country. He tells the Democratic society, that he cannot promise to be a better subject of this government than he has been of that of Great Britain. Let us hope, that he intends us an agreeable disappointment, if not, the sooner he emigrates back again the better.

[*Observations on the Emigration of Dr. Joseph Priestley* (London, 1794), pp. 26–30.]

*

As late as 1806, Cobbett was not convinced that parliamentary reform was the answer to the country's ills brought about by 'Pitt's system'. To those who proposed extensive changes in voting rights, he said he feared the excesses he believed it had produced in France under the Jacobin Terror. Even a reform ensuring that all men of property had some say in the election of members of parliament as suggested by Whigs such as George Tierney would be insufficient to overcome the corruption that had become intrinsic to a corrupt system. It was the responsibility of the House of Commons to prevent the high taxes associated with his real bugbear 'the funding and taxing and paper system' set up by William Pitt. When that system ceased to operate, parliamentary reform would be unnecessary. Until then proposals for reform would prove impractical or might even lead to political upheaval.

Of what has been denominated *Parliamentary Reform*, I have always disapproved; because I never could perceive, in any one of the projects that were broached, the least prospect of producing a *real reform*. Of universal suffrage I have witnessed the effects too attentively and with too much disgust ever to think of it with approbation. That the people of property; I mean *all* persons having real property, should have some weight in the election of members of parliament I allow; but, even if this were provided for by law, the funding and taxing and paper system still continuing in existence to its present extent, I should be glad to hear the reasons, whence anyone is sanguine enough to conclude, that the evil complained of by Mr. Tierney, the evil of leaving the making of laws in the hands of men of mere money, who have little or no connection with or feeling for the people; I should be glad to hear the reasons, whence, the present money-system continuing in full force, any man can conclude that this evil, as to the magnitude of which I agree in opinion with Mr. Tierney, is to be gotten rid of. To me, it appears, that, while the present means of acquiring such immense fortunes, at the expense of the people, remain, there can be found out no effectual cure for this evil [...] Viewing the House of Commons, therefore, as "the guardians of the property of the people," as Mr. Pitt, in his better days, described them; and not as assembled merely to discuss, or, rather, to sanction executive measures, I cannot, with the above facts before my eyes, perceive any ground for hoping that any practical good would, while the funding system exists in its present extent, result from the adoption of any of those projects, which have professed to have in view what is called *Parliamentary Reform*; to which I must add, that, in my opinion, every such project would be found utterly impracticable; that it would, at once, drop lifeless from the hands of the projector, or, which is infinitely worse, would disseminate the seeds of a convulsion, to be freed from the numerous torments and horrors of which, the people would gladly resort to the at once protecting and deadly shield of a military despot. When the funding system, from whatever cause, shall cease to operate upon civil and political liberty, there will be no need of projects for parliamentary reform. The parliament will, as far as shall be necessary, then reform itself; and, until then, no attempt at alteration, in this respect, should, in my opinion, and for the reasons I have above-stated, be made, either in or out of the Houses of parliament.

[*Political Register*, 15 March 1806.]

*

When an election was called in the City of Westminster, a constituency with an exceptionally large electorate by eighteenth-century standards of approaching 20,000 people, Cobbett urged them exercise their vote and resist attempts to coerce them. Cobbett was highlighting the dangers he saw in an electoral system in which bribing and treating electors was commonplace.

To hear some persons talk of an election for Westminster, a stranger to the state of things would believe, that the electors were the bondsmen, or, at best, the mere menial servants of a few great families. The question, upon hearing such persons talk, seems to be, not what man the electors may wish to choose, but what man is preferred by a few of the noblemen, though, by-the-by, it is well known, that the law positively forbids such noblemen to interfere in elections. Notwithstanding this law, we hear the boroughs called after the names of the peers who are the *owners* of them; we hear that such a peer has so many members in the House of Commons, and such a peer so many more; and this we, at last, have come to hear and to talk about with perfect unconcern; but, this is no excuse for *you*. Neither peers nor anybody else can render you dependant if you are disposed to be free. You are nearly *twenty thousand* in number. Your trades and occupations are, generally speaking, full as necessary to your employers as their employment is necessary to you. If you are turned out of one house there is always another ready to receive you; if you lose one customer, you gain another; you need court the smiles, you need fear the frowns, of no man, and no set of men, living. Some few unfortunate dependants there may be amongst you; but, the number is so small as to be unworthy of notice, when compared to the whole. [...] To make use of any interested motive for the purpose of inducing an elector to give, or to withhold, his vote, is a crime in the eye of the law, which has provided injunctions and oaths, which has prepared shame and punishment for every such crime; but, to attempt to induce an elector to vote contrary to his conscience, is also a personal offence, that every honest man will resent with as much indignation as he would an accusation of perjury. How scandalous, then, is it that tradesmen should patiently listen to the commands of their customers, nay, that they should obey those commands, in direct opposition to the dictates of their own minds, from the paltry consideration of gain, which, when compared to the weight of taxes, brought upon them from the want of real representatives, is as a farthing to a pound! [...]

The possessor of the elective franchise is the holder of a trust; he acts not only for himself, but for his country, and more especially for his family and children. To violate his trust, or to neglect the performance of what it imposes upon him, is, therefore, not merely an act of baseness, not merely a degradation of himself, but a crime against others; and, a man so acting, ought to be regarded by his neighbours as a public offender; as an injurer of every other man; as a person to be shunned and abhorred; as a person very little, if at all, less detestable than one who betrays his country into the hands of an enemy. It is no justification of such a man, to say that those who bias him are his superiors, or that his temptation is great. In the case of Westminster there is no temptation at all; and, besides, what crime is there which might not, upon such a principle, be justified? And, as to the "*superiors*" who bias, they may be superior in riches; but in every other respect are they not the basest of mankind, except only those who are biased by them? Are they not violators of the law? Are they not hypocrites of the most odious description? Are they not, with the sound of loyalty and patriotism on their lips, the worst of enemies to their King and their country? I shall be told, that, in some instances, even the Clergy have used the means of corruption at elections. I hope such instances are rare; and it cannot but shock anyone to know that they at all exist; but, if they existed in ever so great a number, no countenance would thereby be afforded to the corrupted; for, of all detestable characters, the most detestable assuredly is what is called "an *electioneering parson*." From the chalice of such a priest one would flee as from a goblet of poison; and if ten such instances could exist, without producing an ecclesiastical censure and punishment, the Church ought to be destroyed, root and branch, for ever.

[*Political Register*, 9 August 1806.]

*

In the summer of 1806, Cobbett decided to contest the seat of Honiton in Devon, as one of its sitting MPs, Mr Cavendish Bradshaw, had to seek re-election having accepted office as part of the government. Cobbett seized on an opportunity to demonstrate the corrupt state of elections. In his election address, published in the *Register*, he took the opportunity to condemn Bradshaw's role as part of the corrupt 'Pitt system' and to declare his own principles of accepting no bribes nor giving any for electoral support.

"Fire shall consume the tabernacles of bribery."–JOB. cap. xv.

GENTLEMEN;—Perceiving that Mr. Cavendish Bradshaw has, since by your voice he was constituted one of the guardians of the public purse, taken care to obtain a place by the means of which he will draw into his own pocket some thousands a year out of that purse, and this, too, at a time when the load of indispensable taxes is pressing his honest and industrious constituents to the earth; perceiving this, and being fully persuaded that, whenever the electors of any place re-choose representatives under similar circumstances, the cause is not so much in their own disposition as in the apathy and lukewarmness of those independent men who may have the ability to rescue them from such hands; with this truth being deeply impressed, I did, upon hearing of the approaching vacancy, use my efforts to prevail upon other men of this description to afford you an opportunity of evincing your good sense and uprightness, and, having failed in those efforts, I have thought it my duty to afford you this opportunity myself; it being manifestly true, that, unless men of independence and of public-spirit will offer themselves as candidates, to rail at electors for choosing and re-choosing the dependent and the mercenary is, in the highest degree, unreasonable and unjust.—As to professions, Gentlemen, so many and so loud, upon such occasions, have they been; so numerous are the instances, in which the foulness and shamelessness of the apostasy have borne an exact proportion to the purity and solemnity of the vow; so completely, and with such fatal effect, have the grounds of confidence been destroyed, that, it is now become necessary, upon all occasions like the present, to give a pledge, such as every man can clearly understand, and such as it is impossible to violate without exposing the violator to detection and to all the consequences of detected hypocrisy and falsehood; and, such a pledge I now give in declaring, that, whether you elect me or not, I never, as long as I live, either for myself, or for, or through the means of, any one of my family, will receive, under any name, whether of salary, pension or other, either directly or indirectly, one single farthing of the public money; but without emolument, compensation, or reward of any kind or in any shape, will, to the utmost of my ability, watch over and defend the property, the liberties and the privileges of the people, never therefrom separating, as I never yet have, the just and constitutional rights and prerogatives of the crown.—This declaration, Gentlemen, is not made without due reflection as to the future as well as to the present, as to public men in general as well as to myself. It proceeds, first, from an opinion, that all the representatives of the people ought never to be exposed to the temptation of betraying their trust; secondly, from long observation that those who live upon the public are amongst the most miserable of men; and, thirdly, from that experience in the various walks of life, which has convinced me of the wisdom of Hagar, who prayed for neither riches nor poverty; not riches, lest he should forget God; not poverty, lest he should be tempted to steal; and, to receive the public money unjustly, is not only stealing, but stealing of the worst and basest sort, including a breach of the most sacred trust, accompanied with the cowardly consciousness of impunity. From reflections like these, Gentlemen, it is, that the declaration now made has proceeded, and, when I depart, in word or in deed, from this declaration, may I become the scorn of my country; wherein to be remembered with esteem, I prize beyond all the riches and all the honours of this world.—But, Gentlemen, as it is my firm determination never to receive a farthing of the public money, so it is my determination, equally firm, never, in any way whatever, to give one farthing of my own money to any man, in order to induce him to vote, or to cause others to vote, for me; and, being convinced, that it is this practice of giving, or promising to give, money, or money's worth, at elections; being convinced, that it is this disgraceful, this unlawful, this profligate, this impious practice, to which are to be ascribed all our calamities and all the dangers that now stare us in the face, I cannot refrain from exhorting you to be, against all attempts at such practices, constantly and watchfully upon your guard. The candidates who have resorted to such means have always been found amongst the most wicked of men; men, who, having, by a life of adultery or of gambling, or of profligacy of some sort, ruined both their character and their fortunes, have staked their last thousand upon an election, with the hope of thereby obtaining security from a jail, and of selling their vote for the means of future subsistence drawn from the sweat of the people at a hundred-fold; and thus expecting to pocket the profit of the corrupt speculation, sneering at their bribed and perjured constituents, as Satan is said to have sneered at the reprobate with whom he had bargained for his soul. [...] WM. COBBETT.

[*Political Register*, 7 June 1806.]

*

But Cobbett was disappointed to find that not only had the previous incumbent of the post been ready to bribe the electors but also that the 400 or so electors of Honiton, many of them quite poor, were themselves now so accustomed to being paid for their votes that they claimed they could not exist without them. Cobbett's discussions with the voters only served to convince him of the need for reform of the electoral system, as the current laws provided no effective disincentive to bribery. Remarkably, Cobbett now claimed bribery at elections as the source of *all* the nation's ills. He conjured up an unspoiled scene of country life to contrast with the corruption he had found. In the event, Cobbett did not contest the election, standing aside for the naval hero, Lord Cochrane, who pledged himself, like Cobbett, not to bribe the electors. Cochrane lost, though was returned for Honiton the following year when he filled a vacancy without a contest.

Now, as to the *state of the borough*, who shall describe it? Who shall describe the gulf wherein have been swallowed the fortunes of so many ancient and once respectable families? There is, the electors will tell you, *no bribery*. They take a certain sum of money each according to their consequence, their degree of influence, and their services to their candidate respectively; "but this," say they, "comes in the shape of a *reward* after the election, and, therefore, the oath may be *safely* taken." Considered as a question of morality, how contemptible this subterfuge is need hardly be noticed; but, to say the truth, they do not deceive themselves, and I must do them the justice to say, that they are not very anxious to deceive any body else. They tell you, flatly and plainly, that the money, which they obtain for their votes, is absolutely necessary to enable them to live; that, without it, they could not *pay their rents;* and that, from election to election, the poor men run up scores at the shops, and are trusted by the shop-keepers, *expressly upon the credit of the proceeds of the ensuing election;* and that, thus, the whole of the inhabitants of the borough, the whole of the persons who return two of the members to every parliament, are bound together in an indissoluble chain of venality!

[*Political Register*, 28 June 1806.]

*

At the end of the Napoleonic Wars Cobbett saw a country loaded with debt and supporting reactionary governments in the aftermath of the Congress of Vienna. He now believed it required radical reform, not his earlier moderate tinkering. He now supported Annual Parliaments, elected each year, rather than the seven-year terms parliament currently enjoyed or the three-year terms suggested by some reformers. Cobbett's aim was to force parliament to respond to the wishes of the taxpaying public as frequently as possible. Like many reformers of the period, Cobbett argued that annually elected parliaments were sanctioned by ancient tradition dating back to Anglo-Saxon times. Cobbett's idea of 'lost' or 'ancient' rights was a staple of reformers like himself and Major John Cartwright who preferred to justify their claims for reform by reference to the past rather than abstract principles. Characteristically, Cobbett cast himself a true rather than a 'sham' reformer.

However, it is necessary to state somewhat of the *outline* of the reform that we seek; because, as is the case in most other good causes, there are *sham* reformers, who mean any thing but that which the people wish for and want. What the people seek is a real reform; a restoration of the whole of their own rights, without violating the rights of others. The rights of the people, according to Magna Carta; according to the constitution and the ancient laws of the kingdom, are, *That they are to be taxed only by their own consent;* and that they *shall* YEARLY *choose their representatives.* These are the essentials. That every man, who pays *a tax*, of any sort, into the hands of a taxgatherer, shall, by his representative, *give his consent to such a tax*, which he cannot do, unless he vote at elections for Members of Parliament, who impose the taxes. It is also an essential, that the election should be *annual;* because the ancient laws say so; and because we know from fatal experience, that a *three years'* parliament, voted themselves into a *seven* years' parliament; and that the seven years' parliament have loaded us with a debt; the interest of which is pressing us to the earth, and the principal of which has been employed in supporting French Emigrants, in subsidizing Germans, in restoring the Bourbons, the Pope, and the Inquisition, and in other ways equally beneficial to the country.

It is quite necessary that the people should be put on their guard against the *Triennial Trick*. It has already been begun to be played off by the hirelings of one of the factions. The object of it is to divide the friends of reform. Mr. Fox played it off *Thirty years ago;* and he at last played a good pension into the hands of Mrs. Fox and her daughters, though he never, *after he was in place*, once, *talked* even, of a parliamentary reform. It is, therefore quite necessary, that the people should be cautioned against the tricks of these sham reformers, who are only so many enemies' spies in the camp of reform.

This is an old, and has often been a very successful trick of a crafty enemy. "*Divide and destroy*" is the maxim of tyrants. First they openly oppose; but, when that is like to fail, they seek to undermine by dividing. They, better than anybody, know the history of the *bundle of sticks;* and they seek to separate the bundle, that they may snap them one at a time. As to the *detail* of reform, it is of little consequence; but the main principles must be adhered to inflexibly; these are, that *every man who pays a tax of any sort into the hands of a taxgatherer, should vote for members of the Commons House; and that parliament should be chosen annually.* To make the right of voting consist in possession of this or that species of property; to make free-hold or copy-hold or lease-hold or life-hold a title to voting, would be to rob the people of their right; and, to allow a man to be a representative for more than a year without being re-chosen, has in it neither justice nor common sense, to say nothing about its being contrary to the spirit of the constitution and to *the very letter* of the ancient laws of England.

['Letter to Sir Francis Burdett', *Political Register*, 19 October 1816.]

*

By 1816 Cobbett's ideas had moved a considerable distance, now he was prepared to espouse an extension of the suffrage to those who paid direct taxes and annually elected parliaments as the reforms necessary to rescue the country from the high taxes and distress of the long wars with France. In his 'Address to the Journeymen and Labourers' he rejected all the palliative schemes being put forward to the general population, including economising on poor rates, reducing the size of their families, and the pious resignation offered by Methodists and evangelicals. He was particularly outraged by the suggestion that labourers should emigrate, urging them instead to seek parliamentary reform. He explained why only direct tax-payers should be included, but recognised that voting arrangements could be altered in due course. Moreover he criticised those who advocated complete overthrow of the system, setting out his ultimately conservative view that he wanted reform not revolution.

No: you will not leave your country. If you have suffered much and long, you have the greater right to remain in the hope of seeing better days. And I beseech you not to look upon yourselves as the *scum;* but, on the contrary, to be well persuaded, that a great deal will depend upon *your exertions*; and, therefore, I now proceed to point out to you what appears to me to be the line of conduct which Journeymen and Labourers ought to pursue in order to obtain *effectual relief*, and to assist in promoting tranquillity and restoring the happiness of their country. [...]

But, this and *all other good things,* must be done by a *reformed Parliament.*—We must have *that first*, or we shall have nothing good; and, any man, who would, *before hand*, take up your time with the detail of what a reformed parliament ought to do in this respect, or with respect to any changes in the form of government, can have no other object than that of defeating the cause of reform, and, indeed, the very act must show, that *to raise obstacles* is his wish.

Such men, now that they find you justly irritated, would persuade you, that, because things have been perverted from their true ends, there *is nothing good* in our *constitution and laws*. For what, then, did Hampden[3] die in the field, and Sydney[4] on the scaffold? And, has it been discovered, at last, that England has *always* been an enslaved country from top to toe? The Americans, who are a very wise people, and who love liberty with all their hearts, and who take care to *enjoy* it too, took special care not to part with any of the great principles and laws which they derived from their forefathers. They took special care to speak with reverence of, and to preserve, Magna Carta, the Bill of Rights, the Habeas Corpus, and not only all the body of the Common Law of England, but most of the rules of our courts, and all our form of jurisprudence. Indeed, it is the greatest glory of England that she has thus supplied with sound principles of freedom those immense regions, which will be peopled, perhaps by hundreds of millions.

I know of no enemy of reform and of the happiness of the country so great as that man, who would persuade you, that we possess *nothing good*, and that *all* must be torn to pieces. There is no principle, no precedent,

---

[3]   John Hampden, opponent of Charles I and prominent parliamentarian, killed in the Civil War at the battle of Chalgrove Field in 1643.

[4]   Algernon Sidney, executed for his part in the Rye House plot of 1683 to assassinate Charles II and the future James II. With his co-conspirator, William Russell, referred to as the 'Whig Martyrs', who aimed to frustrate Stuart pretensions to absolutism.

no regulation (except as to mere matter of detail), favourable to freedom, which is not to be found in the Laws of England or in the example of our Ancestors. Therefore, I say, we may ask for, and we want *nothing new*. We have great constitutional laws and principles, to which we are immovably attached. We want *great alteration*, but we want *nothing new*. Alteration, modification to suit the times and circumstances; but, the great principles ought to be and must be, the same, or else confusion will follow.

It was the misfortune of the French people, that they had no great and settled principles to refer to in their laws or history. They sallied forth and inflicted vengeance on their oppressors; but, for want of settled principles, to which to refer, they fell into confusion; they massacred *each other;* they next flew to a military chief to protect them even *against themselves;* and the result has been what we too well know. Let us, therefore, congratulate ourselves, that we have great constitutional principles and laws, to which we can refer, and to which we are attached.

[*Political Register*, 2 November 1816.]

*

Similarly in his 'Letter to the Luddites', the machine-breakers who had operated across a great swathe of northern England in 1810–12 and who seemed to be reviving in 1816, Cobbett urged the futility of their actions when the cause of their distresses lay with the political system and what it had produced. High taxes and paper money were the cause of distress not machinery. Again, as with the labourers in general, the answer was not direct action but parliamentary reform.

Your distress, that is to say, that which you now more immediately feel, arises from want of employment with wages sufficient for your support. The want of such employment has arisen from the want of a sufficient demand for the goods you make. The want of a sufficient demand for the goods you make has arisen from the want of means in the nation at large to purchase your goods. This want of means to purchase your goods has arisen from the weight of the taxes co-operating with the bubble of paper-money. The enormous burden of taxes and the bubble of paper-money have arisen from the war, the sinecures, the standing army, the loans, and the stoppage of cash-payments at the Bank; and, it appears very clearly to me, that these never would have existed, if the Members of the House of Commons had been chosen annually by the people at large. [...]

Thus, then, my fellow countrymen, it is not *machinery;* it is not the grinding disposition of your employers; it is not improvements in machinery; it is not extortions on the part of Bakers and Butchers and

Millers and Farmers and Corn-Dealers and Cheese and Butter Sellers. It is not to any causes of this sort that you ought to attribute your present great and cruel sufferings; but wholly and solely to the great burden of taxes, co-operating with the bubble of paper-money. And, now, before I proceed any further, let me explain to you how the paper-money, or funding, system has *worked* us all. This is a very important matter, and it is easily understood by any man of plain good sense, who will but attend to it for a moment.

['A Letter to the Luddites', *Political Register*, 30 November 1816.]

*

Cobbett's fears were proved correct, the government of Lord Liverpool passing a raft of repressive legislation in the spring of 1817 and pursuing charges of High Treason against the plotters of the attempt on the Tower in December 1816 and against a further attempted rising in Derbyshire. Its use of spies and informers, some of whom came close to acting as agents provocateurs, created a poisonous atmosphere in which Cobbett, having already served one term of imprisonment, feared for his personal freedom and that of the country as a whole. He urged the people of his home county to petition for repeal of the Act suspending Habeas Corpus and contrasted the government's expedition in passing repressive legislation with its failure to attend to the many petitions demanding reform.

Let no one, therefore, deceive himself with the expectation of a return from this path at *some future time*. The Petitions for a *repeal* must be sent up *now* or *never*. It will be a striking fact in history, that, on the very night that this Bill made its last appearance in the House of Commons, there lay upon the floor of that House, nearly *six hundred petitions* signed by *one million and sixty thousand men*, praying for *Parliamentary Reform*. They had been carried down in *Hackney Coaches*, and had been carried in by Sir Francis Burdett[5] and Lord Cochrane; and when the two Masters in Chancery came in to announce that the Lords had finished the Bill, they were unable to approach the table, the whole space, of several yards, from the Bar to the Table, being filled with this immense heap of Petitions! There had been petitions, with several *hundred thousand* names, presented before, and praying for the same thing; and Sir Francis Burdett, when the Bill came down from the Lords, emphatically observed, "That Bill is the answer to these Petitions;" an observation which History will not forget in recording the occurrences of these disgraceful times. I believe, that, in

---

5   Sir Francis Burdett (1770–1844), radical MP, fellow parliamentary reformer and sometimes ally of Cobbett.

the whole, more than *one million and a half of men* have signed Petitions
for Parliamentary Reform, upon the principles of *Annual Parliaments*
and *Universal Suffrage*; and, this has been done in the most fair and open
manner. In the 11 millions, or thereabouts, of the natives of England and
Scotland, there cannot be more than about two millions of active, sturdy
men. However, suppose the *families* to be *two millions and a half*, and that
there be one *active man* to each family, a *majority* of the active men of
the nation have petitioned upon this occasion, notwithstanding all the
efforts that have been made to prevent petitioning. But, the truth is, that a
considerable part of the petitions are not yet come in; and, if no measures
of prevention, no menaces, no *undue* influence, had been made use of,
there would, I am convinced, have been *nine tenths* of the names, of *all the
men in the country* to these petitions.

This, therefore, is THE PRAYER OF THE PEOPLE. Let our
adversaries say or do what they will, this is the PEOPLE'S PRAYER; and,
though Corruption may call it an attempt to overthrow the Constitution,
this prayer, I am fully convinced, will be *finally* heard. I, for my part, as
far as I have power, will always contend for this as our *right*. We have by
reference to *law* and by an appeal to *reason,* proved it to be our right; and,
we have received *no answer.*

['To the People of Hampshire', *Political Register*, 8 March 1817.]

*

Cobbett returned from America in 1819 to find reform no further advanced
than when he left. He decided, however, to contest the election at Coventry,
a relatively 'open' borough with up to 3,000 voters amongst the freemen. He
found himself, however, faced with the full force of the violent opposition which
open polling permitted, especially when an 'independent' such as Cobbett tried
to break into a borough with well-established representatives. When Cobbett
appeared to be doing well, he was countered by brute force, leaving him to
conclude that the 517 who eventually voted for him were at least honest votes,
and despairing of an evil and corrupt electoral system.

After the polling, on this memorable Friday, had gone on in the manner,
and during the time, above described, the *Rich Ruffians* (several of them
in person) came with their savages, *not less than five hundred in number*,
in regular order, about eight or ten deep, with drums and banners at their
head. They made their approach by the higher part of the ground. The
head of this column of Savages began the attack upon my voters at the
upper end of the Booth. *Fighting* was out of the question. All attempts

to resist were vain. And, in five minutes, *three hundred* of my voters were as completely driven away as if an army had made an attack upon them.

After this, not a man dare to shew his face in order to vote for me, during that whole day. If a man crept in unperceived, he was, as soon as discovered, pulled back, dragged away, jostled, beaten, or cut. The ferocity of the Savages, this day, was such as I thought human beings incapable of. I have seen parcels of drunken soldiers. I have seen gangs of furious and drunken sailors. I have seen roaring mobs in London. I have seen whole bands of American Indians, drunk with rum. But, never did my eyes behold any thing in human shape so ferocious, so odiously, so diabolically ferocious, as those bands of villains, hired, paid, fed, and drenched by the Rich Ruffians of Coventry. I have seen much of the world: I have seen French, Irish, Scotch, Americans, Spaniards, Portuguese, and American Indians. I have always been proud of my native country. Few men, with like means, have boasted more than I have of *English humanity and fair-play*. But, never, since I was born, did I see anything so disgraceful to human nature; so ferocious; so odious; so hateful; as the conduct of the Rich Ruffians and their savages, at Coventry, on Friday, the tenth of March, 1820.

There were about sixty wretches, stationed opposite the poling place for the express purpose of putting forth *execrations* on me. They and all the savages were regularly supplied with gin or brandy. The *execrators* foamed at mouth, till, in some cases, the foam extended itself widely down into their dirty and long beards. I actually saw a wretch, who kept on repeating: "*G—d blast you!*" till the foam, from white, became brown all round his mouth. There were two fellows with broad faces, one of them pocked-marked, who sent forth execrations and foam, till they whitened over the shoulders of a man that stood just before them. One old wretch, who had swallowed a great deal of gin, exhausted himself so much by straining his throat, that he, at last, fell down in a sort of fit, with the curses on his lips! [...]

All the circumstances considered, the wonder is, that 517 men should have been found so full of devotion to principle as to vote for me at that Hell-upon-earth, the Booth of Coventry. My heart ached for them when I saw them approach. When I shook hands with them, it really seemed that I was bidding them adieu upon their death beds. Many of them, and, indeed, the most of them, were sober, religious, men. They were manifestly actuated by a conscientious feeling of duty. I never shall forget the friendship and affection that they demonstrated towards me.

[*Political Register*, 25 March 1820.]

*

Increasingly concerned and vociferous about the plight of the rural labourers, Cobbett was agitating for reform in the midst of the wave of unrest which swept the rural counties from 1830 and was dubbed the 'Captain Swing' riots from the mythical leader of the revolt and the prominence given to the destruction of threshing machines. Charged with inciting the labourers to violence, Cobbett was acquitted in spring 1831, but believed that it was the revolt of the rural poor which had played a vital part in bringing about reform in 1832 and that his writings had led them to understand their true condition.

> Besides suffering from want, the working people were made to endure insults and indignities such as even Negroes were never exposed to. They were harnessed like horses or asses and made to draw carts and wagons; they were shut up in pounds made to hold stray cattle; they were made to work with bells round their necks; and they had drivers set over them, just as if they had been galley slaves; they were sold by auction for certain times, as the Negroes were sold in the West Indies; the married men were kept separated from their wives, by force, to prevent them from breeding; and, in short, no human beings were ever before treated so unjustly, with so much insolence, and with such damnable barbarity, as the working people of England had been. Such were the fruits of public debts and funds! Without them, this industrious and moral and brave nation never could have been brought into this degraded state.
>
> I had seen the cause of Reform fast gaining ground; but, it was not until the month of October, 1830, when the chopsticks set about the work, that I really expected it to come in any reasonable time. Every event must have a beginning; and the greatest events have frequently had their beginnings in trifling causes. I had often used to tell [my] friends, in Long Island and at New York, that no change would ever take place, unless it were begun amongst the hedgers and ditchers and the ploughmen and the thrashers; how often had I told them that people were not formidable when assembled together in great towns. What, then, was it not the meetings and petitions of the great towns that produced Parliamentary Reform? They did good, particularly by their speeches they brought forth, but, the great and efficient cause was, the movements of the chopsticks.

[*The Autobiography of William Cobbett*, ed. William Reitzel (London, 1933), p. 207.]

*

Following the 1832 Reform Act, Cobbett stood for Parliament again, for two boroughs, Manchester and Oldham, as allowed at the time, both of them new seats created under the new provisions which reflected the growing influence of the northern industrial cities. Cobbett dismissed any thought of self-aggrandisement. He recognised the Reform Act as limited but one which would allow for further extension. True to his earlier principles, he prided himself on being elected at Oldham without any of the bribery, treating and rioting he regarded as the characteristics of corruption.

> On my own personal account, I set not the value of a straw upon the seat in Parliament. I had, for a long while, wished to be in the Commons' House; but never for the sake of any advantage or personal pleasure of my own. From a very early age, I imbibed the opinion, that it was every man's duty to do all that lay in his power to *leave his country as good as he found it*. I know that my country presents a scene of wretchedness and disgrace, compared with the scene that it presented at the time that I was born. I hate the life of the great cities; I hate their everlasting noise and bustle; my taste, all my own personal enjoyments, would lead me far away from them for ever. I could, if I had been so minded, have secured, out of my own earnings, much greater possessions and in a state of tranquillity; much greater than I ever had a desire to be master of. But, feeling that I possessed the mind to enable me to assist in restoring my country to the state in which I found it, a sense of duty to that country restrains me from consulting my own ease and my own private enjoyments [...] the invitation to become a candidate for MANCHESTER, came *first*. The people of OLDHAM, which is at about eight miles distant from MANCHESTER, knowing how difficult it would be to carry an election for MANCHESTER, by mere voluntary support, came to the resolution to secure my return for OLDHAM, which, though inferior to MANCHESTER in point of population, is still a very large and opulent town, consisting in the whole *parish*, I believe, of upwards of sixty thousand people. Had the invitation come first from OLDHAM, I should certainly have declined that for MANCHESTER; because my object was not to disturb any place, but to take the seat with as much quietness as possible. [...] I was at the opening of the elections at MANCHESTER; where, having obtained an immense majority upon *the view*, having obtained the decision of the *public* at MANCHESTER; having, upon those hustings, seen hooted off that very Mr. SHARPE [...] who was the boroughreeve that forbade me to enter MANCHESTER, on my return from America, in 1819 [...] [h]aving done this, I went off to OLDHAM, there to remain until I should come back to MANCHESTER a member of Parliament. The election at MANCHESTER was, doubtless, greatly influenced by the decision at OLDHAM, which was known at the former place by *twelve o'clock of the first polling day*. So that after that it was naturally to be expected that the electors of MANCHESTER who intended to vote for me, would either transfer their votes [...] or that

they would not vote at all. Yet, in spite of this, the state of the poll, at its close, on the second day, was as follows:

> PHILLIPS   ... 2,923
> THOMSON ... 2,069
> LOYD   ... 1,832
> HOPE   ... 1,560
> COBBETT ... 1,305

This result, considering the above-mentioned circumstances, alone was sufficiently honourable to me. Not one single pint of beer, or glass of gin, had been given to any human being on my part; no attorney, and no attorney's clerk had been employed; and not a single person hired, I believe, to do any one thing connected with my election. All, except the mere printing, and the hire of a few carriages, was the effect of *voluntary exertion*, chiefly by young men in the middle rank of life, whose zeal and activity I never can sufficiently applaud. [...]

So much for the election at MANCHESTER. With regard to that for OLDHAM [...] [t]he polling was over on the 13th [of December], when the numbers stood as follows:

> FIELDEN[6] ... 670
> COBBETT ... 642
> BRIGHT   ... 153
> BURGE   ... 101
> STEPHEN ...   3

At this election not one single farthing's worth of victuals or drink was given to anybody for any service whatsoever. The committee, composed of sensible and sober manufacturers and tradesmen, paid for the printing that they had done, and paid all the expenses of the hustings, polling places, clerks, &c. They paid also for the entertainment of the candidates at the hotel: and even the carriages to and from MANCHESTER, that I went in, I found paid for; and not a man nor woman in this excellent town attempted to obtain from us either money, drink, or any promise to do anything for them in their private concerns. This was *purity of election*, indeed. It is an honour, indeed, to represent a people like this. Neither [Mr Fielden nor myself] ever canvassed in any shape or form, either individually or collectively; neither of us ever asked the people to give us

---

6   John Fielden (1784–1849), manufacturer and Tory radical, elected alongside Cobbett at Oldham.

a vote; but we contented ourselves with saying, that, if they chose us to represent them, we would be their true representatives to the best of our power.

Of one thing we are both of us particularly proud; and that is, that the people had the good sense; that sense of their own worth, and our rights, as to scorn to attempt to *chair* us, or to drag us through the streets. In my address to them on my RETURN, I besought them not to think of imitating the slaves of the boroughmongers. "Now," said I, "my friends, I shall come down from the hustings, and the first hand-loom weaver I meet with, I shall take by the arm and walk with him up to the hotel from which I came." I did this, Mr. FIELDEN did the same; and thus, in this appropriate manner, we closed this election, which ought to become an example to every borough and every county in the kingdom. Not a disturbance of any sort; not a blow given in anger; scarcely an abusive word from one person to another; not a single drunken man to be seen about the streets; much singing, much playing music, much joy, much triumph; but all was peace and decorum, from the beginning to the end. [...] As a mark of victory, on my own account, over the combined malignity of [...] factions, I set a very high value upon this seat in Parliament. But I set a higher value upon it, as vindicating the character of the *Commons*, or common people of England. I always stood firmly up in defence, not only the rights, but of the character of the common people, who, of late years, were looked upon by both the political factions, and by all the hordes that live upon the taxes, as not being of the same flesh and blood with themselves.

['To the Cobbettites', *Political Register*, 22 December 1832.]

Chapter 5
Villains and Pet Hates

Cobbett might be described, in Samuel Johnson's phrase, as a 'good hater'. William Hazlitt – who wrote an essay 'On the Pleasure of Hating' – gives a vivid account of Cobbett's pugilistic style of journalism:

> As a political partisan, no one can stand against him. With his brandished club, like Giant Despair in the Pilgrim's Progress, he knocks out their brains; and not only no individual, but no corrupt system could hold out against his powerful and repeated attacks [...] In short, wherever power is, there is he against: he naturally butts at all obstacles, as unicorns are attracted to oak-trees.[1]

Hazlitt viewed being a good hater as a political virtue, part of an oppositional tradition in English literature and history that stretched back to John Milton and seventeenth-century republicanism. Cobbett, it might be noted, hated both Johnson and Milton.

A single chapter will inevitably fail to do justice to the full range of Cobbett's prejudices: there are many examples in other chapters and a full Cobbett demonology would run to several volumes. Prominent among his targets are the politicians of his day; first, the radicals who welcomed the French Revolution, and then the defenders of a corrupt status quo. Cobbett belonged to a brilliant age of political satire and his journalism forms a prose equivalent to the caricatures of Gillray and Cruikshank. He was adept at satirising political speeches and invented a new kind of parliamentary sketch writing through his open letters in the *Political Register*. He was also remorseless when he discovered a new target for his anger and many of his feuds ran for several decades. However, aside from these personal feuds, Cobbett's search for the root causes of bad government and economic malaise led him to a more entrenched system of corruption, which he dedicated his life to exposing. A frequently bizarre assortment of bête noires – including potatoes, pianos, paper money, Shakespeare and tea – were all symptoms of what he described, with brilliant simplicity and withering contempt, as 'the THING'. He characterised London as 'the Great Wen', a swelling on the body politic, poisoning everything around it. The political economists associated with the *Edinburgh Review* were the target of countless

---

[1] Hazlitt, 'Character of Cobbett' in *The Complete Works of William Hazlitt*, ed. P.P Howe (21 vols, London, 1931), VIII, pp. 53–4.

diatribes against 'Scotch *feelosofers*', although when he finally visited Scotland in 1832 he was pleased to discover so many supporters there.

There is also a much uglier side to Cobbett's hatred, which forms an uncomfortable but undeniable part of his populism. He often employed virulently anti-Semitic stereotypes, describing Jews as Christ-killers, money-lenders and financiers. In Cobbett's rhetoric, 'Jew' becomes synonymous with 'stock-jobber', part of the corruption he associates with a system of public credit. His anti-Semitism is expressed both with violent intensity and depressing regularity. Cobbett was also a fierce opponent of the abolitionist William Wilberforce, who he viewed as campaigning against slavery abroad at the expense of agricultural labourers and factory workers in Britain. Cobbett sometimes voiced his opposition to Wilberforce through a polemical comparison between different kinds of exploitation, but at other times expressed it in racialised terms that are now abhorrent. Cobbett's admirers have often tried to conceal or dismiss the more disturbing aspects of his work, but the crude bigotry of some of his writing is an integral part of his populism and a troubling aspect of his legacy for British journalism.

*

Thomas Paine, author of *Common Sense* and *Rights of Man*, was one of the primary targets of Cobbett's anti-Jacobin writings. He re-published a scurrilous, government-sponsored *Life of Thomas Paine* and added his own commentary on the text, from which the following extract is taken. Cobbett also includes Rousseau and Sterne as examples of a dangerous form of Sensibility, while the closing passage is particularly ironic in light of Cobbett's later attempt to honour Paine's remains.

> Paine's humanity, like that of all the reforming philosophers of the present enlightened day, is of the speculative kind. It never breaks out into action. Hear these people and you would think them overflowing with the milk of human kindness. They stretch their benevolence to the extremities of the globe: it embraces every living creature—except those who have the misfortune to come in contact with them. They are all citizens of the world: country, and friends and relations are unworthy the attention of men who are occupied in rendering all mankind happy and free.
>
> I ever suspect the sincerity of a man whose discourse abounds in expressions of universal philanthropy. Nothing is easier than for a person of some imagination to raise himself to a swell of sentiment, without the aid of one single feeling of the heart. Rousseau, for instance, is everlastingly babbling about his *genre humain* (human race) and his "*coeur aimant et tendre*" (tender and loving heart). He writes for the human race, his heart bleeds for the distresses of the human race, and in the midst of all

this he sends his unfortunate bastards to the poor-house, the receptacle of misery! Virtuous and tender-hearted and sympathetic Rousseau! Certainly nothing is so disgusting as this, except it be to see the humane and sentimental Sterne wiping away a tear at the sight of a dead jack-ass, while his injured wife and child were pining away their days in a nunnery, and while he was debauching the wife of his friend.* [...]

How Tom gets a living now, or what brothel he inhabits, I know not, nor does it much signify to any body here or any where else. He has done all the mischief he can in the world, and whether his carcass is at last to be suffered to rot on the earth, or to be dried in the air, is of very little consequence. Whenever and wherever he breathes his last, he will excite neither sorrow nor compassion; no friendly hand will close his eyes, not a groan will be uttered, not a tear will be shed. Like *Judas* he will be remembered by posterity; men will learn to express all that is base, malignant, treacherous, unnatural and blasphemous, by the single monosyllable, *Paine*.

* Sterne's writings are most admirably calculated to destroy the morals of the youth of both sexes; but it was reserved for some of the printers in the United States to give those writings the finishing touch. What the lewd author was ashamed to do, they have done for him. They have explained his *double entendres* and *filthy inuendos* by a set of the most bawdy cuts that ever disgraced the pencil.—I was shown a copy of the *Sentimental* Journey in this style at the shop of Citizen Thomas Bradford of Philadelphia, the only place in the city, I believe, where it is to be had.

[*The Life of Thomas Paine* (Philadelphia, 1796), re-printed in *Porcupine's Works*, vol. IV, pp. 79–113.]

*

One of Cobbett's most well-known bête noires was the potato, or – as he described it – the 'root of extreme unction'. His anger was provoked by attempts to replace bread with a cheaper substitute in the labourer's diet, but his hostility also stemmed from his belief that potatoes were associated with dirt, and reduced labourers to the level of hogs.

This root is become a favourite because it is the suitable companion of misery and filth. It can be seized hold of before it be half ripe, it can be raked out of the ground with the paws, and without the help of any utensils, except, perhaps, a stick to rake it from the fire, can be conveyed into the stomach, in the space of an hour. We have but one step further to go, and that is, to eat it raw, side by side with our bristly fellow-creatures, who, by the by, reject it as long as they can get at any species of grain or at any other vegetable.—I can remember when the first acre of potatoes was planted in a field, in the neighbourhood of the place where I was born; and I very well remember, that even the poorest of the people would not eat them. They called them *hog*-potatoes; but now, they are become a considerable portion of the diet, of those who raise the bread for others to eat.—It is not many years ago that a bill was brought into Parliament for the giving of premiums for the cultivation of this ruinous root. It was thrown out, to be sure; but the bare fact of its having been brought in, was a disgrace to the country.

['Price of Bread', *Political Register*, 2 October 1813.]

*

Cobbett was particularly scathing towards the new manufacturing, mercantile and agricultural elite, comparing them unfavourably to an older and, in his eyes, more benevolent, nobility and landed gentry. For Cobbett, the upstart ranks of the new rich represented a grave threat both to ordinary labourers and projects for political reform.

It seems to me, therefore, very wonderful, that those who *have property*, and who do not *share in the taxes*, should not be eager to promote meetings to petition; but the conduct of some of *your* rich neighbours has more than folly in it; it is deeply tinged with tyranny. I allude to the *threats* which they published against all those of their workmen, who should attend the meeting on Brandon Hill,[2] and which threats ought never to be forgotten by *you*. But this hatred to the cause of public liberty is, I am sorry to say it, but too common amongst merchants, great manufacturers, and great farmers; especially those who have *risen suddenly* from the dunghill to a chariot. If we look a little more closely into the influence of riches, in such a state of things as this, we shall be less surprised at this apparently unnatural feeling in men who were, but the other day, merely journeymen and labourers themselves.—As soon as a foolish and unfeeling man gets rich, he becomes desirous of making the world believe, that *he never was poor*. He knows, that he has neither *birth* nor *education* to recommend him to the respect of those who have been less fortunate than himself. Though they pull their hats off to him, he always suspects that they are looking back to his mean origin; and, instead of adopting that kindness towards them, and that affability which would make them cheerfully acknowledge his superiority, he endeavours, by a distant and

---

2   Brandon Hill, Bristol, a popular site for reform meetings.

rigid deportment, to extort from their fears that which he wants the sense to obtain from their love. So that, at last, he verifies the old maxim: "*Set a beggar on horse-back, and he'll ride to the Devil.*"

This is the very worst species of aristocracy. It has all the *pride* and none of the *liberal sentiments* of the nobility and great gentry; and, the *farming* and *manufacturing* aristocracy is worse, a great deal, than the *mercantile*, because the latter must have more knowledge of the world, which is a great corrector of insolent and stupid pride. As to the *farmers*, who have grown into riches all of a sudden, they are the most cruel and hardened of all mankind. There are many of them, who really look upon their labourers as so many brutes; and, though they can scarcely spell their own names or pronounce the commonest words in an intelligible manner, they give themselves airs, which no gentleman ever thought of. I have heard sentiments from men of this description, which would not have disgraced the lips of negro-drivers or of a Dey of Algiers. Such men are always seeking to cause their origin to be forgotten. They would, with their hands, pull down their superiors, and, with their feet, trample down their inferiors; but, as they are frequently *tenants*, and, as their meanness is equal to their upstart pride; as they are afflicted with

"Meanness that soars, and pride that licks the dust,"

their chief aim is to trample into the very ground all who are beneath them in point of pecuniary circumstances, in order that they may have as few equals as possible, and that there may be *as wide a distance as possible between them and their labourers.*

Such men are naturally enemies to any Reform that would restore the great mass of the people to liberty and happiness; and, so blinded are they by these their base passions, that they almost prefer being *ruined themselves* to seeing their labourers enjoy their rights.

['An Address to the Men of Bristol', *Political Register*, 11 January 1817.]

*

Cobbett was a longstanding opponent of the Reverend Thomas Malthus, who argued in *An Essay on the Principle of Population* (1798) that the rate of population growth will always outstrip increases in the food supply. Malthus's theory holds that 'vice and misery' – including war, famine, disease, delayed marriage and prostitution – are the natural results of the tendency towards overpopulation, and irreducible by poor relief.

PARSON,

I have, during my life, detested many men; but never any one so much as you. Your book on POPULATION contains matter more offensive to my feelings even than that of the Dungeon-Bill. It could have sprung from no mind not capable of dictating acts of greater cruelty than any recorded in the history of the massacre of St. Bartholomew. Priests have, in all ages, been remarkable for cool and deliberate and unrelenting cruelty; but it seems to have been reserved for the Church of England to produce one who has a just claim to the atrocious pre-eminence. No assemblage of words can give an appropriate designation of you; and, therefore, as being the single word which best suits the character of such a man, I call you *Parson*, which, amongst other meanings, includes that of Boroughmonger Tool.

It must be very clear to every attentive reader of your book on *Population*, that it was written for the sole purpose of preparing before-hand a justification for those deeds of injustice and cruelty, of which the *Parish Vestry Bill*[3] appears to be a mere prelude. The project will fail: the tyrants will not have the *power* to commit the deeds, which you recommend, and which they intend to commit. But, that is no matter. It is right that the scheme should be exposed; in order that, as we ought to take the will for the deed, we may be prepared to do justice to the schemer and to the intended executors of the scheme.

In your book you shew, that, in certain cases, a *crowded* population has been attended with great evils, a great deal of unhappiness, misery and human degradation. You then, without any reason to bear you out, predict, or leave it to be clearly inferred, that the same is likely to take place in England. Your principles are almost all false; and your reasoning, in almost every instance, is the same. But, it is not my intention to waste my time on your abstract matter. I shall come, at once, to your practical result; to your recommendation to the Boroughmongers to pass laws to *punish the poor for marrying.* [...]

The bare idea of *a law* to punish a labourer and artisan for *marrying*; the bare idea is enough to fill one with indignation and horror. But, when this is moulded into a distinct proposal and strong recommendation we can hardly find patience sufficient to restrain us from breaking out into a volley of curses on the head of the proposer, be he who he may. [...]

To suppose such a thing possible as a Society, in which men, who are able and willing to work, cannot support their families, and ought, with a great part of the women, to be *compelled* to lead a life of celibacy, for fear of having children to be starved; to suppose such a thing possible is monstrous. But, if there should be such a Society, every one will say, that it ought instantly to be dissolved; because a state of nature would be far

---

3   The 1818 Act for the Regulation of Parish Vestries established a voting system in parish vestries, determined by contribution to the poor rates, as part of the reorganisation of parish poor relief.

preferable to it. However, the *laws of England* say, that no person shall be without a sufficiency of food and raiment; and, as we shall see, this part of our laws is no more than a recognition of those principles of the social compact, of which I have just been speaking.

['To Parson Malthus. On the Rights of the Poor; and on the cruelty recommended by him to be exercised towards the Poor', *Political Register*, 8 May 1819.]

*

Cobbett tried to warn his readers that tea and coffee were detrimental to their health, encouraging them to brew their own beer, or replace (taxed) tea and coffee with a cheaper substitute made from roasted wheat. With characteristic precision, he calculated that giving up tea for a year could save £11. 7s. 2d.

The drink, which has come to supply the place of beer has, in general, been *tea*. It is notorious, that tea has no *useful strength* in it; that it contains nothing *nutricious;* that it, besides being *good* for nothing, has *badness* in it, because it is well known to produce want of sleep in many cases, and, in all cases, to shake and weaken the nerves. It is, in fact, a weaker kind of laudanum, which enlivens for the moment and deadens afterwards. At any rate it communicates no strength to the body; it does not, in any degree, assist in affording what labour demands. It is, then, of no *use*. And, now, as to its *cost*, compared with that of *beer*. I shall make my comparison applicable to a year, or three hundred and sixty five days. I shall suppose the tea to be only five shillings the pound; the sugar only seven pence; the milk, only two pence a quart. The prices are at the very lowest. I shall suppose a tea pot to cost a shilling, six cups and saucers two shillings and sixpence, and six pewter spoons eighteen pence. How to estimate the firing I hardly know; but certainly there must, in the course of the year, be two hundred fires made that would not be made, were it not for tea drinking. Then comes the great article of all, the *time* employed in this tea making affair [...] the wretched thing amounts to a good third part of a good and able labourer's wages. For this money, he and his family may drink good and wholesome beer, and in a short time, out of the mere savings from this waste, may drink it out of silver cups and tankards. In a labourer's family, *wholesome* beer, that has a little life in it, is all that is wanted in *general*. [...] I view the tea drinking as a destroyer of health, an enfeebler of the frame, an engenderer of effeminacy and laziness, a debaucher of youth, and a maker of misery for old age.

[*Cottage Economy* (London, 1822), paras 23–9.]

*

In one of his most famous and memorable phrases, Cobbett characterized London as 'the Great Wen'. A 'wen' is a swelling, boil or sebaceous cyst, defined in Johnson's *Dictionary* as 'a dangerous fleshy excrescence'. Cobbett viewed the capital as a poisonous swelling on the body politic and in the following passage describes how London draws a constant stream of people, goods and money towards it, slowly destroying the health of the nation.

> Let me, Sir, beg of you just to take a ride out round this WEN. When you come back you will tell me that you see the foundations and part structure of about *three thousand new houses*. I shall then ask you, whence this can arise? You will hardly have the face to tell me, that it is a proof of increasing *national prosperity;* and I have the vanity to think, that, after getting you to sit down, to forget, for a quarter of an hour, all the allurements of Whitehall, and all the botheration of its neighbourhood; I am really of opinion, that I should make you confess, that there is something radically wrong; and that, at last, some dreadful scenes must arise, unless measures of prevention be adopted. In short, it is to suppose a man an idiot, to suppose him not to perceive, that this monstrous WEN is now sucking up the vitals of the country.
>
> And by what means does it suck up those vitals, but by the means of that enormous taxation, which takes away the capital of the farmer, the rent of the landlord, and the wages of the labourer? Having taken a ride round London, you then ought to take a ride round the country; go into the country towns, see the wasting tradesmen and their families; but, above all things, go to the *villages*, and see the misery of the labourers; see their misery, compared to the happy state in which they lived before the swellings out of this corrupt and all-devouring WEN. When I tell you that the villages, the homesteds, the cottages, are growing daily more and more out of repair, you will say *it is not true;* therefore, let that tell for nothing. But you will not deny the wretchedness of the *labourers!* The landlords and the farmers can tell their own tale. They tell their own tale in remonstrances and prayers, addressed to the House. Nobody tells the tale of the labourer.

['To Mr. Canning', *Political Register*, 22 February 1823.]

*

William Wilberforce led the campaign first for the abolition of the slave trade and then, in the 1820s, for the emancipation of slaves in the West Indies. In this open letter, Cobbett responded to Wilberforce's *Appeal to the religion, justice and humanity of the inhabitants of the British empire in behalf of the negro slaves in the West Indies*, which contrasted the conditions of slaves in the West Indies with those enjoyed by 'free British labourers'. Wilberforce had begun his career as a supporter of parliamentary reform, but from 1812 represented a pocket borough controlled by Lord Calthorpe, his wife's cousin. He supported the repressive measures of Lord Liverpool's government at the end of the Napoleonic Wars and in the wake of the Peterloo Massacre of 1819, in which 11 people were killed and several hundred injured when the yeomanry cavalry charged into a crowd demanding universal suffrage and annual parliaments.

WILBERFORCE,

I HAVE you before me in a canting pamphlet [...] You talk a great deal about the partiality of the laws in the West Indies. What you say about the inhumanity of these laws is right enough; but have you Wilberforce, have you ever done any thing to mitigate the laws which exist in this country with regard to those free British labourers of which you so cantingly talk? Never have you done one single act, in favour of the labourers of this country; but many and many an act have you done against them. In this canting and rubbishy pamphlet, you bring forward in the way of charge against the West India planters and Assemblies, the following: that "the killing of a slave was not to be punished, according to their laws, unless the killing were committed wantonly, or from *bloodimindedness* or *cruel intention*. And," say you, "lest there should be any disposition to visit the crime too severely, it was specially enacted, that, 'if any Negro or other slave, while under punishment by his master, or master's order, for running away, or any other crimes or misdemeanors towards his said master, unfortunately *shall suffer in life* or *member*, which seldom happens, *no person whatever shall be liable to any fine therefore*.'" This is pretty damnable, to be sure: this is tyranny: here is horrible slavery: the tyrants ought to be stricken down by thunderbolts, or to be otherwise destroyed. But, Wilberforce, listen to me a bit; did you never hear of a parcel of people, who were assembled at Manchester on the 16th August, 1819. These were persons whom you call *free British labourers*. Well then, these labourers had not run away from any masters. They had committed no crimes or misdemeanors towards any masters. About five hundred of them were, nevertheless, killed or wounded: they suffered "in *life or member*." And pray, WILBERFORCE, was any body punished for killing and wounding them? Did any body pay any fines for killing and wounding these free British labourers? Were not those who committed the killing and wounding *thanked* for their good conduct on that occasion? Did you ever object to those thanks? Did you not object to any parliamentary inquiry into the conduct of those who caused that killing and wounding? Well then, this was all right, was it?

['To William Wilberforce', *Political Register*, 30 August 1823.]

*

Cobbett's attacks on modern finance and public credit often include violent expressions of anti-Semitism. The following extract from *A History of the Protestant "Reformation"* moves from the beginning of the stock market, Bank of England and national debt, created in the 1690s to fund war with France, to the Catholic prohibition on usury. However, as Leonora Nattrass argues, this passage is more complicated than simple bigotry: here, Cobbett both identifies with medieval prejudices and historicises them, retaining the post-Reformation rise of capitalism as his primary target.[4]

> Thus arose loans, funds, banks, bankers, bank-notes and a NATIONAL DEBT; things that England had never heard or dreamed of, before this war for "preserving the Protestant religion as by law established;" things without which she had had a long and glorious career of many centuries, and had been the greatest and happiest country in the world; things which she never would, and never could, have heard of, had it not been for what is audaciously called the "REFORMATION," seeing that to lend money at interest; that is to say, for gain; that is to say, to receive money for the use of money; seeing that to do this was contrary, and still is contrary to the principles of the Catholic Church; and, amongst Christians, or professors of Christianity, such a thing was never heard of before that which is impudently called "THE REFORMATION." [...] JEWS did it; but, then Jews had no civil rights. They existed only by mere sufferance. They could be shut up, or banished, or even sold, at the king's pleasure. They were regarded as a sort of monsters, who professed to be the lineal descendants and to hold the opinions of those who had murdered the SON OF GOD AND SAVIOUR OF MEN. They were not permitted to practise their blasphemies openly. If they had synagogues, they were unseen by the people. The horrid wretches themselves were compelled to keep out of public view on Sundays, and on Saints' days. They were not allowed to pollute with their presence the streets or the roads of a Christian country, on days set apart for public devotion. In degraded wretches like these USURY, that is, receiving money for the use of money, was tolerated, just for the same cause that incest is tolerated amongst dogs.

[*A History of the Protestant "Reformation" in England and Ireland* (London, 1829), para. 403.]

*

---

[4]   See L. Nattrass, *The Politics of Style* (Cambridge, 1995), pp. 164–7.

Throughout *Rural Rides*, Cobbett's descriptions of the landscape and people of southern England are punctuated with angry tirades. He is particularly angry when he comes across evangelical preachers, accusing them of forcing religion on the poor without doing anything to alleviate their poverty.

> Coming through the village of BENENDEN, I heard a man, at my right, talking very loud about *houses! houses! houses!* It was a Methodist parson, in a house, close by the road side. I pulled up, and stood still, in the middle of the road, but looking, in silent soberness, into the window (which was open) of the room in which the preacher was at work. I believe my stopping rather disconcerted him; for he got into shocking *repetition*. 'Do you KNOW,' said he, laying great stress on the word KNOW: 'do you KNOW, that you have ready for you houses, houses I say; I say do you KNOW; do you KNOW that you have houses in the heavens not made with hands? Do you KNOW this from *experience?* Has the blessed Jesus *told you so?*' And, on he went to say, that, if Jesus had told them so, they would be saved, and that if he had not, and did not, they would be damned. Some girls whom I saw in the room, plump and rosy as could be, did not seem at all daunted by these menaces; and indeed, they appeared to me to be thinking much more about getting houses for themselves *in this world first:* just to *see a little* before they entered, or endeavoured to enter, or even thought much about, those '*houses*' of which the parson was speaking: *houses* with pig-styes and little snug gardens attached to them, together with all the other domestic and conjugal circumstances, these girls seemed to be preparing themselves for. The truth is, these fellows have no power on the minds of any but the miserable.
>
> [*Rural Rides*, ed. I. Dyck (London, 2001), pp. 140–1 (31 August 1823).]

*

Cobbett frequently expressed his animosity towards 'Scotch *feelosofers*', the school of political economy associated with the *Edinburgh Review*. While his changing views towards Scotland are discussed in more detail in a later chapter, the following tirade from *Rural Rides* shows Cobbett's view of 'Scotch' political economy as a cruel and oppressive system of alienated labour.

> I have never been able clearly to comprehend what the beastly Scotch *feelosofers* mean by their '*national wealth*'; but, as far as I can understand them, this is their meaning: that national wealth means, that which is *left* of the products of the country over and above what is *consumed*, or *used*, by those whose labour causes the products to be. This being the notion, it follows, of course, that the *fewer* poor devils you can screw the products

out of, the *richer* the nation is. This is, too, the notion of BURDETT as expressed in his silly and most nasty, musty aristocratic speech of last session. What, then, is to be done with this *over-produce*? Who is to have it? Is it to go to pensioners, placemen, tax-gatherers, dead-weight people, soldiers, gendarmerie, police-people, and, in short, to whole millions *who do no work at all*? Is this a cause of '*national wealth*'? Is a nation made *rich* by taking the food and clothing from those who create them, and giving them to those who do nothing of any use? [...]

What a *twist* a head must have before it can come to the conclusion, that the *nation* gains in *wealth* by the government being able to cause the work to be done by those who have hardly any share in the fruit of the labour! What a *twist* such a head must have! The Scotch *feelosofers*, who seem all to have been, by nature, formed for negro-drivers, have an insuperable objection to all those establishments and customs which occasion *holidays*. They call them a *great inderance*, a great *bar to industry*, a great *drawback from* '*national wealth*'. I wish each of these unfeeling fellows had a spade put into his hand for ten days, only ten days, and that he were compelled to dig only just as much as one of the common labourers at Fulham. The metaphysical gentleman would, I believe, soon discover the *use of holidays!* But, *why* should men, why should *any* men, work *hard?* Why, I ask, should they work *incessantly*, if working part of the days of the week be sufficient? Why should the people at MILTON, for instance, work incessantly, when they now raise food and clothing and fuel and every necessary *to maintain well five times their number?* And, pray, say, thou conceited Scotch feelosofer, how the '*national wealth*' can be increased by making these people work *incessantly*, that they may raise food and clothing, to go to feed and clothe *people who do not work at all?*

[*Rural Rides*, ed. I. Dyck (London, 2001), pp. 291–3 (30 August 1826).]

*

Cobbett grew ever angrier as he grew older, and years of political persecution made him increasingly paranoid. Here, he defends his strident style of journalism.

How many well-meaning people have exclaimed, "It is a pity that Cobbett is so *violent*"; such persons never ask themselves whether they would think a man too violent who should knock down and break the limbs of a ruffian, who is coming, knife in hand, to cut his throat, and that too, without the smallest provocation on earth. This has been my state: when I began to write, I had attacked no writer, I fell foul of nobody in the shape of a "literary gentleman." I was as modest as a maid, and dealt in qualifications, and modifications, and mitigations to the best of my poor powers in the line of palavering; but when I discovered that it was envy that was at work in my assailants, I called to mind the saying of Swift; namely, "The moment a man of real talent makes his first appearance before the public, the whole battalion of dunces beat to arms and sally forth against him; and down he falls for ever, if he have not courage as well as talent." These are nearly his words; and I am infinitely indebted to him for having enabled me to read these words. They occurred to me, when I was first unprovokedly assaulted; and I instantly resolved to proceed in the very way in which I have always proceeded, giving three, four, or ten blows for one; and never, in any case, ceased to pursue the assailant, in some way or other, until he was completely down.

['Cobbett's Egotism', *Political Register*, 26 January 1828.]

Chapter 6
Sound Money and Cottage Economy

Cobbett's views on economic matters fall into two distinct but related categories. On the one hand, at the national level, following the renewal of the war with France in 1803 he became a persistent critic of the economic policy of the government, particularly for its handling of the financing of the Napoleonic Wars and its effects upon the common people. These policies he saw as undermining the prosperity of the world he had known as a youth and his concerns about the effects of the 'funding system' and 'paper money' was to become central to his criticism of the way the country was governed. Cobbett's views, clung to tenaciously throughout the rest of his life, directed his belief in the need for parliamentary reform and the destruction of the system of self-serving corruption he called 'the Thing'. On the other hand, by origins a countryman, Cobbett saw the real wealth of the country in agriculture and the only decent life that people could live in a rural world where they could largely provide for themselves. As a result he had a passionate interest in all things agricultural and horticultural which he saw as central to the nation's wealth and to the lives of its people. One of his most persistent concerns was to improve the standards of farming and husbandry by careful 'economy', meaning good management. As a working farmer for most of his life, combining it to a remarkable extent with an incredibly busy life of journalism and political activism, he was as ready to offer opinions on laying out an asparagus bed or building a farm gate as he was on the national debt and paper money. Moreover, seeking to step aside from the onward march of commercialism and industry, he promoted 'cottage economy', as a self-sufficient and attainable mode of existence which would free the rural labourer from dependence on others, avoid the snares of dubious products such as potatoes and tea, and prevent his having to call on the poor law other than in genuinely unfortunate circumstances. 'Cottage Economy' was an idea which was to have a huge impact long after Cobbett's immediate concerns and his own life were over. The model of peasant-style self-sufficiency was to exercise a powerful impact not only for the rural labourers for whom it was intended but also upon the first wave of industrial workers seeking an alternative to factory life. So too for generations of rural idealists seeking to recreate a better life in the country, making *Cottage Economy* one of Cobbett's most popular and regularly reprinted works.

Living through an era of great economic transformation and the beginnings of the industrial revolution, he continued to see agriculture as the true basis of a country's wealth. As the long wars against revolutionary and Napoleonic France progressed and produced high taxes, poor harvests and periods of acute distress,

Cobbett increasingly viewed the common people as the victims of politicians and financiers. He evoked the traditional argument of earlier eighteenth-century Tory writers such as Jonathan Swift and Viscount Bolingbroke who blamed the ruin of the country on the politicians and their corrupt supporters in the City. One of the fixations of 'country Tories' was the National Debt, created as long ago as the 1690s to finance the wars against Louis XIV, which allowed the government to raise long-term and, in effect, perpetual loans, providing it could meet the interest payments out of the taxes it levied upon the country. For some it was a pernicious system which benefited the financiers and bankers, who earned the interest at the expense of the landed classes who paid taxes upon their land and everyone who paid excise duties on a wide range of commodities. As its first critics – like Jonathan Swift – were quick to notice, debts incurred in temporary circumstances produced a permanent burden upon the taxpayer. Hopes that the National Debt would be paid off faded as the eighteenth century wore on and further wars added to it. At the outbreak of the wars with France in 1793 it stood at £243 million pounds against a government income of only £17 million, by the time war resumed in 1803 the debt had more than doubled to £516 million as war expenditure had ballooned during the 1790s with the cost met by loans and taxes. By 1816 it stood at nearly £800 million where the debts incurred to defeat Napoleon burdened the country and its people with extra taxation for decades to come. It was little wonder that previous criticisms of the National Debt by earlier writers and statesmen should turn into a roar of disapproval from Cobbett who saw both the impoverishment of his countrymen and the enrichment of the financiers proceeding apace. Moreover, he increasingly saw politicians, such as Pitt, in an unholy alliance with the money men, supporting each other to their mutual benefit at the expense of the nation.

Ironically, Cobbett owed his views on public finance not only to an older generation of 'Country' opinion, but also to the writings of his once arch-enemy, Thomas Paine. Paine's *Decline and Fall of the English System of Finance* (1796), which he had read and once disparaged, fitted in well with Cobbett's growing unease with the implications of the British government's methods in financing the war. Paine had argued that the debt had grown with each succeeding war in the eighteenth century, the circulation of paper money increased, producing depreciation and higher prices, forcing in turn large loans, more notes and further depreciation. A point would be reached when faith in paper money would be lost and people would find that there was nothing like enough bullion to back up the currency. On his calculation, there were in 1796 at least £60 million of banknotes in circulation but no more than £2 million in gold at the Bank of England. Britain's whole system of credit and war finance, he believed, was entering a terminal phase which would lead to financial collapse and political revolution. When, a year later, in 1797, Pitt's government was forced to suspend cash payments in gold from the Bank of England, it almost seemed that Paine's predictions were about to be realised. In fact, they were not, as the British financial and credit system proved more robust than anticipated. Initially, too, Cobbett had dismissed Paine's views as those of an 'arch rebel' and was prepared to take on trust the financial operations of the government at least up to 1802 and the short-lived Peace of Amiens. From 1803, however, Cobbett began to believe national bankruptcy was looming, using arguments which he later acknowledged came from Paine. To the old fear of a ballooning National Debt was added the growth of paper money and the prediction that when confidence in paper money fell below that of bullion, financial collapse would follow. While out of this wreckage he hoped a system purified of its corrupt money-men and stock-jobbers might emerge, he also feared that in that crash much of the traditional order might be overwhelmed.[1] As he became more radical in his denunciations of the government after the Napoleonic Wars were over, he was readier to acknowledge Paine's influence, claiming in 1819 that from his 'expiring flambeau I lighted my taper and from the year 1803 to the present hour I have been warning the Parliament and the Government against the consequences of this fatal system, which has at last produced in this once happy country, misery such as never was witnessed before in the world...'.[2] In *Paper Against Gold* in 1815 he collected 32 articles from the *Political Register* since 1810 to 'trace the paper-money system to its deadly root'.[3] Cobbett's preoccupations with the fiscal system gave rise to his famous offer to be broiled alive on a gridiron if his prophecies of financial ruin were not proved true. He persuaded himself that he was in the right, though many commentators at the time and subsequently accused Cobbett of being both naïve and alarmist. It was incontrovertible, however, that almost 25 years of war had saddled the country with enormous debts which required servicing through taxation. To the end of his life, when Parliamentary Reform was being passed in 1832, he saw it as an opportunity for the final triumph over 'the Thing' and over a nexus of economic and political policies which had ruined the prosperity the country had once enjoyed.

Cobbett always had an alternative to this record of mismanagement and corruption in the financial world; it was a prosperous agriculture, alive to improvements in crops and providing everyone, farmers and labourers alike, with the 'good living' he remembered from the time of his youth. His interest in agriculture never wavered, irrespective of the huge burden of his journalistic output, his constant publishing ventures, and his political activism. A working

---

[1]   See D.A. Wilson, *Paine and Cobbett: the Transatlantic Connection* (Kingston, 1988), pp. 153–7.

[2]   *Political Register*, 18 December 1819.

[3]   Its fuller title was *Paper Against Gold and Glory Against Prosperity. Or, An account of the Rise, Progress, Extent, and Present State of the Funds, and of the Paper-Money of Great Britain; etc.* (London, 1815). For its evolution see M.L. Pearl, *William Cobbett: A Bibliographical Account of his Life and Times* (reprint edition Westport, Conn. 1971), pp. 89–92.

farmer, he was part of the general movement of agricultural improvement known to historians as the 'agricultural revolution'. Interest in farming and farming methods was both fashionable and big business. George III kept a model farm at Windsor and pioneer improvers such as Jethro Tull and 'Turnip' Townsend were national names even before Cobbett was born. During Cobbett's lifetime Coke of Norfolk was holding annual meetings on his Norfolk estates to demonstrate progressive farming methods. Farming was an essential industry, the annual harvest still dictating the wellbeing of the whole economy and making up the largest component of the domestic economy even at the time of his death. Although commerce and industry were growing apace during his lifetime, Cobbett's gaze remained predominantly towards agriculture and traditional domestic manufacture. Moreover his 'opinions' on agriculture were as strong as his views on politics, both in regard to its place in national life and the detail of its techniques and practices. Cobbett was always ready to pass comment on the state of agriculture and agricultural practice wherever he was, occupying a considerable part of his most famous work, *Rural Rides*, as well as his tours of Scotland and Ireland. Inevitably, as shown elsewhere, his experience in America had a powerful influence too. Producing a passionate advocacy of crops such as maize, 'Cobbett's Corn', whose manifold uses he not only wrote about but demonstrated. His private correspondence switched naturally and without effort between reform politics and breeds of sheep and his role as a practising farmer and horticulturalist gave his views a 'hands on' quality which makes them still relevant. While some of Cobbett's horticultural writings, such as *The American Gardener* (1821) and *The English Gardener* (1829) were aimed at the larger gardens of gentlemen, entering a market shared by many other writers, and others more specific, such as *A Treatise on Cobbett's Corn* (1828), *Cottage Economy* was aimed at 'the conducting of the affairs of a Labourer's family'. It promoted an ideal of self-sufficiency which proved immensely influential both as a vindication of a rural life and a powerful allure for those seeking escape from an urban industrial world. Although the idea of a world of rural self-sufficiency was ultimately to be eclipsed by urbanisation and industrialisation, within 10 years of Cobbett's death, Chartists were attempting to set up co-operative, peasant smallholdings under their Land Plan, subscribed to by hundreds of industrial workers seeking to return to the land. A myriad of experiments in 'back to the land', at home and abroad, owed much to Cobbett's original classic of self-sufficiency which also influenced early socialists such as William Morris and Robert Blatchford.[4] He influenced too, late nineteenth-century attempts to settle the unemployed with 'four acres and a cow', provide urban workers with allotments, settle ex-servicemen on smallholdings after the First World War and

---

[4]   See A. Hadfield, *The Chartist Land Company* (Newton Abbott, 1970); J. Marsh, *Back to the Land: the Pastoral Impulse in Victorian England from 1880 to 1914* (London, 1982).

had a role in the emergence of self-sufficiency and rural communes as part of the counter-culture of the twentieth century.

*

Cobbett's debt to Jonathan Swift (1667–1745), the Tory writer best known for his *Gulliver's Travels* but as a political writer a fierce opponent of the National Debt, was acknowledged in the heading for Cobbett's denunciation of the financial system. In a series of articles for the *Register* in 1810, written while imprisoned in Newgate, Cobbett set out his systematic assault on the way the public finances had been mismanaged. The articles were later collated under the same title, 'Paper Against Gold', that he had used in the *Register*, as a two volume publication in 1815.

> "I ever abominated that scheme of politics, (now about 30 years old) of setting up a monied interest in opposition to the landed. For I conceived, there could not be a truer maxim in our government than this, that the possessors of the soil are the best judges of what is for the advantage of the kingdom. If others had thought the same way, funds of credit and South Sea projects would neither have been felt nor heard of.'–SWIFT, 1720.

> ['Paper Against Gold: being an examination of the Bullion Committee: in a series of letters to the Tradesmen and Farmers in and near Salisbury. Letter I', *Political Register*, 1 September 1810.]

*

Cobbett blamed Pitt the Younger, First Lord of the Treasury and effectively Prime Minister, for the escalation of debt during the first series of wars against France. For Cobbett this was a particularly bitter example of betrayal, because Pitt had laid claim before the wars began to be a financial reformer and had staked his political position on schemes to reduce government indebtedness.

> How many times were we told, that it required but *one* more campaign; *one* more; only *one* more *vigorous* campaign, to put an end to the war; to destroy, to annihilate, for ever, the *resources* of France. Alas! those resources have not been destroyed. They have increased in a fearful degree; while we have accumulated hundreds of millions of Debt in the attempt. How many writers have flattered us, from time to time, with the hope, nay, the certainty (if we would but persevere) of triumphing over the French by the means of our *riches!* To how many of these deceivers have we been so foolish as to listen! It is this credulity, which has led to the present state of things; and, unless we shake it off at once, and resolve to look our dangers in the face, we shall, I greatly fear, experience that fate which our deceivers

told us would be experienced by our enemy. PITT, it is well known, grew into favour with the nation in consequence of his promises and his plans to pay-off the National Debt; and, this same PITT, who found that Debt 257 millions, left it upwards of 600 millions, after having, for twenty years, had the full power of managing all the resources of the nation; after having, for nearly the whole of that time, had the support of three fourths, if not more, of the Members of the House of Commons; after having, of course, adopted whatever measures he thought proper, during the whole of that time. He found the Debt *two hundred* and fifty odd millions, and he left it *six hundred* and fifty odd. This was what was done for England by that PITT, whose own *private debts* the *people* had to pay, besides the expense of a *monument* to his memory! This is what every man in England should bear constantly in mind.

['Paper Against Gold ... Letter III', *Political Register*, 12 September 1810.]

*

The growth of the National Debt was ineluctably linked for Cobbett to the growth of that twin evil of the growth of paper money. The recipients of interest were seen by Cobbett as directly responsible for the expanding circulation of banknotes.

When the Stock owners, or Public Creditors, as they are sometimes called, went to the Bank to receive their dividends, or interest, they might have either bank notes, or Gold and Silver, according to their choice. Some persons chose the coin, and some the paper. But, as the Debt increased, and, of course, the amount of the dividends, or interest, it was evident, from what has already been said, that the Bank would possess a less and less quantity of Gold and Silver in proportion to the quantity of its paper. [...]
    This the Bank could bear before the Anti-Jacobin war; but, when that war had nearly doubled the Debt, the Interest, and the number of the payments, on account of Interest; when this increase had taken place, the Bank found it necessary, not only to augment the general quantity of its notes; it found it necessary not only to add to the total amount of its notes; that is to say, to put out a greater sum in notes, than it had out before the Anti-Jacobin war; but, it also found it necessary to put out some notes of *lower amount* than it already had, in order to pay *the parts of ten pounds,* which we have just mentioned.

['Paper Against Gold ... Letter X', *Political Register*, 10 October 1810.]

*

For Cobbett, paper money was an unnecessary evil and one which, with the National Debt, created new ones, allowing the government to erode traditional liberties, fund a standing army and pauperise the people through its inflationary effects. In effect, Cobbett identified the deterioration of the country with the mismanagement of the financial system. He had no fears about ending it.

> Why, Gentlemen, should the total destruction of the paper-money produce any of these effects? Why should it destroy all *property;* why produce *bloodshed;* why destroy our *holy religion?* I have before told you, that the paper-money was unknown in England, till within about 107 years. England did very well before that time. The people of England were brave and free, happy at home and dreaded abroad, long before paper-money was heard of. Why, then, should they now believe, that, without paper-money, they would be reduced to a state of barbarism and slavery? The Church, as it is now established, existed long before paper-money was thought of, and so did *all these laws*, which we yet *boast* of as the great bulwarks of our freedom; and, what is more, I defy any man to show me one single law, *in favour of the liberties of the people,* which has been passed *since* the establishment of the Paper-Money System, while numerous laws have been passed hostile to those liberties. Before the existence of the National Debt and the Bank, the House of Commons used frequently to refuse to grant the money called for by the Crown; since they have existed, no grant of the kind has ever been refused by the House. Before the Paper System existed, there was no standing army in England; before the Paper System existed, there were not more than *two hundred thousand paupers* in England and Wales; there are now *twelve hundred thousand.*

['Paper Against Gold ... Letter XXIX', *Political Register*, 3 August 1811.]

*

Cobbett explained to the machine-breakers of the post-war period, the Luddites, that the origins of the distresses lay in the inflation caused by paper money.

> Before the wars against the French People, which wars have ended in replacing our king's and country's *old enemies*, the family of *Bourbon*, on the thrones of France, Spain and Naples, and which have restored the Inquisition that Napoleon had put down; before those wars, the chief part of the money in England was *Gold and Silver*. But, even the first war against the people of France cost so much money, that bank-paper was used in such great abundance, that, in 1797, people became alarmed, and ran to the Bank of England to get real money for the notes which they

held. Then was fulfilled the prophecy of Mr. PAINE. The Bank *could not pay their notes!* The Bank Directors went to PITT and told him their fears. He called a Council, and the Council issued an *order* to the Bank to *refuse* to pay their promissory notes in specie, though the notes were all payable to the *bearer* and on *demand*. The parliament *afterwards* passed an Act to *protect* Pitt, the Council, and the Bank Directors *against the law,* which had been violated in these transactions!

From this time, there has been little besides paper-money. This became plenty, and, of course, wages and corn and every thing became *high in price.*

['A Letter to the Luddites', *Political Register*, 30 November 1816.]

*

Cobbett argued in the year after the war that the political and financial systems were so mutually interdependent that reform could never come before the system of paper money and debt were destroyed. He criticised those who saw reform as possible without tackling the fiscal system.

This is the subject of real importance to the country. A bawling Speech-maker, who always ends without saying anything, and who never thinks of attempting to *do* any of those things which he declares to be necessary, has observed that to talk of *this* matter, until a Reform be accomplished, is like *putting the cart before the horse*. If this wise person be correct, all that I can say is, that the horse must come after the cart; for there never will be a Reform of the Parliament as long as the Paper System can be carried on. We may laugh at the release of Sir Massah Menassah Lopez; we may laugh at the childish, snivelling stuff about Grampound; but these are the only Reforms that we shall see as long as the Paper System shall continue to prevail. And, though I hold it to be just and laudable to contend for a Reform; though I know that the nation never can be itself again without a Reform; still I must despise the man who affects to believe that there ever can be a Reform of the Commons House as long as the Paper System remains whole and entire; and I cannot help deeming those to be very great hypocrites, or very weak men indeed, who are constantly bawling about Reform, and who turn from the subject of Paper Money as something too small for the grasp of their amazing capacities.

[*Political Register*, 17 February 1821.]

*

For Cobbett, the way to cut through the interdependence of what he called 'the Thing' was simply to cease to pay the interest owed to those who had loaned money to the government. Cobbett believed that this could be done without calamitous effects.

Having now, Sir, swept away this childish stuff, let us come *to the point:* let us come to the question of *public faith,* two words very much used, very little understood in their application to this matter, but capable of doing an enormous quantity of mischief to the nation. I assert that, whether the Nation pay the whole of the interest as it is now paid, or whether it cease to pay any interest at all, is merely, like every other question of state, a question of EXPEDIENCY. We have so long called the thing a Debt; we have so long called the funds *property;* we have so long talked of a *mortgage* which the Fundholders have upon the Nation; we have so long called the Fundholders *Creditors;* that, at last, we have confounded a matter of State with a private transaction; two things wholly distinct in their origin, in their progress, and in all their bearing and effects.

It is pretty enough to hear Mr. BARING talk of *dishonesty* in not continuing to pay to the full nominal amount; it is pretty enough to hear him appeal to *morals* and *religion* on behalf of the Fundholder. It is pretty enough to hear him dash along so glibly and say that the Debtor is not to plead *inability* to pay, until he has given up his all. But, if the Fundholder now receives from the Farmer two bushels of wheat instead of the price of the one bushel which he lent; if the mortgagee receives, in fact, double interest, when he contracted only for single interest; if the man who lent nine and twenty shillings in the shape of a guinea, now demands a guinea and eight shillings back in return; if this be the case, where is the *honesty,* where the *morality,* where the *religion,* of these harpies of Loanmakers; and where is the justice, where the wisdom, where even the common prudence of the government that will pass and enforce Laws for compelling the borrowers to submit to such lenders? [...]

We are now approaching the time, when this subject will force itself upon the country. I foresaw that it would so force itself, and I fully and boldly discussed it many years ago, in spite of reproaches and calumnies. In 1806, just about this time fifteen years ago; when the interest of the Debt was not much more than half what it is now, I insisted upon the *justice* and *necessity* of ceasing to pay that interest. I maintained that it was just and wise to cease to pay any part of the interest; this doctrine I still hold; and, I think it is high time that I receive some answer other than that of abuse, if I am to receive any answer at all.

[*Political Register*, 17 February 1821.]

*

When it appeared in 1819 that the government was attempting to do what Cobbett had long-believed impossible, reintroduce the backing of the currency with bullion, he forecast disaster, offering his famous boast to be broiled alive if proved wrong.

> The Borough-mongers, seeing the danger of continuing a paper-bubble, as Grenville now himself calls it. Seeing that a bubble is a thing that may, at any moment, burst, have "*resolved*" to return to cash-payments; that is to say, they have *resolved*, that the nation shall, with a currency greatly diminished in quantity, continue to pay to the pawn to the former nominal amount of payment; that is to say, to make the nation pay, in fact, two, or, perhaps, three time as much in taxes as it paid before; that is to say, to give to the sinecure placeman the price of two or three bushels of wheat instead of that of one which was given him before. To resolve, my friends, is an easy matter; but, as our pretty fellows will find, to *execute* a resolution is sometimes a very difficult matter; and, if they execute their *resolution*, though it has now assumed the shape of a law, I will give Castlereagh leave to put me upon a gridiron, while Sidmouth stirs the fire, and Canning stands by making a jest of my writhing and my groans.[5] And yet, *if they do not execute it,* what a figure will they *then* make? Will anyone *then* have the impudence to pretend to believe, that they are the men to extricate England from her difficulties? And will those little bands of rapacious miscreants, called PITT CLUBS, any longer dare to show their faces before the oppressed and insulted people, whom they assisted to plunge into ruin, misery, and degradation?

[*Political Register*, 13 November 1819.]

*

Cobbett remained true to his principles of sound money to the end of his life. His Address to the electors of Manchester when seeking election in the reformed parliament in 1832 concentrated heavily upon his proposals for cutting a swathe through government expenditure, including ceasing payment of the interest on the National Debt.

> GENTLEMEN,
>
> IN all cases where men are about to form engagements with each other, it is, before all things, necessary for them to start with a clear

---

[5]   Charles Canning, Viscount Castlereagh (Robert Stewart), and Viscount Sidmouth (Henry Addington) were leading members of Lord Liverpool's government.

understanding with regard to what each party shall do, in consequence of the engagement.

I will therefore clearly state to you the things which I will do (God giving me life and health), if you choose me for one of your representatives. I have always found, that the short way to arrive at any just object, in the accomplishment of which you stand in need of the co-operation of others, is to declare to those others, at the outset, openly and explicitly *what the object is;* and therefore I will now, in the most open and plain manner, state the things which I wish to see accomplished, and which, if you send me to the Parliament, I will use my utmost endeavours to cause to be accomplished; and which things are as follows:

1. To put an end to all pensions, sinecures, grants, allowances, half-pay, and all other emoluments now paid out of the taxes, except for such public services as, upon a very scrupulous examination, shall be found fully to merit them; and to reduce all salaries to the American standard.

2. To discharge the standing army, except such part of the ordnance and artillery as may be necessary to maintain the arsenals at the seaports in a state of readiness for war; and to abolish the military academies, and dispose of all barracks and other property now applied to military uses.

3. To make the counties, each according to its whole number of members of parliament, maintain and equip a body of militia, horse as well as foot and artillery, at the country expense, and to have these bodies, as they are in America, mustered at stated periods; so that, at any time, a hundred thousand efficient men may be ready to come into the field, if the defence of the kingdom require it.

4. To abolish tithes of every description; to leave to the clergy the churches, the church-yards, the parsonage houses, and the *ancient* glebes; and, for the rest, leave them to the voluntary contributions of the people.

5. To take all the rest of the property, commonly called church-property; all the houses, lands, manors, tolls, rents, and real property of every kind, now possessed by bishops, chapters, or other ecclesiastical bodies, and all the misapplied property of corporate bodies of every sort; and also all the property called crown-lands, or crown-estates, including that of the Duchies of Cornwall and Lancaster; and sell them all, and apply the proceeds to the discharge of the Debt which the late parliaments contracted with the fundholders.

6. To cease, during the first six months after June 1832, to pay interest on a fourth part of the Debt; second six months, to cease to pay

interest on another fourth; and so on for the other two fourths; so that no more interest, or any part of the Debt would be paid, after the end of two years.

['To the Electors of Manchester', *Political Register*, 10 September 1831.]

*

But Cobbett believed when the worst abuses of 'the Thing' had been rectified, there would be scope to give the labourer a chance to live a better life.

As long as the parliament remained unreformed, there was no hope of better days for the labourer; the farmer was unable to give him a sufficiency of wages without ruin to himself, owing to the enormous burdens which had to bear. The reform of parliament will, and must diminish these burdens. It was useless for men to be industrious, sober, and frugal, while misery was still their lot in spite of the constant practice of these virtues. They laboured in despair; and therefore when idleness was as well rewarded as industry, why should they labour? *Things will now be changed:* we shall have encouragement to practise care and frugality. I am about to teach you how each of you who has a little piece of ground in his hands may greatly add to his wellbeing; but even this I was discouraged from doing as long as the parliament remained unreformed. I, some years ago, wrote a little book called "COTTAGE ECONOMY", of which book scores of thousands of copies have been sold. It teaches the brewing of beer, the making of bread, the rearing of pigs and poultry, the keeping of a cow, the curing of bacon; and, in short, everything necessary to teach a small family how to make the most of a little bit of ground, and how to live well by good management. Particularly how to dispense with the everlasting pot hung over the fire to cook the soul-degrading potatoes.

[*Two-Penny Trash*, 1 April 1831.]

*

In contrast to the evils wrought by high finance upon the economy Cobbett advocated his vision of a decent competence for everyone. In his introduction to *Cottage Economy* Cobbett outlined the advantages to the labourer of being able to provide for himself with the essentials of life. Ever the practical horticulturalist, he set out the means by which an ordinary labourer could provide himself with much of what he required for an adequate subsistence.

The laws, the economy, or management, of a state may be such as to render it impossible for the Labourer, however skilful and industrious, to maintain his family in health and decency; and, such has, for many years past, been the management of the affairs of this once truly great and happy land. A system of paper money, the effect of which was to take from the labourer the half of his earnings, was what no industry and care could make head against. I do not pretend, that this system was done *by design*. But, no matter for the *cause;* such was the effect.

Better times, however, are approaching. The Labourer now appears likely to obtain that hire of which he is worthy; and, therefore, this appears to me to be the time to press upon him the *duty* of using his best exertions for the rearing of his family in a manner that must give him the best security for happiness to himself, his wife and children, and to make him, in all respects, what his forefathers were. The people of England have been famed, in all ages, for their *good living;* for the *abundance of their food* and *goodness of their attire.* The old sayings about English roast beef and plum-pudding, and about English hospitality, had not their foundations in *nothing.* And, in spite of all refinements of sickly minds, it is *abundant living* amongst the people at large, which is the great test of good government, and the surest basis of national greatness and security. [...]

And, bear in mind, that, if the state of the labourer has its disadvantages when compared with other callings and conditions of life, it has also its advantages. It is free from the torments of ambition, and from a great part of the causes of ill-health, for which not all the riches in the world and all the circumstances of high rank are a compensation. The able and prudent labourer is always *safe*, at the least, and that is what few men are who are lifted above him. They have losses and crosses to fear, the very thought of which never enters his mind, if he act well his part towards himself, his family and his neighbour.

But, the basis of good to him, is *steady and skilful labour.* To assist him in the pursuit of this labour, and in the turning of it to the best account, are the principal objects of the present little work. I propose to treat of Brewing Beer, making Bread, keeping Cows and Pigs, rearing Poultry, Rabbits, Pigeons, keeping Bees and the uses of the Honey; and to all these things, too, in a mere Cottage Establishment; and to show, that, while, from a very small piece of ground, a large part of the food of a considerable family may be raised, the very act of raising it will be the best possible foundation of *education* of the children of the labourer; that it will teach them a great number of useful things, *add greatly to their value when they go forth from* their father's home, make them start in life with all possible advantages, and give them the best chance of leading happy lives. And, is it not much more rational for parents to be employed in teaching their children how to cultivate a garden, to feed and rear animals, to make bread, beer, bacon, butter, and cheese, and to be able to do these things for themselves, or for others, than to leave them to prowl about the lanes and commons or to mope at the heels of some crafty, sleek-headed pretended saint, who while he extracts the last penny from their pockets, bids them be contented with their misery, and promises them, in exchange for their pence, ever-lasting glory in the world to come? It is upon the hungry and wretched that the fanatic works. The dejected and forlorn are his prey. As an ailing carcass engenders vermin, a pauperized community engenders teachers of fanaticism, the very foundation of whose doctrines is, that we are to care nothing about this world, and that all our labours and exertions are in vain.

The man who is doing well, who is in good health, who has a blooming and dutiful and cheerful and happy family about him, and who passes his day of rest amongst them, is not to be made to believe, that he was born to be miserable, and that poverty, the certain reward of laziness, is to secure him a crown of glory.

[*Cottage Economy* (London, 1822), 'Introduction'.]

Chapter 7
Religion, Medievalism and the Gothic

Cobbett wrote about religion in primarily social and political terms, evaluating religious institutions in terms of their influence on the welfare of individuals and communities. He insisted that religion was less a question of belief than of material wellbeing, and opposed what he saw as the attempts of Evangelicals to placate the poor with spiritual consolation, or make the distribution of charity conditional on displays of piety.

As a result, his own individual beliefs are hard to fathom. He was brought up within the Church of England and declared he would never abandon the faith of his parents. However, he was highly critical of the Anglican clergy – viewing them as greedy, corrupt and generally uninterested in their flock – and conducted a long-running public feud with the local parson at Botley. His eventual re-assessment of Thomas Paine, one of his bête noires during the 1790s, included an interest in Paine's *Age of Reason*, an attack on revealed religion and religious institutions. Cobbett's series of articles on Paine shows a brave, even reckless, attempt to discuss Paine's deism at a time when these ideas were anathema to most of Cobbett's audience. By contrast, Cobbett's prejudices towards Methodists, Evangelicals and Jews were expressed in crude and highly offensive terms.

A significant aspect of Cobbett's later career is his sympathetic treatment of Catholicism. This was based on a distinctive and characteristically contrarian historical vision, set out most fully in *A History of the Protestant "Reformation"*. For Cobbett, the Reformation – kept within inverted commas, or 'scare' quotes – was the beginning of an inexorable process of national decline, which had destroyed the social fabric of medieval England and replaced a generous system of monastic charity with the more miserly Poor Laws. Cobbett's idealisation of medieval society became an important part of his Victorian legacy, and his influence can be seen in the writings of Carlyle, Pugin, Disraeli, Ruskin and Morris. As Raymond Williams suggests, Cobbett bears,

> [a] surprising share of responsibility for that idealization of the Middle Ages which is so characteristic of nineteenth-century social criticism [...] Its most important aspect, for Cobbett, was its use of the monasteries as a standard for social institutions: the image of the working of a communal society as a welcome alternative to the claims of individualism.[1]

---

[1]   R. Williams, *Culture and Society 1780–1950* (Harmondsworth, 1971; first pub. 1957), p. 37.

Cobbett's *History of the Protestant "Reformation"* became part of the campaign for Catholic Emancipation, which was finally secured in 1829. In his final years, Cobbett re-iterated his long-held view that the true test of Christianity was doing good in this world:

> The *Christian religion*, then, is not an affair of preaching, or prating, or ranting, but of taking care of the bodies as well as the souls of the people, not an affair of belief and faith and of professions, but an affair of doing good, and especially to those who are in want; not an affair of fire and brimstone, but an affair of bacon and bread, beer and a bed.[2]

*

Cobbett was particularly opposed to the system of tithes, which he contrasted with the religious freedoms of the United States.

> I have talked to several farmers here about the tithes in England, and, they *laugh*. They sometimes almost make me angry; for they seem, at last, not to believe what I say, when I tell them, that the English farmer gives, and is compelled to give, the Parson a tenth part of his whole crop, and of his fruit and milk and eggs and calves and lambs and pigs and wool and honey. They cannot believe this. They treat it as a sort of *romance*. [...]
>
> But, my Botley neighbours, you will exclaim, "*No tithes!* Why, then, there can be not *Churches* and no *Parsons!* The people must know nothing of God or Devil; and must all go to hell!" By no means, my friends. Here are plenty of Churches. No less than three Episcopal (or English) Churches; three Presbyterian Churches; three Lutheran Churches; one or two Quaker Meeting-houses; and two Methodist Places; all within *six miles* of the spot where I am sitting. And, these, mind, not poor shabby Churches; but each of them larger and better built and far handsomer than Botley Church, with the Church-yards all kept in the neatest order, with a head-stone to almost every grave. As to the Quaker Meeting-house, it would take Botley Church into its belly, if you were first to knock off the steeple.
>
> Oh, no! Tithes are not necessary to promote *religion*. [...] Religion means *a reverence for God*. And, what has this to do with tithes? Why cannot you reverence God, without Baker and his wife and children eating up a tenth part of the corn and milk and eggs and lambs and pigs and calves that are produced in Botley parish? The Parsons, in this country, are supported by those who choose to employ them. A man belongs to what congregation he pleases. He pays what is required by the rules of the congregation. And, if he thinks that it is not necessary to belong to any

---

2   *Political Register*, 15 February 1834.

congregation, he pays nothing at all. And, the consequence is, that all is harmony and good neighbourhood.

[*A Year's Residence in the United States of America* (London, 1819), paras 429–33.]

*

Cobbett appropriated Edmund Burke's lament for a lost 'age of chivalry' in his campaign for Queen Caroline, the estranged wife of the Prince Regent. In 1820, following the death of George III, the new king tried to divorce his wife through act of parliament. Cobbett uses Burke's defence of Marie Antoinette, from *Reflections on the Revolution in France* (1790), to present the radical campaign for Queen Caroline as the chivalrous defence of an injured queen.

Surely, amongst 658 members of Parliament, there are some to be found with zeal to undertake, and talent to conduct, a cause like that of her Majesty. Shall it be said of England, that all her Commoners and all her Nobles produce not one man of great talent, and of heart flowing with true ambition, to fly to the defence of an injured Queen? When the late Queen of France was only gently constrained by the populace to join her husband in a procession from Versailles to Paris, BURKE exclaimed that the days of chivalry were gone, or thousands of swords would have flown from their scabbards, to prevent what he, in his insolence towards the people, called an indignity offered to this Queen of France! What, then, shall be said now, when apparently not an unhired tongue is, in any eminent station, moved in defence of this injured Queen of England? BURKE, if he had lived till these days, would have seen somebody on the part of the Countess FITZWILLIAM, publicly contradicting, in print, a statement that her Ladyship had *condescended* to call upon the Queen! If thousands of swords ought to have flown from their scabbards to avenge the insult offered to the Queen of France, what ought to be the feelings of the people of England, at the insult offered to their Queen at St. Omers? However, the age of chivalry is not wholly gone. The spirit of that age is still left in England, but it appears to live only in the breasts of the people; that people, which have been charged with a want of loyalty, with a want of reverence for the Throne, with a want of attachment to Kings and Queens; and who now are charged with factitiousness and sedition, because they set up an unanimous shout of "GOD SAVE THE QUEEN!"

[*Political Register*, 17 June 1820.]

*

Passing through the villages around Stratton Park, Hampshire, the country estate of the Baring banking family, Cobbett observed what he saw as signs of a paternalistic and hypocritical form of religion.

> A little girl, of whom I asked my way down into East Stratton, and who was dressed in a camlet gown, white apron and plaid cloak (it was Sunday), and who had a book in her hand, told me that Lady Baring gave her the clothes, and had her taught to read and to sing hymns and spiritual songs.
>
> As I came through the Strattons I saw not less than a dozen girls clad in this same way. It is impossible not to believe that this is done with a good motive; but, it is possible not to believe that it is productive of good. It *must* create *hypocrites*, and hypocrisy is the great sin of the age. Society is in a *queer* state when the rich think, that they must *educate* the poor in order to insure their *own safety:* for this, at bottom, is the great motive now at work in pushing on the education scheme, although in this particular case, perhaps, there may be a little enthusiasm at work. When persons are glutted with riches; when they have their fill of them; when they are surfeited of all earthly pursuits, they are very apt to begin to think about the next world; and, the moment they begin to think of that, they begin to look over the *account* that they shall have to present. Hence the far greater part of what are called '*charities*'. But, it is the business of *governments* to take care that there shall be very little of this *glutting* with riches, and very little need of 'charities'.

[*Rural Rides*, ed. I. Dyck (London, 2001), p. 43 (17 November 1822).]

*

Elsewhere on his *Rural Rides* he noticed a decline in the influence of the established church, comparing present-day services with the Sundays of his childhood.

> It is very true, that the *labouring* people have, in a great measure, ceased to go to church. There were scarcely any of that class at this great country church to-day. I do not believe that there were *ten*. I can remember when they were so numerous, that the parson could not attempt to begin, till the rattling of their nailed shoes ceased. I have seen, I am sure, five hundred boys and men in smock-frocks coming out of church at one time. To-day has been a *fine day:* there would have been many at church to-day, if ever there are; and here I have another to add to many things that convince me, that the labouring classes have, in great part, ceased to go to church; that their way of thinking and feeling with regard to both church and clergy are

totally changed; and that there is now very little *moral hold* which the latter possess.

[*Rural Rides*, ed. I. Dyck (London, 2001), p. 139 (31 August 1823).]

*

Cobbett defended his 'political' view of religion, arguing that the Church of England had been established by law, and that his *History of the Protestant "Reformation"* was motivated by a sense of patriotic duty.

> A parson said to me, once, by letter, 'your religion, Mr Cobbett, seems to me to be altogether *political*.' 'Very much so indeed,' answered I, 'and well it may, since I have been furnished with a *creed which makes part of an Act of Parliament*.' And, the fact is, I am no Doctor of Divinity, and like a religion, *any religion*, that tends to make men innocent and benevolent and happy, by taking the best possible means of furnishing them with plenty to eat and drink and wear. I am a Protestant of the Church of England, and, as such, blush to see, that *more than half* the parsonage-houses are *wholly gone*, or are become *mere hovels*. What I have written on the 'PROTESTANT REFORMATION', has proceeded entirely from a sense of justice towards our calumniated Catholic forefathers, to whom we owe *all* those of our institutions that are worthy of our admiration and gratitude. I have not written as a Catholic, but as an Englishman; yet, a sincere Catholic must feel some little gratitude towards me.

[*Rural Rides*, ed. I. Dyck (London, 2001), pp. 357–8 (25 September 1826).]

*

At the opening of his *History of the Protestant "Reformation"* Cobbett asked his readers to re-examine received wisdom about the English Reformation and take a dramatically revisionist view.

> Now, my friends, a fair and honest inquiry will teach us, that this was an alteration greatly for the worse; that the "REFORMATION," as it is called, was engendered in beastly lust, brought forth in hypocrisy and perfidy, and cherished and fed by plunder, devastation, and by rivers of innocent English and Irish blood; and that, as to its more remote consequences, they are, some of them, now before us in that misery, that beggary, that nakedness, that hunger, that everlasting wrangling and spite, which now stare us in the face and stun our ears at every turn, and which the "Reformation" has given us in exchange for the ease and happiness and

harmony and Christian charity, enjoyed so abundantly, and for so many ages, by our Catholic forbears.

Were there, for the entering on this inquiry, no motive other than that of a bare love of justice, that motive alone would, I hope, be sufficient with the far greater part of Englishmen. But, besides this abstract motive, there is another of great and pressing practical importance. A full third part of our fellow-subjects are still Catholics; and when we consider, that the principles of the "Reformation" are put forward as the ground for excluding them from their civil rights, and also as the ground for treating them in a manner the most scornful, despiteful and cruel; when we consider, that it is not in human nature for men to endure such treatment, without wishing for, and without seeking, opportunities for taking vengeance; when we consider the present formidable attitude of foreign nations, naturally our foes, and how necessary it is that we should all be cordially united in order to preserve the independence of our country; when we consider, that such union is utterly impossible as long as one-third part of the people are treated as outcasts, because, and only because, they have in spite of two hundred years of prosecutions unparalleled, adhered to the religion of their and of our fathers: when we consider these things, that fair and honest inquiry, on which a bare love of justice might well induce us to enter, presses itself upon us as a duty which we owe ourselves, our children, and our country.

[*A History of the Protestant "Reformation" in England and Ireland* (London, 1829), paras 4–5.]

*

Cobbett signed a presentation copy of the *History of the Protestant "Reformation"* to Pope Pius VIII, 'the present head of that Holy Church under the influence of which England enjoyed so many ages of Plenty, Freedom, Happiness and Renown...'.[3] He also published an open letter to the Pope on politics and religion in contemporary England, from which the following two extracts are taken.

Barn-Elm Farm, 10th Nov. 1828.

MAY IT PLEASE YOUR HOLINESS,

I, who am the author of the "HISTORY OF THE PROTESTANT REFORMATION," having been informed by a Catholic gentleman, of undoubted veracity, that, at an interview, some time ago, with your Holiness, at the Vatican, you, after some praises bestowed on my work,

---

3   Quoted in P. Manning, 'The History of Cobbett's "A History of the Protestant 'Reformation'"', *The Huntington Library Quarterly*, 64.3/4 (2001), 429–43, p. 434.

expressed to him your wonder how it was that the Catholics of this Kingdom *did not cause me to be a Member of the Parliament;* and that you hoped, that a considerable part of the *rent,* collected from the Catholics in Ireland, *went, at any rate, to be the reward of my unparalleled services to the Catholics in every part of the world.* This information has induced me to make a statement of the true reasons for that which excited the wonder of YOUR HOLINESS; and, in order to do this satisfactorily, it will be necessary for me to describe the character, conduct, and views of the Catholic Aristocracy and Lawyers of England and Ireland; after which description Your Holiness will cease to wonder upon the subject of the seat in Parliament, and also on the subject of the Catholic Rent. [...] It is notorious that my work has softened all those asperities against the Catholics that heretofore existed in the breasts of numerous Protestants; that it has dissipated a great part of the prejudices that existed against the ancient church; that it has caused the Catholics in this kingdom to carry their head aloft, and openly pride themselves in their religion, instead of sneaking about and shunning the acknowledgement that they were of it; that the Catholic chapels are much more frequented than they were before the work was published, and that numerous converts, in every populous part of England, have been amongst its effects. These things are notorious: the celebrity of the book is also notorious: it is equally notorious that, in every Catholic country, it has been honoured with the eulogiums of the highest dignitaries of the Catholic church: and it is also notorious that it has received the sanction of YOUR HOLINESS, and has been printed at the press of the Vatican: it is notorious, further, that the Catholic priests in England and Ireland, together with all their flocks, in every part of the kingdom, with the exception of the aristocracy and the lawyers, feel and express towards me, upon all occasions, gratitude the most profound.

[*A Letter to His Holiness the Pope, on the Character, the Conduct and the Views, of the Catholic Aristocracy and Lawyers of England and Ireland* (London, 1828), pp. 1–14.]

*

I was, what is called, born and bred at the plough tail, and received no book-learning of any sort, except that which I myself acquired, during eight years that I was in the army, part of the time a private soldier, and the larger part a non-commissioned officer. I have now been *twenty-seven years* the author of a Weekly Publication, called the POLITICAL REGISTER. I was born at FARNHAM, in the county of SURREY, which town is over-looked by that very palace which was formerly inhabited by WILLIAM of WICKHAM, and by so many other munificent Catholic Bishops of Winchester; and out of which palace a late *Protestant Bishop* SOLD SMALL BEER TO THE PEOPLE, as stated by me in paragraph 124, vol. I. of the History of the Protestant Reformation, where the fact will remain for ages to warm the heart of the Catholic with just pride, and to make the Protestant cheek burn with shame. At about a mile from this town of FARNHAM, stand, at a place called WEVERLY, the ruins of an abbey, which was formerly the abode of CISTERCIAN MONKS. When I was a little boy, I worked in the grounds near these ruins, of the former magnificence of which some traces still are left. I frequently prowled amongst these ruins by myself, climbed up on the ivy which partly covered the walls, where I found birds' eggs, or young birds, to take. Persons so young have very little thought; but I used to wonder why such ruin had been made. At the age of about ten, I saw, by accident, the fine Cathedral of Winchester, about twenty miles from my own home. Little impression was made on my mind by the sight, other than a sort of a vague idea, that England must have had a different people living in it, in the days when such buildings were raised. At the age of fourteen, or thereabouts, I saw the Cathedral at Salisbury, which strengthened the idea that I had formerly imbibed, that it must have been a very different race of people that inhabited England, in former days. These thoughts were, however, banished from my mind by the passions, the noise, and the bustle of that sort of life in which I arrived at manhood; and, as "*Popery* and *Slavery*," and "*Slavery* and *Popery*," had been continually dinned into the ears of us all; and as it was not my business to dive into the question, I went on taking the assertion upon trust until the year 1818, when I arrived at the age of fifty-two years. At this time the people of England were in very great distress; and those *poor rates*, which rose out of the "Reformation," and the history of which poor-rates your Holiness has read in paragraph 331 to paragraph 338, vol. I. of my work; these poor-rates having become very burthensome to the owners and occupiers of the land, one MALTHUS, a Protestant Church Parson, wrote a book to show that the poor *had no claim upon the land for relief; and that they ought to be left to that law of nature which doomed them and their families to perish, if they had no lawful means of their own whereby to obtain sustenance;* and he actually called upon the Parliament to *pass a law to this horrid effect.* I, who had been bred amongst the labouring classes, read, with indignation, of a project like this; and I wrote and published a letter to the Parson upon the subject.

In order to overset his assertion, *that the poor have no claim upon the land for relief,* it was necessary for me to look back into History. I knew very well that the laws for the relief of the poor had their origin in the forty-third year of the reign of the horrible Elizabeth; but it was necessary to ascertain the sources whence the poor were provided for *previous to that bloody reign*. I went back to the very origin of the common law of England; I examined the cannons of the Catholic church; I read all the acts of parliament relative to the subject. This enquiry, while it recalled from banishment my early thoughts about the ruins of Weverly Abbey, and about the Cathedrals, brought me acquainted with the causes, the progress, and the effects, of the Protestant Reformation: it enabled me to lay prostrate the cruel doctrines of PARSON MALTHUS; but it did a great deal more than that; it made me ashamed of having been, for so many years of my life, deluded by crafty and designing hypocrites to make one amongst the revilers, or the contemners, at least, of the religion of my fathers; of that religion which fed the poor out of the tithes and other revenues of the church; of that religion which had inspired men with piety and generosity, to erect every edifice now remaining in the country, worth the trouble of walking a hundred yards to see, and had created every seminary of learning, and caused to be enacted every law, and to be framed every institution, of which England has a right to be proud.

[*A Letter to His Holiness the Pope, on the Character, the Conduct and the Views, of the Catholic Aristocracy and Lawyers of England and Ireland* (London, 1828), pp. 18–23.]

Chapter 8
Love and Marriage

Cobbett met his future wife, Anne Reid, in 1787, while stationed in New Brunswick. She was the daughter of an artillery sergeant and, at 13 years old, 10 years Cobbett's junior (although he always believed he had been born in 1766 and therefore describes himself as being 'within about a month of twenty-one' at their first meeting). They were married in England five years later and had seven children who survived childhood: Anne, William, John, James, Eleanor, Susan and Richard. Cobbett's family frequently appear in his published writings, and he invests great significance in an ideal of rural life identified with domesticity and 'cottage economy'. The family were all heavily involved in Cobbett's agricultural projects and he describes a close-knit and industrious household.

However, what appears to be a traditional and conservative way of life was in many ways radically unconventional. During Cobbett imprisonment in Newgate, Anne (15 years old), William (11) and John (9) all took turns to stay with him and take dictation of the *Political Register*. Following the suspension of Habeas Corpus in 1817, the family went with him into political exile in America and in the 1820s one or more of the children often accompanied him on his 'Rural Rides'. In 1830, James and William were sent to Paris as foreign correspondents for the *Political Register*, following the overthrow of King Charles X in the July Revolution. However, it is Anne who seems to have been the strongest supporter of her father's political campaigns, and she played a particularly important role in his campaign for Queen Caroline.

Cobbett's views on love, marriage and family also carried wider resonance, at a time when the 'domestic affections' were often at the centre of political debate. In 1790, Edmund Burke described love for the 'little platoon' of the family as the seeds of patriotism: 'To be attached to the subdivision, to love the little platoon we belong to in society, is the first principle (the germ as it were) of public affections. It is the first link in the series by which we proceed towards a love to our country, and to mankind.'[1] Cobbett agreed with Burke on the relationship between family and public life, but differed from him in his ideas of patriotism. Cobbett was also a vociferous critic of Thomas Malthus's theory of population, which he saw as a barbaric attack on the rights of the poor to early marriage, large families and independent living.

In 1829, Cobbett set out his views on love and marriage in *Advice to Young Men*, which was divided into six letters: to a youth, young man, lover, husband,

---

[1]   Edmund Burke, *Reflections on the Revolution in France*, ed. C.C. O'Brien (London, 2004), p. 135.

father and citizen. However, while Cobbett dispensed advice for a happy and productive domestic life, this ideal was increasingly far removed from his own reality. The final years of his life were shadowed by bitter family disputes, which were only fully revealed in George Spater's 1982 biography. From 1827, he spent increasing amounts of time living alone and only allowed his eldest son, William, to see him. Thomas Macaulay, his fellow MP in the reformed Parliament, wrote in his diary about the paranoia of Cobbett's final years:

> In truth his faculties were impaired by age; and the late hours of the House probably assisted to enfeeble his body & consequently his mind. His egotism & his suspicion that everybody was in a plot against him increased and at last attained such a height that he was really as mad as Rousseau. Poor creature![2]

*

Cobbett always distinguished himself from writers of romance, so realised that his letters of 'Advice to a Lover' and 'Advice to a Husband' might cause some surprise.

> Some persons will smile, and others laugh outright, at the idea of "Cobbett's giving advice for conducting the affairs of *love*." Yes, but I was once young, and surely I may say with the poet, I forget which of them,
>
> > "Though old I am, for ladies' love unfit,
> > The power of beauty I remember yet."[3]
>
> I forget, indeed, the *names* of the ladies as completely, pretty nigh, as I do that of the poets; but I remember their influence, and of this influence on the conduct and in the affairs and on the condition of men, I have, and must have, been a witness all my life long. And, when we consider in how great a degree the happiness of all the remainder of a man's life depends, and always must depend, on his taste and judgment in the character of a lover, this may well be considered as the most important period of the whole term of his existence.
>
> [*Advice to Young Men* (London, 1829), para. 9.]

*

---

[2]   G. Spater, *William Cobbett: The Poor Man's Friend*, 2 vols (Cambridge, 1982), vol. 2, p. 522.

[3]   'Old as I am, for Ladies Love unfit,/ The Pow'r of Beauty I remember yet', John Dryden, *Cymon and Iphigenia, from Boccace* (1700), ll. 1–2.

Cobbett always liked to describe his own experience of any subject he wrote about, and this applies as much to marriage as it does to politics or farming. In *Advice to Young Men* he moved from theory to practice by recalling the first time he saw his future wife.

> You should never forget, that marriage, which is a state that every young person ought to have in view, is a thing to last *for life*; and that, generally speaking, it is to make life *happy*, or *miserable*; for, though a man may bring his mind to something nearly a state of *indifference*, even *that* is misery, except with those who can hardly be reckoned amongst sensitive beings. Marriage brings numerous *cares*, which are amply compensated by the more numerous delights which are their companions. But, to have the delights, as well as the cares, the choice of the partner must be fortunate. I say *fortunate*; for, after all, love, real love, impassioned affection, is an ingredient so absolutely necessary, that no *perfect* reliance can be placed on the judgment. Yet, the judgment may do something; reason may have some influence; and, therefore, I here offer you my advice with regard to the exercise of that reason.
>
> The things which you ought to desire in a wife are, 1. Chastity; 2. sobriety; 3. industry; 4. frugality; 5. cleanliness; 6. knowledge of domestic affairs; 7. good temper; 8. beauty. [...] if I could not have found a *young woman* (and I am sure I never should have married an *old* one) who I was not *sure* possessed *all* the qualities expressed by the word sobriety, I should have remained a bachelor to the end of that life, which, in that case, would, I am satisfied, have terminated without my having performed a thousandth part of those labours which have been, and are, in spite of all political prejudice, the wonder of all who have seen, or heard of, them. Scores of gentlemen have, at different times, expressed to me their surprise, that I was "*always in spirits*;" that nothing *pulled me down*; and the truth is, that, throughout nearly forty years of troubles, losses, and crosses, assailed all the while by more numerous and powerful enemies than ever man had before to contend with, and performing, at the same time, labours greater than man ever before performed; all those labours requiring mental exertion, and some of them mental exertion of the highest order; the truth is, that, throughout the whole of this long time of troubles and of labours, I have never known a single hour of *real anxiety*; the troubles have been no troubles to me; I have not known what *lowness of spirits* meaned; have been more gay, and felt less care, than any bachelor that ever lived. "You are *always in spirits*, Cobbett!" To be sure; for why should I not? *Poverty* I have always set at defiance, and, I could, therefore, defy the temptations of riches; and, as to *home* and *children*, I had taken care to provide myself with an inexhaustible store of that "*sobriety*," which

I am so strongly recommending my reader to provide himself with; or, if he cannot do that, to deliberate long before he ventures on the life-enduring matrimonial voyage. [...]

When I first saw my wife, she was *thirteen years old*, and I was within about a month of *twenty-one*. She was the daughter of a Serjeant of artillery, and I was the Serjeant-Major of a regiment of foot, both stationed in forts near the city of St. John in the Province of New Brunswick. I sat in the same room with her, for about an hour, in company with others, and I made up my mind, that she was the very girl for me. That I thought her beautiful is certain, for that I had always said should be an indispensable qualification; but I saw in her what I deemed marks of that sobriety of *conduct* of which I have said so much, and which has been by far the greatest blessing of my life. It was now dead of winter, and, of course, the snow several feet deep on the ground, and the weather piercing cold. It was my habit, when I had done my morning's writing, to go out at break of day to take a walk on a hill at the foot of which our barracks lay. In about three mornings after I had first seen her, I had, by an invitation to breakfast with me, got up two young men to join me in my walk; and our road lay by the house of her father and mother. It was hardly light, but she was out on the snow, scrubbing out a washing-tub. "That's the girl for me," said I, when we had got out of her hearing.

[*Advice to Young Men* (London, 1829), paras 88–94.]

*

Following their engagement, Anne Reid returned to England with her parents, while Cobbett remained in New Brunswick. Cobbett's memories of this period produce one of his most remarkable autobiographical passages, imagining an alternative life in which he never returned to Anne and never achieved political celebrity.

The Province of New Brunswick, in North America, in which I passed my years from the age of eighteen to that of twenty-six, consists, in general, of heaps of rocks, in the interstices of which grow the pine, the spruce, and various sorts of fir trees, or, where the woods have been burnt down, the bushes of the raspberry or those of the huckleberry. The province is cut asunder lengthwise, by a great river, called the St. John, about two hundred miles in length, and, at half way from the mouth, full a mile wide. Into this main river run innumerable smaller rivers, there called CREEKS. On the sides of these creeks the land is, in places, clear of rocks; it is, in these places, generally good and productive; the trees that grow here are the birch, the maple, and others of the deciduous class; natural meadows here and there present themselves; and some of these spots far surpass in rural beauty any other that my eyes ever beheld; the creeks, abounding towards their sources in water-falls of endless variety, as well in form as in magnitude, and always teeming with fish, while water-fowl enliven their surface, and while wild-pigeons, of the gayest plumage, flutter, in thousands upon thousands, amongst the branches of the beautiful trees, which, sometimes, for miles together, form an arch over the creeks.

I, in one of my rambles in the woods, in which I took great delight, came to a spot at a very short distance from the source of one of these creeks. Here was every thing to delight the eye, and especially of one like me, who seem to have been born to love rural life, and trees and plants of all sorts. Here were about two hundred acres of natural meadow, interspersed with patches of maple-trees in various forms and of various extent; the creek (there about thirty miles from its point of joining the St. John) ran down the middle of the spot, which formed a sort of dish, the high and rocky hills rising all round it, except at the outlet of the creek, and these hills crowned with lofty pines: in the hills were the sources of the creek, the waters of which came down in cascades, for any one of which many a nobleman in England would, if he could transfer it, give a good slice of his fertile estate; and in the creek, at the foot of the cascades, there were, in the season, salmon the finest in the world, and so abundant, and so easily taken, as to be used for manuring the land.

If nature, in her very best humour, had made a spot for the express purpose of captivating me, she could not have exceeded the efforts which she had here made. But I found something here besides these rude works of nature; I found something in the fashioning of which *man* had had something to do. I found a large and well-built log dwelling house, standing (in the month of September) on the edge of a very good field of Indian Corn, by the side of which there was a piece of buck-wheat just then mowed. I found a homestead, and some very pretty cows. I found all the things by which an easy and happy farmer is surrounded: and I found still something besides all these; something that was destined to give me a great deal of pleasure and also a great deal of pain, both in their extreme degree; and both of which, in spite of the lapse of forty years, now make an attempt to rush back into my heart.

Partly from misinformation, and partly from miscalculation, I had lost my way; and, quite alone, but armed with my sword and a brace of pistols, to defend myself against the bears, I arrived at the log-house in the middle of a moonlight night, the hoar frost covering the trees and the grass. A stout and clamorous dog, kept off by the gleaming of my sword, waked the master of the house, who got up, received me with great hospitality, got me something to eat, and put me into a feather-bed, a thing that I had been a stranger to for some years. I, being very tired, had tried to pass the night in the woods, between the trunks of two large trees, which had fallen side by side, and within a yard of each other. I had made a nest for myself of dry fern, and had made a covering by laying boughs of spruce across the trunks of the trees. But unable to sleep on account of the cold; becoming sick from the great quantity of water that I had drank during the heat of the day, and being, moreover, alarmed at the noise of the bears, and lest one of them should find me in a defenceless state, I had roused myself up, and had crept along as well as I could. So that no hero of eastern romance ever experienced a more enchanting change.

I had got into the house of one of those YANKEE LOYALISTS, who, at the close of the revolutionary war (which, until it had succeeded, was called a rebellion) had accepted of grants of land in the King's Province of New Brunswick; and who, to the great honour of England, had been furnished with all the means of making new and comfortable settlements. I was suffered to sleep till breakfast time, when I found a table, the like of which I have since seen so many in the United States, loaded with good things. The master and the mistress of the house, aged about fifty, were like what an English farmer and his wife were half a century ago. There were two sons, tall and stout, who appeared to have come in from work, and the youngest of whom was about my age, then twenty-three. But there was *another member* of the family, aged nineteen, who (dressed according to the neat and simple fashion of New England, whence she had come with her parents five or six years before) had her long light-brown hair twisted nicely up, and fastened on the top of her head, in which head were a pair of lively blue eyes, associated with features of which that softness and that sweetness, so characteristic of American girls, were the predominant expressions, the whole being set off by a complexion indicative of glowing health, and forming, figure, movements, and all taken together, an assemblage of beauties, far surpassing any that I had ever seen but *once* in my life. That *once* was, too, *two years agone;* and, in such a case and at such an age, two years, two whole years, is a long, long while! It was a space as long as the eleventh part of my then life! Here was the *present* against the *absent:* here was the power of the *eyes* pitted against that of the *memory:* here were all the senses up in arms to subdue the influence of the thoughts: here was vanity, here was passion, here was the spot of all spots in the world, and here were also the life, and the manners and the habits and the pursuits that I delighted in: here was every thing that imagination can conceive, united in a conspiracy against the poor little brunette in England! What, then, did I fall in love at once with this bouquet of lilies and roses? Oh! by no means. I was, however, so enchanted with *the place;* I so much enjoyed its tranquillity, the shade of the maple trees, the business of the farm, the sports of the water and of the woods, that I stayed at it to the last possible minute, promising, at my departure, to come again as often as I possibly could; a promise which I most punctually fulfilled.

Winter is the great season for jaunting and *dancing* (called *frolicking*) in America. In this Province the river and the creeks were the only *roads* from settlement to settlement. In summer we travelled in *canoes;* in winter in *sleighs* on the ice or snow. During more than two years I spent all the time I could with my Yankee friends: they were all fond of me: I talked to them about country affairs, my evident delight in which they took as a compliment to themselves: the father and mother treated me as one of their children; the sons as a brother; and the daughter, who was as modest and as full of sensibility as she was beautiful, in a way to which a chap much less sanguine than I was would have given the tenderest interpretation; which treatment I, especially in the last-mentioned case, most cordially repaid.

It is when you meet in company with others of your own age that you are, in love matters, put, most frequently, to the test, and exposed to detection. The next door neighbour might, in that country, be ten miles off. We used to have a frolic, sometimes at one house and sometimes at another. Here, where female eyes are very much on the alert, no secret can long be kept; and very soon father, mother, brothers and the whole neighbourhood looked upon the thing as certain, not excepting herself, to whom I, however, had never once even talked of marriage, and had never even told her that I *loved* her. But I had a thousand times done these by *implication*, taking into view the interpretation that she would naturally put upon my looks, appellations and acts; and it was of this, that I had to accuse myself. Yet I was not a *deceiver;* for my affection for her was very great: I spent no really pleasant hours but with her: I was uneasy if she showed the slightest regard for any other young man: I was unhappy if the smallest matter affected her health or spirits: I quitted her in dejection, and returned to her with eager delight: many a time, when I could get leave but for a day, I paddled in a canoe two whole succeeding nights, in order to pass that day with her. If this was not love, it was first cousin to it; for as to any *criminal* intention I no more thought of it, in her case, than if she had been my sister. Many times I put to myself the questions: "What am I at? Is not this wrong? *Why do I go?*" But still I went.

Then, further in my excuse, my *prior engagement*, though carefully left unalluded to by both parties, was, in that thin population, and owing to the singular circumstances of it, and to the great talk that there always was about me, *perfectly well known* to her and all her family. It was matter of so much notoriety and conversation in the Province, that

GENERAL CARLETON[4] (brother of the late Lord Dorchester), who was the Governor when I was there, when he, about fifteen years afterwards, did me the honour, on his return to England, to come and see me at my house in Duke Street, Westminster, asked, before he went away, to see my *wife*, of whom *he had heard so much* before her marriage. So that here was no *deception* on my part: but still I ought not to have suffered even the most distant hope to be entertained by a person so innocent, so amiable, for whom I had so much affection, and to whose heart I had no right to give a single twinge. I ought, from the very first, to have prevented the possibility of her ever feeling pain on my account. I was young, to be sure; but I was old enough to know what was my duty in this case, and I ought, dismissing my own feelings, to have had the resolution to perform it.

The *last parting* came; and now came my just punishment! The time was known to every body, and was irrevocably fixed; for I had to move with a regiment, and the embarkation of a regiment is an *epoch* in a thinly settled province. To describe this parting would be too painful even at this distant day, and with this frost of age upon my head. The kind and virtuous father came forty miles to see me just as I was going on board in the river. *His* looks and words I have never forgotten. As the vessel descended, she passed the mouth of *that creek* which I had so often entered with delight; and though England, and all that England contained, were before me, I lost sight of this creek with an aching heart.

On what trifles turn the great events in the life of man! If I had received a *cool* letter from my intended wife; if I had only heard a rumour of any thing from which fickleness in her might have been inferred; if I had found in her any, even the smallest, abatement of affection; if she had but let go any one of the hundred strings by which she held my heart: if any of these, never would the world have heard of me. Young as I was; able as I was as a soldier; proud as I was of the admiration and commendations of which I was the object; fond as I was, too, of the command, which, at so early an age, my rare conduct and great natural talents had given me; sanguine as was my mind, and brilliant as were my prospects: yet I had seen so much of the meannesses, the unjust partialities, the insolent pomposity, the disgusting dissipations of that way of life, that I was weary of it: I longed, exchanging my fine laced coat for the Yankee farmer's home-spun, to be where I should never behold the supple crouch of servility, and never hear the hectoring voice of authority, again; and, on the lonely banks of this branch-covered creek, which contained (she out of the question)

---

[4]   Thomas Carleton (c. 1735–1817), Lieutenant-Governor of New Brunswick from 1786, returned to England in 1805.

every thing congenial to my taste and dear to my heart, I, unapplauded, unfeared, unenvied and uncalumniated, should have lived and died.

[*Advice to Young Men* (London, 1829), paras 142–51.]

*

Cobbett travelled to England, obtained his discharge from the army in December 1791 and married Anne Reid in Woolwich on 5 February 1792. They fled to France following the publication of *The Soldiers Friend*, spent six happy months near St Omer, and then went on to America as the French Revolution descended into violence. This letter describes the domestic tragedies they experienced during their first years in America.

When I wrote to you before, I lived at Wilmington, a town about 30 miles from here, but since that I have found it to my advantage to remove to the capital.[5] It is generally said, and often with much justice, that a rolling stone never gathers moss; this, however, has not been the case with me; for though my rambles in France and this Country cost me above a hundred and ninety guineas, and though I was reduced to about eighteen at my arrival at Wilmington, I am now better off than ever, notwithstanding my expences in my family have been enormous. But I must not take the merit of this entirely upon myself; My dear Nancy is entitled to her share of it; it perhaps is intirely owing to her care, industry and sweetness of temper that I owe all my success.

   I told you before that we had a little boy;—my wife was brought to bed of a second boy about the middle of last March, but it was still born, though alive a few minutes before.—She suffered a great deal.—But, now prepare your tender heart to pity us—On the 3rd. of June our other dear little fellow was snatched from us.—Oh, Miss Smither! I hope you will never experience a calamaty [sic] like this—All I ever felt before was nothing—nothing at all, to this.—The dearest sweetest beautifulest little fellow that ever was seen.—We adored him—Every body admired— When we lived at Wilmington people came on purpose to see him for his beauty.—he was just beginning to prattle, and to chace [sic] the flies about the floor with a fan.—I am sure I shall never perfectly recover his loss—I feel my spirits altered—A settled sadness seems to have taken possession of my mind; nor do I wish to be diverted from it.—For my poor Nancy, I cannot paint to you her distress—for several days she would take no nourishment—We were even afraid for her —never was a child so adored—I had two of the ablest physicians in the place—but I was not to

---

5   Philadelphia was the capital of the United States between 1790 and 1800.

be blessed.—I am happy, however, that my Nancy is reistablished—thank God our means enabled me to change houses directly, and we are come a little into the country for the summer, where I hope we may recover, at least, tranquillity.

[William Cobbett to Rachel Smither, Philadelphia, 6 July 1794, Nuffield XXX/2/1–2.]

*

Cobbett later looked back affectionately to their early married life in Philadelphia, placing great emphasis on the care and attention he showed to Nancy.

Women are all patriots of the soil; and when her neighbours used to ask my wife whether *all* English husbands were like hers, she boldly answered in the affirmative. I had business to occupy the whole of my time, Sundays and weekdays, except sleeping hours; but I used to make time to assist her in the taking care of her baby, and in all sorts of things: get up, light her fire, boil her tea-kettle, carry her up warm water in cold weather, take the child while she dressed herself and got the breakfast ready, then breakfast, get her in water and wood for the day, then dress myself neatly, and sally forth to my business. The moment that was over I used to hasten back to her again; and I no more thought of spending a moment *away from her*, unless business compelled me, than I thought of quitting the country and going to sea. The *thunder* and *lightning* are tremendous in America, compared with what they are in England. My wife was, at one time, very much afraid of thunder and lightning; and as is the feeling of all such women, and, indeed, all men too, she wanted company, and particularly her husband, in those times of danger. I knew well, of course, that my presence would not diminish the danger; but, be I at what I might, if within reach of home, I used to quit my business and hasten to her, the moment I perceived a thunder storm approaching. Scores of miles have I, first and last, *run* on this errand, in the streets of Philadelphia! The Frenchmen, who were my scholars, used to laugh at me exceedingly on this account; and sometimes, when I was making an appointment with them, they would say, with a smile and a bow, "*Sauve la tonnere toujours, Monsieur Cobbett.*"

[*Advice to Young Men* (London, 1829), para. 167.]

*

The following extract is taken from a letter Cobbett wrote to his political ally William Windham after the birth of his and Nancy's second daughter, Eleanor.

With a rapidly growing family, Cobbett described his educational plans for the children.

Botley, 6th December, 1805.

Sir,

I have the pleasure to tell you that my hours of anxiety may, for the present, at least, be said to be over; for Mrs. Cobbett was, early this morning, delivered of a girl; and both are as well as is usual in similar cases.—I was very much alarmed, some most anxious appearances taking place for several days back. [...]

I propose, if all is tolerably well, to be in town early in the next week. But, I must come back again; for, we have been so constantly beside each other, that I am sure that my absence, except in case of indispensable necessity, would be taken not kindly; and I owe her too much ever to risk the suffering of such a though[t] to enter her mind. My three eldest children I shall now put to school. Spring was the time intended; but this unexpected stoppage here alters the plan. Bishop's Waltham is the place to begin with. My intention is to make the boys fit to *fight* their way through life; for, who can be so weak as to imagine, that we shall, or, that they will, ever see many days of tranquillity! To write English; to speak French; to read a little Latin, perhaps; to ride, to play at single-stick,[6] and, above all things to *work at husbandry*, it is my intention to teach them, in all by precept & in the most instances, if please God to spare me, by example. I have seen too many proofs of the inefficacy of riches to the obtaining of happiness & too many instances of the misery to which a dependance upon patronage leads, to think of making them either rich men, or pretenders to distinction through high favour. They *may* have minds that will bear them upwards from the humble walk that I have in view: if so, it is well. I shall do nothing to stifle genius, but, if it be not of a stamp to rise of itself, there is no raising it.

[William Cobbett to William Windham, British Library Add. MSS. 37,853, f. 191.]

*

Cobbett's idealisation of love and marriage in rural life sometimes becomes a source of sentimental comedy in his writings, as in the following passage from *Rural Rides*.

---

[6]   Cobbett was a champion of the sport of single-stick, in which two combatants, each armed with a wooden pole and with one hand tied behind their back, competed to be the first to draw an inch of blood from his opponent's skull.

It was dark by the time that we got to a village, called EAST WOODHAY. Sunday evening is the time *for courting*, in the country. It is not convenient to carry this on before faces, and, at farm-houses and cottages, there are no spare apartments; so that the pairs turn out, and pitch up, to carry on their negociations, by the side of stile or a gate. The evening was auspicious; it was *pretty dark*, the *weather mild*, and *Old Michaelmas* (when yearly services end) was fast approaching; and, accordingly, I do not recollect ever having before seen so many negociations going on, within so short a distance. At WEST WOODHAY my horse *cast a shoe*, and, as the road was abominably flinty, we were compelled to go at a snail's pace; and I should have gone crazy with impatience, had it not been for these ambassadors and ambassadresses of Cupid, to every pair of whom I said something or other. I began by asking the fellow *my road;* and, from the tone and manner of his answer, I could tell pretty nearly what prospect he had of success, and knew what to say to draw something from him. I had some famous sport with them, saying to them more than I should have said by day-light.

[*Rural Rides*, ed. I. Dyck (London, 2001), pp. 385–6 (2 October 1826).]

*

Cobbett was a fierce critic of the theory proposed by T.R. Malthus in *An Essay on the Principle of Population* (1798) that population always grows faster than increases in food production. By contrast, Cobbett believed that rural labourers should have the right to early marriage and large families.

Music, indeed! Give me a mother singing to her clean and fat and rosy baby, and making the house ring with her extravagant and hyperbolical encomiums on it. That is the music which is *"the food of love;"* and not the formal, pedantic noises, an affectation of skill in which is now-a-days the ruin of half the young couples in the middle rank of life. Let any man observe, as I so frequently have, with delight, the excessive fondness of the labouring people for their children. Let him observe with what pride they dress them out on a Sunday, with means deducted from their own scanty meals. Let him observe the husband, who has toiled all the week like a horse, nursing the baby, while the wife is preparing the bit of dinner. Let him observe them both abstaining from a sufficiency, lest the children should feel the pinchings of hunger. Let him observe, in short, the whole of their demeanour, the real mutual affection, evinced, not in words, but in unequivocal deeds. Let him observe these things, and, having then cast a look at the lives of the great and wealthy, he will say, with me, that, when a man is choosing his partner for life, the dread of poverty ought to be cast to the winds. A labourer's cottage, on a Sunday; the husband or wife having a baby in arms, looking at two or three older ones playing between the flower-borders going from the wicket to the door, is, according to my taste, the most interesting object that eyes ever beheld; and, it is an object to be beheld in no country upon earth but England. In France, a labourer's cottage means *a shed* with a *dung-heap* before the door; and it means much about the same in America, where it is wholly inexcusable. In riding once, about five years ago, from Petworth to Horsham, on a Sunday in the afternoon, I came to a solitary cottage which stood at about twenty yards distance from the road. There was the wife with the baby in her arms, the husband teaching another child to walk, while *four* more were at play before them. I stopped and looked at them for some time, and then, turning my horse, rode up to the wicket, getting into talk by asking the distance to Horsham. I found that the man worked chiefly in the woods, and that he was doing pretty well. The wife was then only *twenty-two*, and the man only *twenty-five*. She was a pretty woman, even for *Sussex*, which, not excepting Lancashire, contains the prettiest women in England. He was a very fine and stout young man. "Why," said I, "how many children do you reckon to have at last?" "I do not care how many," said the man: "God never sends mouths without sending meat." "Did you ever hear," said I, "of one PARSON MALTHUS?" "No, sir." "Why, if he were to hear of your works, he would be outrageous; for he wants an act of parliament to prevent poor people from marrying young, and from having such lots of children." "Oh! the brute!" exclaimed the wife; while the husband laughed, thinking that I was joking. I asked the man whether he had ever had *relief from the parish;* and upon his answering in the negative, I took out my purse, took from it enough to bait my horse at Horsham, and to clear my turnpikes to WORTH, whither I was going in order to stay awhile, and gave him all the rest. Now, is it not a shame, is it not a sin of all sins, that people like these should, by acts of the government, be reduced to such misery as to be induced to abandon their homes and their country, to seek, in a foreign land, the means of preventing themselves and their children from starving? And this has been, and now is, actually the case with many such families in this same county of Sussex!

[*Advice to Young Men* (London, 1829), para. 99.]

*

Cobbett's opposition to 'the damnable Malthusian doctrine' drove him to write *Surplus Population: A Comedy in Three Acts*, which presents clear moral contrasts through characters such as 'Sir Gripe Grindum, of Grindum Hall, in the County of Grindum' – a possible influence for Dickens's creation of Mr. Gradgrind in

Hard Times. In the final months of his life Cobbett tried to direct performances of the play on a tour of Surrey and Sussex, but was frustrated by local magistrates. In the following extract, Squire Thimble, 'a great Anti-Population Philosopher' – based on the utilitarian Francis Place (1771–1854) – talks to Mrs Stiles, a farmer's wife, about the forthcoming marriage of Betsey Birch, who is betrothed to Stiles's servant Dick Hazle.

Squire Thimble.	*Married*, did you say! *Married!* That girl going to be *married!*
Mrs. Stiles.	Yes, Sir; they have been courting a long while, and they be desperate fond of one another.
Squire Thimble.	*Desperate*, indeed! But do you encourage such things, then?
Mrs. Stiles.	What things, Sir?
Squire Thimble.	Why, the coupling together of these poor creatures to fill the country with beggars and thieves.
Mrs. Stiles.	[*With warmth.*] I'm sure there isn't a better young man in the parish than Richard Hazle; and as for Betty Birch, young as she is, she shall make bread, butter, cheese, or beer, with any woman in the whole county, let the next be who she will. Beggars and thieves, indeed!
Squire Thimble.	Well, if these be good people, so much the more reason to keep them from being plunged into misery; and....
Mrs. Stiles.	[*Interrupting him.*] Misery, Sir!
Squire Thimble.	Yes, and from adding to that great national disease, the *surplus population*.
Mrs. Stiles.	Never heard of that disease before, Sir; we ben't troubled with't in these parts, though we have the small-pox and measles terrible bad sometimes; and our poor neighbour, Chopstick, lost four as fine children last week as....
Squire Thimble.	So much the better! so much the better!
Mrs. Stiles.	What, Sir!
Squire Thimble.	Yes; so much the better, I say, and [*aside*] if it had taken you off too, it would have been better still. [*To her.*] Go, good woman, and tell the girl to come and speak to me.
Mrs. Stiles.	She's going to her mother's to get ready for her wedding; but I'll call her in for a minute. [*Exit. Enter Betsey.*]

Squire Thimble.	So, young woman, you are going to be married, I understand?
Betsey.	Yes, Sir.
Squire Thimble.	How old are you?
Betsey.	I'm nineteen, Sir, come next Valentine's eve.
Squire Thimble.	That is to say, you are *eighteen!* [*Aside.*] No wonder the country is ruined! And your mother now; how old is she?
Betsey.	I can't justly say, Sir; but I heard her say she was forty some time back.
Squire Thimble.	And how many of you has she brought into the world?
Betsey.	Only seventeen, Sir.
Squire Thimble.	Seventeen! *Only* seventeen!
Betsey.	Seventeen now alive, Sir; she lost two and had two still-born and....
Squire Thimble.	Hold your tongue! Hold your tongue. [*Aside.*] It is quite monstrous! Nothing can save the country but plague, pestilence, famine, and sudden death. Government ought to import a ship-load of arsenic. [*To her.*] But, young woman, cannot you impose on yourself *"moral restraint"* for ten or a dozen years?
Betsey.	Pray what is that, Sir?
Squire Thimble.	Cannot you keep single till you are about thirty years old?
Betsey.	[*Stifling a laugh.*] Thirty years old, Sir!

['Surplus Population', *Political Register*, 28 May 1831.]

Chapter 9
Poverty and the Poor Laws

Cobbett was a pioneer of what the nineteenth century would come to call 'the Condition of England' question. A great part of his writing had its source in the effects that misgovernment and corruption were having upon the living standards of the common people and, in particular, the people he saw as his own, the agricultural labourers. It was the long wars against Revolutionary France and then Napoleon, running for almost a generation, from 1793 to 1815, with only two small breaks, which gradually alerted him to the growing poverty of his fellow countrymen. He became convinced that high taxes, expensive loan-financing and paper money were combining to impoverish the ordinary labourers while supporting a corrupt and bloated establishment of government fund-holders, financiers and politicians. By the second phase of the wars, after 1803, Cobbett moved decisively into opposition, feeling betrayed by his one-time hero, William Pitt, the Prime Minister during the 1790s until 1801 and again from 1804–6. He identified Pitt with what he saw as the virtually ruinous explosion of the national debt and the introduction of paper money to ease the shortage of bullion from 1797. High taxes and inflation he saw as reducing the common labourers to a poverty they had not experienced in his youth. Cobbett saw poverty as the direct result of the wars and Pitt's mismanagement of war finance.

Cobbett reflected a reality. The wars with France quadrupled the national debt and involved government in borrowing on an unprecedented scale. New taxes on almost every commodity were introduced and war-time bad harvests in 1795–6 and 1800–1 drove food prices to unprecedented heights. Economic warfare with France and conflict with America brought disruption to trade and the ending of the wars brought riots and machine-breaking. There was widespread unemployment because of the ending of war contracts, a trade and agricultural depression and a flood of demobilised soldiers and sailors. Taxation also remained high to pay off the massive burden in interest now owing on government debt. It was no surprise then that the immediate post-war period, the years between 1815 and 1819 – 'Waterloo to Peterloo' – were marked by widespread distress and political agitation.

But as well as the exigencies of war and its associated upheavals, the country was also undergoing immense longer-term changes as population growth, agricultural change, industrialisation and urbanisation had their effects upon the living standards of the labouring classes. Cobbett's beloved agricultural labourers were being affected by population growth which swelled the local force without necessarily providing extra employment in the agricultural areas. Enclosure and agricultural improvement had mixed effects upon the rural labour force, driving some independent smallholders into the ranks of landless labourers, at a time when low agricultural prices were already putting intense pressure on wages. As Cobbett noted too, factory production was now destroying the market for the domestic crafts upon which many agricultural families had depended for extra income. By the 1820s the situation was becoming desperate in some of the agricultural districts with many parishes carrying a permanent body of underemployed or unemployed labourers. Cobbett was enraged that in these 'hard parishes' where the labourers were entirely dependent upon their wages, their conditions had deteriorated from what he remembered as a youth.

Urban conditions were little better. Cobbett blamed taxes and corruption for the discontents of factory workers and machine-breaking weavers in the midst of the post-war depression, urging them to petition for reform in order to obtain reduced taxes and a cull of corruption to better their position. Though less familiar to him, the desperation in London parishes where children were being deserted by their parents produced some of his most sentimental observations about what poverty was doing to the normal decencies of family life. Moreover, when he ventured north to the manufacturing districts Cobbett was horrified by his first encounters with the factory system. He anticipated almost all the criticisms which became familiar in subsequent decades in parliamentary commissions and critics of the new industrial world. Atrocious working conditions, rigid time-discipline, and wages diluted by 'truck' systems and company shops, meant that the industrial workers were at least as badly off as their country cousins.

But it was the conditions of Cobbett's 'chopsticks' which dominated the last years of his life as rural conditions failed to improve and exploded from 1830 in the great wave of incendiarism, riots and machine-breaking which became known as the 'Captain Swing' disturbances. Cobbett set out to establish as a principle the right of the labourers to a basic subsistence and to poor relief as well as organising petitions on behalf of some of the most distressed amongst them. As a farmer and employer he was ready to defend the rights of property against the charge of 'levelling', but he inveighed against the growing luxury of farmers while their labourers suffered distress and repression when they protested. Parliamentary reform, Cobbett believed, would relieve farmers and labourers alike of the taxes and tithes levied to support a corrupt political, financial and religious establishment. Cobbett found himself on trial for incitement to violence because of his activities in urging the labourers to petition for reform. Triumphantly acquitted, Cobbett remained the most vehement supporter of fair treatment for the labourers and their right to relief, as well as continuing to campaign for parliamentary reform to reduce the burden of taxation.

The last great campaign of his life was in response to the introduction of the New Poor Law in 1834. Cobbett was enraged in the 1820s that it was the

Poor Rates that became the target for reform rather than the corruption of the establishment. Under the existing poor law, people born in a parish had a right to subsistence when old, infirm or unable to work. A rate collected in the parish from all inhabitants of any substance provided the money required. New conditions had increased the burdens of poor rates. For example, modification during the high prices of the 1790s had tied the rate of relief to the price of bread. When prices rose to the new heights as they did in 1800–1, or after the Napoleonic Wars, costs inevitably rose and a growing population threatened the system in rural areas with collapse. Poor relief was normally given to parishioners as a payment without entering a workhouse, which many parishes did not possess. The 'Old' Poor Law came under attack from the new generation of political economists, who saw it as distorting wages and inhibiting the free movement of labourers. The farmers and well-to-do also increasingly resented the rising cost of poor rates. What was planned was a system in which poor relief would only be given in workhouses under conditions so severe that only the genuinely destitute would seek to apply. Cobbett's fulminations against the rationale and justice of the New Poor Law proved in vain, the Act passing into law, provoking lasting hostility in both rural and industrial areas.

*

Cobbett's early preoccupations with defending Britain against the French Revolution and its supporters in Britain and America, supporting the war effort, and organising resistance to invasion gradually gave way to an even more fundamental issue and an abiding concern for the rest of his life, namely that the condition of the ordinary people had deteriorated markedly from what he had known in his youth. A visit to the parish of Horton Heath in Hampshire and the examination of some cottage interiors confirmed what his examination of the movement of wages and prices at this stage of the wars had led him to suspect.

> I myself, in the early part of my writing life was deceived [...] but, when, in [1804], I revisited the English Labourer's dwelling, and that, too, after having so recently witnessed the happiness of labourers in America; when I saw that the *clock* was gone; that even the *Sunday-coat* was gone; when I saw those whom I had known the most neat, chearful and happy beings on earth, and these my own countrymen too, had become the most wretched and forlorn of human beings, I looked seriously and inquired patiently into the matter; and this inquiry into the causes of an effect which had so deep an impression on my mind, led to that series of exertions, which have *occupied my whole life, since that time, to better the lot of the Labourers.*

[*Political Register*, 19 May 1821.]

*

By the end of the Napoleonic Wars Cobbett was clear that the poverty and distress of the people was the result of how the wars had been financed with expensive loans and paper money, which led to onerous taxes and high prices. When in reply to an Address from the City of London the government protested that the distress evident in the country was 'unavoidable', Cobbett had his answer.

Oh, no! The distress and difficulties have *not* arisen from *unavoidable* causes; for the weight of taxes might have been avoided. However, let me ask the Ministers a few questions here. I will not ask them whether it was unavoidable for the Bank to stop payment in cash in 1797; whether it was unavoidable to renew the war in 1803, whether it was unavoidable to persevere in the war with America after the war in England ceased, and, at last, to make peace without attaining any object of war; whether it was unavoidable to renew the war in 1815 for the purpose of compelling the French people to give up Napoleon and submit to the Bourbons; whether it was unavoidable to keep up an army to maintain the Bourbons on the throne of France, at a time when thousands of the protestants of the country were butchered or burnt by those who called themselves the *loyal*. I will not put any of these questions to the Ministers; but with the Official Accounts before me, I will ask them a few questions applicable to the present moment. I ask them, then,

	POUNDS
Was it *unavoidable* to keep up an army at the expense, including the Ordnance, of	26,736,027
Was it *unavoidable* that the Expense of the Civil List should, in last year, amount to	1,028,000
Was it *unavoidable* for us to pay in the same year, on account of the *deficiencies* of the Civil List	534,713
Was it *unavoidable* that the other additional allowances to the Royal Family, in that year, should amount to	366,660
Was it *unavoidable* that the Civil List for Scotland should amount to	126,613
Was it *unavoidable* to give for the *relief* of *suffering* French and Dutch Emigrants, in that year, after the *Bourbons* and the *"Orange Boven"* had been restored, the sum of	79,581
Was it *unavoidable* to expend in that year (including an arrear of the former year) in SECRET SERVICE Money, the sum of	158,442

Was it *unavoidable* to pay, *last year*, out of the taxes for
the relief of the *Poor* Clergy of the Church of England,
the sum of   100,000

I could ask them a great many more questions of a similar nature and
tendency, but here are enough for the present; and, if the Citizens of
London should happen to be satisfied, that all these expenses were
unavoidable, all the taxes, of course, are unavoidable, and then it is clear,
that the present distress and difficulty of the country are to be attributed
to unavoidable causes. But, if the Citizens should think, that a very large
part, nine tenths for instance, of these expenses might have been *avoided*,
then they will come to the opposite conclusion, and, if they be not beaten
at a single blow, they will not fail to communicate that conclusion to His
Royal Highness.

['A Letter to Henry Hunt, Esq.', *Political Register*, 14 December 1816.]

*

Cobbett measured the distress of the country in the post-war years from a notice
in one of the London parishes warning of the penalties for parents who deserted
their children.

But, in the general Subscription for the poor creatures of Spital-fields
you see only a small part of the effects of your labours. There have been
Meetings in almost *all the parishes* of the Metropolis for similar purposes.
Large Subscriptions are going on in every direction. Just as if the poverty
and misery were not as great a *month ago* as they are now! Great indeed
they are, and they are producing symptoms so horrible that one sickens
but to think of them. Amongst others, take the facts described in a *placard*
now sticking against the walls. "PUBLIC NOTICE.–United Parishes of
Saint Andrew Holborn—above Bar, and St. George the Martyr, Queen's
Square. At a Meeting of the Overseers held this day in consequence
of MANY PERSONS DESERTING THEIR FAMILIES–it was
resolved, That, in future, all persons, who desert their Families, whereby
they become chargeable to these Parishes, or when the reputed Parents
of an illegitimate child abscond, *such persons shall be advertised in the
public papers* or in *posting bills,* with a full description of their persons,
residence, and calling, and other particulars, and a Reward offered for
their apprehension. And all Inhabitants *harbouring persons for the night,*
for the like purpose; will be *prosecuted* accordingly."
     To what are we come at last! And this is the age of our *glory*, is it? This
is the situation we are in, when immense sums are voted for the erection of

monuments to commemorate the deeds of the last twenty-five years! This is the state which not to be *proud* of Mr. VANSITTART said was a proof of baseness in an Englishman! It is in this situation of the country, that PITT CLUBS have the insolence to hold their triumphal carousals!—Shall we *never* see those men in sackcloth? These insolent men, while wallowing in wealth, do not reflect on the pangs which must wring the poor man's heart before he can so far subdue the feelings of the husband and the father as to make him "*desert his family;*" or, if they do reflect on them, they must be more cruel than the storm and the waves. The labouring men in England, generally speaking, are the kindest and most indulgent of husbands and of parents. It has often been observed by me, that they are generally so to a fault. If a boy or girl belonging to them behave ill towards their employers, the father and mother are very hard to be convinced of the fact.—I have often to remonstrate with them upon this subject, and to remind them of how much more indulgent they are to their children than I am to mine. "Aye, Sir," said a very good woman to me a little while ago, "but your children have *their belly full of victuals.*" The answer was a *silencer.* And this is the true cause of their indulgence, and of their excessive affection too. They see their children in want; they grow up in continual suffering; they are incessantly objects of compassion over and above the love which nature has implanted in the parent's breast. Their obstinate perseverance in justifying the conduct of their children upon all occasions is a fault; but it arises from the most amiable of human weaknesses; and though it may, and often is, injurious in its effects, it is the least censurable of all the frailties of the heart.

If I have here, as I am sure I have, given the true character of the English Labourer, as a parent and a husband, what must that state of things be, which has rendered the *desertion of family* so frequent an offence as to call forth a hand-bill and *placard* such as that which I have quoted above?

['A Letter to Henry Hunt, Esq.', *Political Register*, 14 December 1816.]

*

But it is the poverty of the agricultural labourers, Cobbett's 'Chopsticks', which excited his most visceral concern. In the *Rural Rides* he highlighted those areas where poverty and indigence were at their worst, identifying them with the corn-growing districts where the farmers, 'the big bull frogs', did well but the labourers fared worst of all. On the Isle of Thanet he compared the labourers' situation unfavourably with the labourers in 'mixed' areas where they retained more independence and a share of the work available.

When I got upon the corn land in the Isle of Thanet, I got into a garden indeed. There is hardly any fallow; comparatively few turnips. It is a country of corn. Most of the harvest is in; but there are some fields of wheat and of barley not yet housed. A great many pieces of lucerne, and all of them very fine. I left Ramsgate to my right about three miles, and went right across the island to Margate; but that place is so thickly settled with stock-jobbing cuckolds, at this time of the year, that, having no fancy to get their horns stuck into me, I turned away to my left when I got within about half a mile of the town. I got to a little hamlet, where I breakfasted; but could get no corn for my horse, and no bacon for myself! All was corn around me. Barns, I should think, two hundred feet long; ricks of enormous size and most numerous; crops of wheat, five quarters to an acre, on the average; and a public-house without either bacon or corn! The labourers' houses, all along through this island, beggarly in the extreme. The people dirty, poor-looking; ragged, but particularly *dirty*. The men and boys with dirty faces, and dirty smock-frocks, and dirty shirts; and, good God! what a difference between the wife of a labouring man here, and the wife of a labouring man in the forests and woodlands of Hampshire and Sussex! Invariably have I observed, that the richer the soil, and the more destitute of woods; that is to say, the more purely a corn country, the more miserable the labourers. The cause is this, the great, the big bull frog grasps all. In this beautiful island every inch of land is appropriated by the rich. No hedges, no ditches, no commons, no grassy lanes: a country divided into great farms; a few trees surround the great farm-house. All the rest is bare of trees; and the wretched labourer has not a stick of wood, and has no place for a pig or cow to graze, or even to lie down upon. The rabbit countries are the countries for labouring men. There the ground is not so valuable. There it is not so easily appropriated by the few. Here, in this island, the work is almost all done by the horses. The horses plough the ground; they sow the ground; they hoe the ground; they carry the corn home; they thresh it out; they carry it to market; nay, in this island, they *rake* the ground; they rake up the straggling straws and ears; so that they do the whole, except the reaping and the mowing. It is impossible to have an idea of anything more miserable than the state of the labourers in this part of the country.

[*Rural Rides*, ed. I. Dyck (London, 2001), pp. 162–3 (4 September 1823).]

*

One of the changes Cobbett lamented was the loss of rural industry and crafts which had supported agricultural families. He believed it had provided women and children with work and income to the labourers' family; now overtaken by the rise of manufacturing in the north, its loss was responsible for depopulating the countryside. In contradiction to the Rev. Thomas Malthus who had highlighted the dangers of population growth, Cobbett believed the countryside was being depopulated and rural workers forced into the new manufacturing towns and London. Once again he lashed out at the 'funding system' for undermining the former prosperity of the labourers.

MALTHUS and his crew of hard-hearted ruffians; those cool calculators of how much "*national wealth*" can be made to arise out of the misery of millions, wholly overlook the frightful *depopulation* which has taken place in consequence of the destruction of *seven-eighths*, at least, of the farmhouses, and a similar destruction of cottages, in consequence of the enclosure of wastes. This destruction has, in part, arisen from the total ruin of the agricultural manufactories. These profitable labours having been taken from the women, girls, and little boys, it became hardly possible for a large family to live upon a small farm. The profit of the small farm received a great addition from the fruit of the labours of spinning, knitting, and the like; but, when these were taken away by the lords of the loom; when flagrant impolicy had thrown all these profits into the hands of a very few persons, who had converted the manufacturing labourers into the slaves that we shall presently see them, the little farm itself did not afford a sufficiency of means to maintain a considerable family. The occupiers of such farms became poor; became unable to pay their rents, and, in a short time, were driven from their healthy habitations; were huddled into sheds and holes, became mere labourers, and a large part of them paupers. MALTHUS and his crew never look at this cause of depopulation. The landowner naturally sought to get rent for his land, and he could now get it from nobody but one who had made money sufficient to hold nine or ten farms. The women, girls and little children having now lost their natural employment for the greater part of the year, became a mere burden upon the land; and the farmer and the landowner resorted to all sorts of expedients to diminish that burden. To diminish the burden, there were no means but that of reducing the number of the labouring class of country people as much as possible. The man and the boy were necessary to agriculture, agriculture could not have them without the women and the girls; it became necessary, therefore, to do without the men and the boys as much as possible.

To do without them all sorts of schemes were resorted to. To make horses perform that which was before performed by men, was one of the methods pursued, and with most destructive success. So, at last, the agricultural parts of the country have been stripped of a very large part of their population. Every scheme that the ingenuity of greediness could devise has been put into practice; but, after all, there remains a mass of pauperism and of misery which the law-makers themselves declare is frightful to behold; and, whatever else their reports may contain; however widely they may differ from one another; and however completely each may be at variance with itself, every one declares that the *evil is constantly increasing*.

While this is the case, and while the country is going on becoming more and more depopulated, and more and more miserable, the great towns, and particularly the manufacturing districts, are daily increasing in numbers. If the people, thus drawn together in masses, were happily situated there might be less ground for lamentation; but, so far from this being the case, these masses are still more miserable than the wretches left behind them in the agricultural districts.

['To the Landowners on the Evils of Collecting Manufacturers into Great Masses', *Political Register*, 17 November 1824.]

*

When Cobbett began to visit the manufacturing districts in the 1820s he became acquainted for the first time with the other side of the poverty from what he had already encountered in his more familiar stamping-ground of the agricultural districts. In the cotton districts of Lancashire and Cheshire he was confronted with full-scale industrialisation, involving large, steam-driven factories, employing hundreds of workers. He was horrified by the conditions he found in this totally alien environment which was already beginning to attract the attention of investigators into the new factory system.

Some of these lords of the loom have in their employ thousands of miserable creatures. In the cotton-spinning work, these creatures are kept, fourteen hours in each day, locked up, summer and winter, in a heat of from EIGHTY TO EIGHTY-FOUR DEGREES. The rules which they are subjected to are such as no negroes were ever subjected to. I once before noticed a statement made on the part of these poor creatures, relative to their treatment in the factories of Lancashire. This statement is dated on 15th of February 1823, and was published at Manchester by J. PHENIX, No. 12, Bow-street, in that blood-stained town. This statement says, that the heat of the factories is from *eighty to eighty-four degrees*. A base agent of the Cotton-Lords, who publishes a newspaper at Stockport, has lately accused me of exaggeration, in having stated the heat at *eighty-four degrees*.

Now, the statement of which I am speaking was published at Manchester; and does any man believe that such a statement would have been published there, if it had not been founded in fact? There was a controversy going on at the time of the publishing of this statement. I read very carefully the answer to this statement; but this answer contained no denial of the heat being from *eighty to eighty-four degrees.*

Now, then, do you duly consider what a heat of *eighty-two* is? Very seldom do we feel such a heat as this in England. The 31st of last August, and the 1st, 2d and 3d of last September, were very hot days. The newspapers told us that men had dropped down dead in the harvest fields, and that many horses had fallen dead upon the road; and yet the heat during those days never exceeded eighty-four degrees in the *hottest part of the day.* We were retreating to the coolest rooms in our houses; we were pulling off our coats, wiping the sweat off our faces, puffing, blowing, and panting; and yet we were living in a heat nothing like eighty degrees. What, then, must be the situation of the poor creatures who are doomed to toil day after day, for three hundred and thirteen days in the year, fourteen hours in each day, in an average heat of eighty-two degrees? Can any man, with a heart in his body, and a tongue in his head, refrain from cursing a system that produces such slavery and such cruelty?

Observe, too, that these poor creatures have no cool room to retreat to, not a moment to wipe off the sweat, and not a breath of air to come and interpose itself between them and infection. The "door of the place wherein they work, is *locked,* except *half an hour,* at tea-time; the workpeople are not allowed to send for water to drink, in the hot factory; even the *rain water is locked up,* by the master's order, otherwise they would be happy to drink even that. If any spinner be found with his *window open,* he is to pay a fine of a shilling"! Mr MARTIN of Galway has procured Acts of Parliament to be passed to prevent *cruelty to animals.* If horses or dogs were shut up in a place like this, they would certainly be thought worthy of Mr. MARTIN's attention.

['To the Landowners on the Evils of Collecting Manufacturers into Great Masses', *Political Register,* 17 November 1824.]

*

With great prescience, Cobbett identified many of the features which would attract the attention of generations of social reformers and trade unionists, who became concerned about the conditions of the workers in the first flush of industrialisation. Unhealthy and dangerous conditions, inhuman discipline, immorality, and the unnatural separation of workers from their families were amongst the things he was one of the first to identify as features of the new industrial world. He also recognised the evils of the 'truck' system, paying the workers' wages in kind or tokens. Another example, he felt, of his fellow countrymen being treated as worse than slaves.

When the pay, the miserable pittance of pay, gets into the hands of these poor creatures, it has to be laid out at a SHOP. That shop is, generally, directly or indirectly, the master's. At this shop the poor creatures must lay out their money, or they are very soon turned off. The statement that I have just mentioned relates an instance, where, "If any workman's wife purchase but a trifling matter at another shop, the shopkeeper tells the *bookkeeper*, and the latter says to the workmen, that the master *will not allow of such work*, and that they must tell their wives neither to go to another shop nor *give saucy language to the shopkeeper*'!

It must be manifest to everyone, that, under such circumstances, the *pay* is nearly nominal. The greedy master takes back again as much of it as he pleases. Another mode of despoiling the poor creatures is this: The master is the owner of cottages, or, rather, holes, which the workpeople have to rent. The statement says, "That cottages of exceedingly small dimensions are let to the workmen at NINE POUNDS A-YEAR. But, though the rent is by the year, it is stopped from them at the end of every fortnight. A *cellar* is *two shillings and sixpence a-week;* and if a house or cellar be empty, and a workman come to work, and have another house or cellar already, he must *pay rent for the empty one*, whether he occupy it or not."

Nine hundred and ninety-nine thousandths of the people of England have not the most distant idea that such things are carried on in a country calling itself free; in a country whose Minister for Foreign Affairs is everlastingly teasing and bothering other Powers to emulate England in *"her humanity*," in abolishing the slave trade in the blacks. The blacks, when carried to the West Indies, are put into a paradise compared with the situation of these poor white creatures in Lancashire, and other factories of the North.

['To the Landowners on the Evils of Collecting Manufacturers into Great Masses', *Political Register*, 17 November 1824.]

*

Cobbett turned his wrath upon the leading free trade writers of the day, such as David Ricardo (1772–1823), who he saw as promoting the factory system and all its evils. He viewed the position of the 'cotton slaves' as worse than had ever been endured by his countrymen even in the past.

Not a word do we ever hear from all these famous witnesses brought before committees, about the immoralities of those monstrous heaps of human bodies. Nay, the Scotch Economists are everlastingly singing forth the praises of these horrible establishments, which they are pleased to look upon as so many proofs of *"natural wealth*." RICARDO, who got half a million of money by "*watching the turn of the market*," very frequently had the impudence to say, even in the House of Commons, that it was no matter to the country how small a portion of its food it raised from its own land, and that if it could buy all its food from foreign countries, and give them manufactures in exchange, it would be as well for England. So say all the Scotch Economists. They seem to care about nothing but the *money*. Their vulgar, huckstering notion is that *money is to be got from other nations*. They care nothing about the means. They always look upon the labouring classes as they do upon sheep, or pigs, or any other "useful animals."

The poor cotton slave is held in bondage as complete as that of the negro. Our histories contain accounts of *vassals* and *villeins* of old times, and affect to *pity* them. Nothing but the basest hypocrisy, or the grossest ignorance, can place those *villeins* beneath the miserable creatures in the North. The villeins belonged to the estate on which they were born. If the estate were transferred, they were transferred along with it. They could not go away and live where they liked. The fruit of their labour belonged to their lords. Their lords could do almost what they liked with them. Now, supposing all this to be literally true, are not the cotton-slaves fast bound to the spot where they are? Can they quit that spot to go and live where they like? Are they not transferred with the factory? Do not their lords take to themselves the fruit of their labour, leaving them the bare means of the most sorry existence? The *villeins* were not, at any rate, shut up in a heat of *eighty-four degrees*. If they were ill, or crippled, the interest of their lords necessarily induced them to take care of them; and they were not packed off to be dealt with by an "*Overseer*," to be lugged away in a cart, upon a bundle of straw, and frequently dying in the road.

['To the Landowners on the Evils of Collecting Manufacturers into Great Masses', *Political Register*, 17 November 1824.]

*

During the 1820s Cobbett became increasingly concerned about the pressures being placed upon the poor and the widespread complaint about the rising costs of supporting the poor through the poor rates. In an extensive discourse he set out what he believed to be the fundamental rights of the labourer, that is to the produce of their own work at a fair rate. Much would be made later, by Marx amongst others, of the implications of what Cobbett asserted, dubbed as the 'labour theory of value', that all wealth was the product of labour. Cobbett's intention at the time, however, was to ensure that labourers had an entitlement to a basic living and to poor relief when unable to work.

There was a time when, in every country in the world, there were no laws, and no such thing as property. The people used the earth and all its produce as they pleased; that is to say, each man took whatever he wanted, if his strength or cunning would allow him to do it. No one acknowledged the superiority of any other: might gave right; strength and wisdom were superior to weakness and folly; and there was no other superiority or inferiority acknowledged amongst men. This was called living under the law of nature. When God put it into the hearts of men to change this state of things, and to make rules and laws for the observance of the whole, they agreed that the whole of the community or body of people should enforce these laws, against any one or more that broke them. The great law of all was this; that, in future, every man should keep to himself; should call *his own;* should be able to apply to his own use solely; that which he had got by his labour. For instance, John Stiles, when living under the law of nature, might take a piece of land, and cultivate it, and have a crop of wheat growing on it; but, when fit for sickle, Tom Nokes, a great deal stronger man than Stiles, might come and cut the wheat and carry it away and let Stiles have none of it. It is not likely that men would be so villanously unjust as this, or that the rest of the people would be so base as to stand by and to see Stiles thus bereft of his wheat, and have nothing left to exist upon, perhaps, but a few wheel-barrows full of damned potatoes; this is not likely; but it might happen, and sometimes did happen, perhaps, and therefore, all the people agreed to enter into a society, to make rules that should give Stiles an exclusive right to his crop, and that should punish such a fellow as Nokes as a robber, if he came to take the crop away.

Here, my friends, you see the origin of *property*, which word means a thing which belongs to a person's self, and a thing that nobody else has any right to. But observe, Stiles had no property in the crop till he created it by his *labour;* and that, therefore, labour, and labour only, is the sole foundation for any property whatsoever. Man's first duty, then, is to labour in some way or other in order to raise his means of living. If his father, for instance, have laboured before him, and has given or left him the fruit of his labour, he has as good a right to that as if it were the fruit of his own labour; a man's next duty is, to refrain from taking by force or by fraud the property of another man; for, to protect men in the enjoyment of their property was the great end in forming civil society. Perhaps it would not be difficult to prove, that men who are compelled to work for their bread, are, provided they earn a sufficiency of food and of raiment and other necessaries of life, as happy and even happier than those who are not compelled to work for their bread; but at any rate, such is the nature of things, such is the order of the world, that there always have been and always must be some very rich and some very poor, and great multitudes not rich; but in a just state of things, there never will be great multitudes steeped in poverty. The order of the world demands that some shall think, while others work; that some shall make and execute the laws to which all are to yield obedience. Poverty, therefore, even in its extreme state, gives no man a right to view his rich neighbour with an evil eye, much less to do him mischief on account of his riches. If the laws be impartial in themselves, and be executed with impartiality, every man's conscience will tell him, that it is his bounden duty to yield them a cheerful obedience, and further, to yield respect and honour to those who are charged with the execution of the laws.

Such are the great duties of all men in civil society; and God forbid that these principles should ever be rooted out of the hearts of the very best and most virtuous of all mankind, the agricultural labourers of this land, so favoured by God Almighty, and for so many ages the freest and happiest country in the world. But, my friends, men did not enter into civil society for the purpose of bringing upon themselves *duties only:* they had another object; namely, that of creating and enjoying *rights*. Just, indeed, as we have seen in the case of John Stiles, who had his crop of wheat taken away by the stronger man Nokes, who left him nothing but a few wheel-barrows full of accursed potatoes, and all their natural consequences, poverty of blood, leprosy, scrofula, pottle belly, and swelled heels! Now, whenever civil society produces such a state of things, when a laborious man like John Stiles is treated in the same way that Nokes treated him, that civil society has not answered its purpose. Labour, as we have seen, was the foundation of all property, and must always be the foundation of property. The labourer, therefore, has a property in his labour; and, as St. James says in his Epistle, and as Moses and his Apostles and Jesus Christ himself say, to rob the labourer of his hire, that is to say, to take from him or to withhold from him the due reward of his labour, is the greatest crime that man can commit against God.

[*Two-Penny Trash*, 1 February 1831.]

*

Cobbett, however, was at pains to show that he was no 'leveller'. A property-owner himself who employed others, he justified the differences between rich and poor and different stations in life.

With regard to the other topic; namely, the notion that all men ought to be *equally rich and live in the same sort of way*, it is not necessary for me to say much, or, indeed, any-thing, to the far greater part of you; and it would not have been necessary to say one word to any of you on the subject, had it not been for the stupid industry of those who have been living on your labours, to give you what they call education; that is to say, book-knowledge, which they have been cramming down your throats by the means of *their schools* and *their tracts*, all having one and the same tendency; namely, to make you live contentedly upon potatoes, while their tables were covered with the best of bread and of meat, and some of them eating strawberries at a guinea an ounce. In this work of *educating*, however, they have, without intending it, produced a pretty prevalent opinion that there ought to be an equal distribution of riches as well as knowledge; and that all men ought to live in the same sort of way. This, a bare survey of the world will convince you, never can be. If there were no rich farmers, there could be no store of corn or of meat in the country; if there were no gentlemen to be magistrates, there could be neither peace nor property; if there were no legislators of great integrity and knowledge, the country must be torn to pieces for want of laws; if there were no men of great learning and experience, there could be no judges to execute the laws; if there were no statesmen, there could be no state, and the nation would have no means of providing for its independence and safety. If all men were upon an equality in point of means, England would become what the wilds of America are, inhabited by wild men, nobody would work except just to provide food and raiment for the day; and our country would become the most beggarly upon the earth; instead of being what it formerly was (and I hope and trust will be again) the pride of its own people and the envy of the world.

[*Political Register*, 2 April 1831.]

*

Cobbett was concerned, however, to assert the rights of labourers to poor relief when necessary, based upon Christian principles and long-established practice at a time when these entitlements were under what he saw as concerted attack.

The *rights* of the labourer, [are] first to have food, raiment, fuel, lodging, medical and spiritual comfort, in return for his labour, and all these, too, in quantity and quality sufficient for the preservation of his life, health, and vigour. Next, if he be unable to work, unable to earn a sufficiency for his family, or unable to obtain work so as to obtain that sufficiency; in either of these cases, he and his family have a right to have a sufficiency supplied out of the superfluities of those to whom the law of civil society has secured more than they want. This claim of the poor man is, as Judge Blackstone states, founded in the very first principle of civil society; for it cannot be believed that men can have assented to enter civil society for any purpose other than that of the benefit of the whole: it cannot be believed that a million of men for instance, entered into civil society in order that a couple of thousand should have all the meat and all the bread and all the good clothing, and that all the rest should live upon potatoes and go covered with miserable rags. No man upon earth, unless he be one who lives upon the labour of others, will pretend to believe that men entered into civil society, in order that those who did no work, that led idle lives, that created nothing, should have bread and flour and beer and clothing and all sorts of good things a hundred times more than they wanted; while those that laboured and made all these things, were compelled to live upon a miserable watery root or die with starvation.

Such are the *duties* and such the *rights* of labouring men. Our forefathers, who well understood those duties and those rights, cheerfully performed the one and amply enjoyed the other. They had an abundance of meat, of bread, and of all the fruits of the earth; they were clothed throughout in good woollen and linen; they had great store of household goods and of everything to make life easy and pleasant; and when old age or widowhood, or the orphan state, or accident, or any circumstance producing indigence, befel them, the priest of the parish maintained them out of the tithes, administering to their wants as the law enjoined, "with his own hands in charity, humility, and mercy." And this, observe, was a RIGHT which they enjoyed, and that, too, a right as perfect as that of any man to his house or his land. When our country was bereft, by means which I have not now the room to describe, of that species of protection for the poor, the poor-law was passed to supply the place of that protection; to parochial relief, therefore, the aged, the widow, the orphan, the infirm, amongst the labouring people, have just the *same* right as their forefathers had to that which was administered to them in so just and kind and Christian-like a manner.

[*Two-Penny Trash*, 1 February 1831.]

*

Cobbett's commitment to the plight of the agricultural labourers was demonstrated in 1832 by his petition on behalf of a group of adjacent parishes in the North of Hampshire: Micheldever, Stoke Charity, Wonston, Sutton Scotney, and Bullington. These parishes, 'hard parishes' as Cobbett called them, represented the kind of conditions that he had found on the Isle of Thanet. He presented the petition at the behest of some educated labourers in the village who provided him with information of their grievances. Attached to the 1,500-word petition were 176 signatures from three of the parishes. In calling for parliamentary reform, the petitioners delineated the poverty of the labourers and the abuses of taxes and tithes which supported a corrupt and expensive civil and religious establishment. Organised in the midst of wave of rioting, rick-burning and machine-breaking in the southern counties, known as the 'Captain Swing' disturbances, 18 of those signing were eventually to be indicted for offences by the judicial Special Commission set up to deal with the outbreaks.

That Kings and Governments were instituted for the happiness, welfare, and for the better regulating, civil society; to protect the weak against the strong, the rich against the poor, the poor against the unjust encroachments of the rich, in short, to watch over and protect the welfare and happiness of the people, and this we doubt not will be your Majesty's endeavour, so long as your Majesty sway the royal sceptre.

That, relying on this, and availing ourselves of the liberty the laws of our country afford us, namely, that of "petitioning the King," we humbly implore your Majesty to cast an eye of pity to the misery and wretchedness that at this moment pervade every part of this country, and of which your Majesty's petitioners have their full share. That many of us have not food sufficient to satisfy our hunger; our drink is chiefly the crystal element; we have not clothes to hide the nakedness of ourselves, our wives, and our children, nor fuel wherewith to warm us; while at the same time our barns are filled with corn, our garners with wool, our pastures abound with cattle, and our land yields us an abundance of wood and coal; all of which displays the wisdom, the kindness, and mercy of a great Creator on the one hand, and the cruelty, the injustice, and the depravity of his creatures on the other. Nearly to this state of misery have your Majesty's humble petitioners long lived, anxiously looking forward for better days; but to our great sorrow and disappointment, we find oppression daily press heavier and heavier on our shoulders, till at length we are driven to the brink of despair. This misery and wretchedness do not proceed from any fault on the part of your Majesty's petitioners, as we use every exertion in our power to subdue these bitter evils; but experience tells us that "all is vain." Some of your Majesty's wealthy subjects impute this prevailing depression to an "over-population," which we positively deny, seeing there is an abundance for the lowest of your Majesty's subjects, if possessed of the ability to purchase. But your Majesty's petitioners more reasonably and justly impute it to a misapplication of the produce of talent and industry; and this proceeds from a misrepresentation in the Commons House of Parliament. [...]

That, in consequence of this misrepresentation in the Commons or People's House of Parliament, we have to complain that upwards of £50,000,000 annually are extorted from that part of Great Britain called England, and of which sum the middle and labouring classes pay the greatest part; whilst the Government of the United States of America cost the 12,000,000 of people they govern not so many thousands, in consequence of which the people so governed, live in the greatest state of ease and happiness. We complain that this tax lie most heavy on those articles which are the necessary of the poor man's life; such as malt, hops, tea, sugar, tobacco, soap, candles, &c. &c.: which cause the price of those articles to be twice their real value; that our wages at this time are not more than nine shillings-a-week (at Barton Stacey but eight shillings), out of which we have to pay, one shilling for the rent of our house, and one for fuel, leaving but seven shillings per week, or one shilling per day for the support of a man, his wife, and three children. That at this time the tax on a bushel of malt, or a pound of tea, amount to as much as the labouring man's wages do in two days and a half. We complain that part of the money extorted from us go to pay the interest of a debt, part of which was contracted by the unnecessary wars, and a part by our fathers' fathers' great grandfathers. We complain that another part of the fruit of our labours go to pay grants, pensions, sinecures, &c. &c., wantonly heaped on the heads of the aristocracy and their relations, whose names are known only by the vast sums they receive, and who has never rendered the country any service whatever. We complain that (according to the statement of Sir James Graham), 113 of his late Majesty's Privy Councillors receive amongst them £650,000 per annum, some of whom are members of the Commons House of Parliament, this being contrary to Magna Carta, which says, "That no person who has an office, or place of profit under the King, or who receives a pension from the Crown, shall be capable of serving as a member of the House of Commons." We complain that notwithstanding a peace of sixteen years, we have a standing army of nearly 100,000 men, fed and clothed out of the fruit of our labour; part of which force is kept to compel us to pay the dreadful burdens heaped on our shoulders; we complain that, among this force, is twice as many officers as is necessary, such as generals, admirals, colonels, captains &c., who receive immense salaries, and what chiefly are in some way or other related to the aristocracy; we complain that we never had a voice in the legislature, though, by the law, we are all liable to serve as soldiers, and shed our blood in the defence of our country, in any war the legislature please to engage in; we complain, that that property, commonly called church-property, is applied to very bad and useless purposes, purposes which have no concern whatever with religion; that whilst many poor clergy have scarce enough to maintain the dignity of their calling, others have four, five, six, and seven livings and places of profit; and whilst some of the bishops have revenues amounting to from ten to thirty, thirty-five, and £40,000 annually; that notwithstanding their immense revenues, the bishops, and other rich men in the church, are often calling on us to "subscribe liberally" towards funds for erecting and enlarging churches and chapels, and for propagating the gospel in foreign parts. As to the uselessness of this church-property, we would cite one instance; that in this parish of Barton Stacey, the great-tithes, which in most part are sold from the church, are worth nearly £1,000 per annum, the small tithes, £450 and which belong to the Dean of Winchester. A curate is hired for about £100 per annum, and who does duty twice on every Sabbath day; that the £1,350 between the money collected and the curate's salary has no more concern with religion than the sturdy ox has with the pretty affairs of the bees; nearly half as much as all the labourers in the parish earn, and which is as much loss to the parish as though taken and thrown into the sea; we complain that trial by jury, so highly valued by our ancestors as to be deemed almost sacred, has been, in many cases, abolished from our courts of justice, placing it in the power of magistrates to imprison and otherwise punish us, and who are chiefly members of the aristocracy, officers under the crown, or clergy of the established church, who, notwithstanding live on the fruit of our labour, often insult and haughtily treat us; so that Sir John Pollen, who is the present member for Andover, in the vicinity of which town we live, and a magistrate, did, at a meeting in that town, call us "poor devils;" and who, he said, "had hardly a rag to cover them." We complain, that, notwithstanding the misery and half starvation to which we are reduced, the law, under severe imprisonment and heavy fine, forbids us to take for our own use the wild birds and animals that inhabit the woods and fields, or the fish that swim in the water; those being kept not for the service, but for the sports of the rich.

['The Petition of the Hard Parishes', *Two-Penny Trash*, 1 July 1832.]

*

Cobbett's last great campaign was against the introduction of the New Poor Law which he saw as threatening the very rights of the poor he had been championing so consistently for decades.

I was in hopes that the "*Reformed* Parliament" would, at once, have set to work to sweep away [...] innovations. Not only did it not do this, but it set itself to work to add to them in number, and to enlarge those that already existed. I pass over twenty instances of this, and come to that great and terrible innovation the POOR-LAW BILL. Long before I was in parliament, I saw the deep-laid scheme gradually preparing for execution. When it was matured and brought before us, I opposed it with all my might. I did everything that I could do to prevent it from being passed.

In this case how stood the matter? There was a proposition to abrogate (though not by name), in effect, those rights of the poor which had always existed, since England had been called England; which rights had been so solemnly recognised by the Act of the 43rd of ELIZABETH; which act had existed upwards of two hundred years, and which had seen, during its existence, the most orderly, the most independent, yet the most obedient; the best fed and the best clad, and, at the same time, the most industrious, and most adroit working people that ever lived upon the face of the earth, being, along with these qualities, the best parents, the best children, the most faithful servants, the most respectful in their demeanour towards superiors, that ever formed a part of any civil community.

And, sir, what was THE GROUND stated for abrogating this law; for uprooting the old and amiable parochial governments of England? What was the ground stated for the doing of this thing; for the sweeping away of this government, carried on by neighbours for their mutual good and happiness; what was the ground stated for the tearing to pieces of this family government, and subjecting thirteen thousand parishes to the absolute will of three commissioners, stuck up in London by the servants of the king, and removable at their pleasure? Why, the grounds were as follow, as stated by the Lord Chancellor, who was backed by Lord RADNOR, and by the Duke of WELLINGTON, and a majority of the two Houses, you, sir, being in the majority of one of those Houses.

There were many pretences urged; many assertions made; but the main ground, which, like the rod of AARON, devoured all the rest, was, that, *if this Bill were not passed, the poor-rates would soon swallow up the estates of the lords and the gentlemen;* and that it was necessary to be passed, in order *to save their estates;* for that, unless it were passed, there was *no security for property.*

Often as I have disproved these assertions; often as I have shown that the increased amount of poor-rates has not been so great, not anything like so great, as the increased amount of rent and taxes. Often as I have shown that the inevitable tendency of the Bill is, to bring down the farmers and labourers of England to the state of those in Ireland; often as I have shown these things, I must show them again here.

[*Cobbett's Legacy to Labourers* (London, 1835), pp. 7–9.]

*

With characteristic vigour he took up the charge that poor rates were 'swallowing up' the property of the country, finding examples of waste and unnecessary expenditure on every side.

It is true, that the nation is burdened, even to the breaking of it down: it is true that the farmers are ruined by prices equal to the prices of forty years ago; but, are they ruined by the six millions (allowing it to be the six millions); or, are they ruined by the fifty-two millions? It is also true that a very large part, and the greater part, of landlords are upon the point of utter ruin; but have they been ruined by the six millions, or by the fifty-two millions? Have they been ruined by the poor-rates; or by the expense of the standing army in time of peace; by the pensions, sinecures, grants and allowances, half-pay, amounting altogether to between six and seven millions a year paid to the usurers, more than doubled in real amount by the passing of your bill?

Monstrous! Stupendous stock of impudence, even in a half-drunk mountebank, to pretend, that the ruin has arisen from the working people! It has been established for fact, that a hundred and thirteen of your brother privy-councillors, not including bishops or royal family, swallow up *six hundred and fifty thousand pounds a year* out of the taxes; a sum equal to the aggregate amount of the poor-rates of Bedfordshire, Berkshire, Buckinghamshire, Huntingdonshire, Cumberland, Monmouthshire, Rutlandshire, Westmoreland, another county or two into the bargain! Yet this is nothing: this is no swallowing up! We vote every year a sum of money to be sent to Hanover, to be given to half-pay officers and their widows and children there, equal to the poor-rates of Cumberland and Westmoreland! There were grants *to augment the livings of the clergy in England*, to the amount of the poor-rates for one year of ten counties in England, standing the first on the alphabetical list. We have just voted, to be given to lords, baronets, and 'squires, to induce them to free their slaves in the West Indies, as much money as would keep the poor of England and Wales for *five years!* All these are not "*swallowings up*," I suppose; but the working people know that they are *swallowings up*; and that they themselves are compelled to pay the far greater part of these sums out of the fruits of their labour.

[*Cobbett's Legacy to Labourers* (London, 1835), pp. 13–15.]

Chapter 10

America

Cobbett spent a total of 10 years in the United States, first in Philadelphia (1792–1800), where he began his career as a political writer, and later on Long Island (1817–19), where he took refuge after the suspension of Habeas Corpus in Britain. In 1800, the emigrated theologian and scientist Joseph Priestley – the target of Cobbett's first American pamphlet – acknowledged him as 'by far the most popular writer in this country', while Cobbett was regarded in Britain as one of the leading experts on the United States.[1]

Cobbett arrived in America in 1792, believing in the republican ideas of Thomas Paine and – as he described himself in a letter to Thomas Jefferson – 'ambitious to become a citizen of a free state'. However, what he saw around him led to a rapid disillusionment with American democracy. In a series of witty, vituperative pamphlets, published under the pen name 'Peter Porcupine', and in his daily newspaper, *Porcupine's Gazette*, Cobbett warned of an international Jacobin conspiracy to subvert the Washington administration and construct a Franco–American alliance against Britain. Against this threat, he championed Tory and Federalist principles, giving vivid descriptions of the revolutionary violence in France, and attacking Republican politicians, Democratic Societies and transatlantic radicals from Britain and Ireland. He supported John Adams as the Federalist candidate in the 1796 presidential election, but later criticised Adams for pursuing peace with France. After losing a libel case, and facing financial ruin, he fled for Britain in 1800. The same year, the election of the pro-French Republican Thomas Jefferson seemed to represent the ascendancy of everything he hated and feared.

However, Cobbett's conversion to radicalism in Britain during the early 1800s led to a corresponding reassessment of the United States. He was the only English journalist to oppose the War of 1812 and he energetically promoted the publication of his writings in America, sending his nephew to New York to act as his American agent. Returning to the United States in 1817, he decided to stay away from the centres of American politics and instead took a lease on a Long Island farm. From there he continued the *Political Register*, sending articles back across the Atlantic, and offered advice on American agriculture to prospective English emigrants. He now viewed America as a land of liberty and opportunity, where English farmers could escape a corrupt political system and enjoy low taxes, cheap living and a more egalitarian culture. When he returned home,

---

[1] Joseph Priestley to Thomas Lindsey, 1 May 1800, *Life and Correspondence of Joseph Priestley*, 2 vols (London, 1832), vol. 2, p. 432.

he sought to introduce American trees to Britain through a transatlantic seed business, while his continued interest in American politics can be seen in the short biography of Andrew Jackson (who he praised as a fellow critic of paper money and modern finance) that he published in 1834. Despite his reputation as an archetypal English writer, the United States is one of the major themes of Cobbett's writing.

*

In his 1796 autobiography, *Life and Adventures of Peter Porcupine*, Cobbett identified the American War of Independence as a seminal event in his early life.

> As to politics, we were like the rest of the country people in England; that is to say, we neither knew or thought any thing about the matter. The shout of victory or the murmurs at a defeat, would now-and-then break in upon our tranquillity for a moment; but I do not remember ever having seen a newspaper in the house; and, most certainly, that privation did not render us less industrious, happy, or free.
>
> After, however, the American war had continued for some time, and the cause and nature of it began to be understood, or rather misunderstood, by the lower classes of the people in England, we became a little better acquainted with subjects of this kind. It is well known, that the people were, as to numbers, nearly equally divided in their opinions, concerning that war, and their wishes respecting the result of it. My father was a partizan of the Americans: he used frequently to dispute on the subject with the gardener of a nobleman who lived near us. This was generally done with good humour, over a pot of our best ale; yet the disputants sometimes grew warm, and gave way to language that could not fail to attract our attention. My father was worsted, without doubt, as he had for antagonist, a shrewd and sensible old Scotchman, far his superior in political knowledge; but he pleaded before a partial audience: we thought there was but one wise man in the world, and that that one was our father. He who pleased the cause of the Americans, had an advantage, too, with young minds: he had only to represent the king's troops as sent to cut the throats of a people, our friends and relations, merely because they would not submit to oppression, and his cause was gained. Speaking to the passions, is ever sure to succeed on the uninformed.
>
> Men of integrity are generally pretty obstinate, in adhering to an opinion once adopted. Whether it was owing to this, or to the weakness of Mr. Martin's arguments, I will not pretend to say; but he never could make a convert of my father: he continued an American, and so staunch a one, that he would not have suffered his best friend to drink success to the king's arms at his table. I cannot give the reader a better idea of his

obstinacy in this respect, and of the length to which this difference in sentiment was carried in England, than by relating the following instance.

My father used to take one of us with him every year, to the great hop-fair at Wey-Hill. The fair was held at Old Michaelmas-tide, and the journey was, to us, a sort of reward for the labours of the summer. It happened to by my turn to go thither, the very year that Long-Island was taken by the British.[2] A great company of hop-merchants and farmers were just sitting down to supper as the post arrived, bringing in the Extraordinary Gazette which announced the victory. A hop-factor from London took the paper, placed his chair upon the table, and began to read with an audible voice. He was opposed, a dispute ensured, and my father retired, taking me by the hand, to another apartment, where we supped with about a dozen others of the same sentiments. Here Washington's health, and success to the Americans, were repeatedly toasted, and this was the first time, as far as I can recollect, that I ever heard the General's name mentioned. Little did I then dream, that I should ever see the man, and still less, that I should hear some of his own countrymen reviling and execrating him.

[*The Life and Adventures of Peter Porcupine*, pp. 21–4, in G.D.H. Cole (ed.) *Life and Adventures*.]

*

William and Nancy Cobbett fled to France in 1792 after the publication of *The Soldier's Friend*. They soon 'perceived the storm gathering' and, on hearing news of the massacre of the Swiss Guard at the Tuileries, sailed for America. Cobbett secured an introduction from the American Ambassador at the Hague to Thomas Jefferson, then Secretary of State, and wrote the following letter asking for employment.

Wilmington, Delaware State, 2nd Nov. 1792.

Sir,

My friend, whom Mr. Short has mentioned in the enclosed letter, procured it for me thinking you might have it in your power to serve me upon my landing in this country: but, conscious that I can have no other pretension to your notice at present than merely that founded on a recommendation, and wishing to avoid the importunate part too often acted by men in my situation, I have chosen this as the least troublesome way of paying my respects to you.

---

[2]   British forces under General Howe took Long Island from George Washington's Continental Army in the Battle of Long Island, fought on 27 August 1776.

Ambitious to become the citizen of a free state, I have left my native country, England, for America: I bring with me youth, a small family, a few useful literary talents and that is all.

Should you have an opportunity of serving me, my conduct shall not show me ungrateful, or falsify the recommendation I now send you. Should that not be the case, I shall feel but little disappointment from it, not doubting but my industry and care will make me a happy and useful member in my adopted country.

      I am, with great respect,
          Sir,
               Your most obedient Servant,
                 Wm. Cobbett

Thomas Jefferson
Secretary of State
Philadelphia
P.S. Sir, I am but a few days landed in America, and am settled here for the Winter, if no employment offers itself during that time.

[Cobbett to Thomas Jefferson, Wilmington, Delaware, 2 November 1792, Pierpont Morgan Library, New York, Department of Literary and Historical Manuscripts, Misc. English, 206247.]

*

Cobbett's letter to Jefferson did not lead to an offer of employment and, 18 months later, he described his complete disenchantment with America. The final part of the following extract alludes to his first, anonymously published, pamphlet.

This country is good for getting money, that is to say if a person is industrious and enterprising. In every other respect the country is miserable. Exactly the contrary of what I expected it.—The land is bad—rocky—houses wretched—roads impassable after the least rain.— Fruit in quantity, but good for nothing—One apple or peach in England or France is worth a bushel of them here.—The seasons are detestable—All is burning or freezing.—There is no spring or Autumn.—The weather is so very inconstant that you are never sure for an hour, a single hour at a time—Last night we made a fire to sit by—and to-day it is scorching hot.—The whole month of March was so hot that we could hardly bear our cloths [sic], and three parts of the month of June there was a frost every night, and so cold in the day time, that we were obliged to wear great coats.—The people are worthy of the country—[a] cheating, sly, roguish gang. Strangers make fortunes here in spite of all this, particularly the

English. The natives are by nature idle, and seek to live by cheating, while foreigners, being industrious, seek no other means than those dictated by integrity, and are sure to meet with encouragement even from the idle and roguish themselves; for, however roguish a man may be, he always loves to deal with an honest man.—You have perhaps heard of the plague being at Philadelphia last year.—It was no plague; it was a fever of the country, and is by no means extraordinary among the Americans.—In the fall of the year almost every person, in any place, has a spell of the fever that is called the fall-fever[3]—it is often fatal, and the only way to avoid it is to quit the country. But this fever is not all—Every month has its particular malady.—In July, for example, every body almost, or at least one half of the people, are taken with vomittings for several days at a time; they often carry off the patient, and almost always children.—In short the country altogether is detestable.

The greatest part of my acquaintance in this country are french merchants from St. Domingo and Martinies. To one of those Islands I shall probably go in about 8 or 9 months; and in that case, if I live so long, I shall be in England in about three years. For I do not intend to stay much above a couple of years in the Islands.—Take care of my trunk and box if you please, till you see me or hear from me. My Nancy's kind love to you all, and accept of mine at the same time. Doctor Priestley is just arrived here from England. He has attacked our English laws and Constitution in print, and declared his sentiments in favour of those butchers in France. He has however been attacked in his turn by an Englishman here.

[William Cobbett to Rachel Smither, Philadelphia, 6 July 1794, Nuffield XXX/2/1–2.]

*

Cobbett's first American publication attacked the Unitarian scientist, philosopher and political radical Joseph Priestley, whose Birmingham house and laboratory had been destroyed by a 'Church and King' mob in 1791. In 1794, Priestley left Britain for America, where he was warmly welcomed by democrats and republicans in New York and Philadelphia – a reception that provoked Cobbett's rage.

I am one of those who wish to believe that foreigners come to this country from choice, and not from necessity. America opens a wide field for enterprize; wages for all mechanics are better, and the means of subsistence proportionably cheaper than in Europe. This is what brings

---

3   Another name for leptospirosis, a type of bacterial infection.

foreigners amongst us: they become citizens of America for the honest purposes of commerce, of turning their industry and talents to the best account, and of bettering their fortunes. By their exertions to enrich themselves, they enrich the state, lower the wages, and render the country less dependent upon others. The most numerous as well as the most useful are mechanics; perhaps a cobler with his hammer and awls, is a more valuable acquisition than a dozen philosophi-theologi-political empericks with all their boasted apparatus.

Of all the English arrived in these States (since the war) no one was ever calculated to render them less service than Doctor Priestley; and what is more, perhaps no one (before or since, or even in the war) ever intended to render them less [...]

It is to be hoped that the Doctor's anger against his country is by this time nearly assuaged: dear bought experience has at last taught him, that an Utopia never existed any where but in a delirious brain. He thought, like too many others, to find America a Terrestrial Paradise; a land of Canaan, where he would have nothing to do, but open his mouth and swallow the milk and honey; but, alas! he is now convinced, I believe, that those who cultivate the fertile Lesowes of Warwickshire,

> Where all around the gentlest breezes play
> Where gentle music melts on every spray,[4]

have little reason to envy him his rocks and his swamps, the music of his bull-frogs and the stings of his musquitoes.

In the preface, so often mentioned, the Doctor expresses a desire of one day returning to "the land that gave him birth;" and, no offence to the New-York addressers, I think we ought to wish that this desire may be very soon accomplished. He is a bird of passage that has visited us, only to avoid the rigour of an inclement season; when the re-animating sunshine of revolution shall burst forth on his native clime, we may hope to see him prune his wings, and take his flight from the dreary banks of the Susquehannah to those of the Thames or the Avon.

[*Observations on the Emigration of Dr. Joseph Priestley* (Philadelphia, 1796), pp. 61–81.]

*

---

4   'There all around the gentlest breezes stray,/ There gentle music melts on every spray', Oliver Goldsmith, *The Traveller* (1764), ll. 321–2.

Having written several pamphlets as 'Peter Porcupine', Cobbett decided to reveal his true identity. His characteristically foolhardy actions caused further controversy, though not the mob violence his friends feared.

IN the Spring of the year 1796, I took a house in Second Street, Philadelphia, for the purpose of carrying on the bookselling business, which I looked upon as being at once a means of getting money, and of propagating writings against the French. I went into my house in May, but the shop could not be gotten ready for some time; and, from one delay and another, I was prevented from opening till the second week in July.

Till I took this house, I had remained almost entirely unknown, as a writer. A few persons did, indeed, know that I was the person, who had assumed the name of PETER PORCUPINE; but the fact was by no means a matter of notoriety. The moment, however, that I had taken a lease of a large house, the transaction became a topic of public conversation, and the eyes of the Democrats and the French, who still lorded it over the city, and who owed me a mutual grudge, were fixed upon me.

I thought my situation somewhat perilous. Such truths as I had published, no man had dared to utter in the United States, since the rebellion. I knew that these truths had mortally offended the leading men amongst the Democrats, who could, at any time, muster a mob quite sufficient to destroy my house, and to murder me. I had not a friend, to whom I could look with any reasonable hope of receiving efficient support; and, as to the *law*, I had seen too much of republican justice, to expect any thing but persecution from that quarter. In short, there were, in Philadelphia, about ten thousand persons, all of whom would have rejoiced to see me murdered; and there might, probably, be two thousand, who would have been very sorry for it; but not above fifty of whom would have stirred an inch to save me.

As the time approached for opening my shop, my friends grew more anxious for my safety. It was recommended to me, to be cautious how I exposed, at my window, any thing that might provoke the people; and, above all, not to put up any *aristocratical portraits*, which would certainly cause my windows to be demolished.

I saw the danger; but also saw, that I must, at once, set all danger at defiance, or live in everlasting subjection to the prejudices and caprice of the democratical mob. I resolved on the former; and, as my shop was to open on a Monday morning, I employed myself all day on Sunday, in preparing an exhibition, that I thought would put the courage and the power of my enemies to the test. I put up in my windows, which were very large, all the portraits that I had in my possession of *kings, queens, princes*, and *nobles*. I had all the English Ministry; several of the Bishops and Judges; the most famous Admirals; and, in short, every picture that I thought likely to excite rage in the enemies of Great Britain.

Early on the Monday morning, I took down my shutters. Such a sight had not been seen in Philadelphia for twenty years. Never since the beginning of the rebellion, had any one dared to hoist at his window the portrait of George the Third.

[*Porcupine's Works* (London, 1801), vol. 4, pp. 3–4.]

*

In the 1790s, Cobbett often assumed an American identity to warn 'fellow Americans' of the disastrous consequences of war with Britain. Instead, he urged an Anglo–American alliance against revolutionary France.

War is at all times and to all countries dreadful in its effects, but to no country and at no time was it ever so dreadful as it would be now to America. This is not a warlike nation, nor has this nation a warlike Government. In a war with any nation whatever, this country can gain nothing, and in a war with Great Britain it has everything to lose. [...] The *warriors* do not pretend that we could go and take Great Britain; they do not pretend that we could take Jamaica; they do not pretend even that we could take Bermuda. What then can we take? Why—*Canada*. This is the burden of their song, or rather *war-whoop*. With this they divert the rabble, and sharpen their fangs for war and conquest. If you ask them *how* they would do this, they tell you that men are not wanting; that *four hundred thousand* would turn out volunteers against Great Britain. I believe that twice that number would turn out for a field-day, with sticks and staves, and return very peaceably home to supper; but would they do this two days running? [...]

I have hitherto proceeded upon the supposition that the people of this country would be all united in the cause of the war. But how far would this be from the case! Almost all the rich, almost all the people of property, would be opposed to it. There is another and still more dangerous kind of division, which would finally end in a dissolution of the Union: I mean the division of the North from the South.

[*Political Censor*, April 1796.]

*

In 1804, Cobbett described his career as a political journalist in Philadelphia in an open letter to William Pitt. Defending his own patriotism and consistency, he argued that it was Pitt who had deserted the patriotic cause by pursuing peace with France.

It is now, Sir, ten years since I first took up the pen with an intention to write for the press, on political subjects; and the occasion of my so doing is too curious in itself, as well as of too much importance as to the sequel, not to be described somewhat in detail. At the memorable epoch of Doctor Priestley's emigration to America, I followed, in the city of Philadelphia, the profession of teacher of the English language to Frenchmen. Newspapers were a luxury for which I had little relish, and which, if I had been ever so fond of, I had not time to enjoy. The manifestoes, therefore, of the Doctor, upon his landing in that country, and the malicious attacks upon the monarchy and the monarch of England which certain societies in America thereupon issued through the press, would, had it not been for a circumstance purely accidental, have escaped, probably for ever, not only my animadversion, but my knowledge of their existence. One of my scholars, who was a person that we in England should call a Coffee-house Politician, chose, for once, to read his newspaper by way of lesson; and, it happened to be the very paper which contained the addresses presented to Doctor Priestley at New York, together with his replies. My scholar, who was a sort of republican, or, at best, but half a monarchist, appeared delighted with the invectives against England, to which he was very much disposed to add. Those Englishmen who have been abroad, particularly if they have had time to make a comparison between the country they are in and that which they have left, well know how difficult it is, upon occasions such as I have been describing, to refrain from expressing their indignation and resentment; and there is not, I trust, much reason to suppose, that I should, in this respect, experience less difficulty than another. The dispute was as warm as might reasonably be expected between a Frenchman, uncommonly violent even for a Frenchman, and an Englishman not remarkable for *sang froid;* and, the result was, a declared resolution, on my part, to write and publish a pamphlet in defence of my country, which pamphlet he pledged himself to answer: his pledge was forfeited: it is known that mine was not.—Thus, Sir, it was, that I became a writer on politics. "Happy for you," you will say, "if you had continued at your verbs and your nouns!" [...] From this time (the summer of 1794) to the year 1800 my labours were without intermission [...] during the whole of which time, I can truly say, that I lived not for myself or my family, but exclusively for my country and my King. I enjoyed nothing that the world calls pleasure, fortune was entirely neglected, and personal safety but very little attended to. When I began to write, the prejudice, the hatred, against England were so great, that scarcely any Englishman would publicly own his country. If asked of what country he was, his answer was evasive; he came from "the old country," or he called himself an Irishman or a Scotchman; for *English* was the hated epithet.

['To the Rt. Hon. William Pitt, On the Causes of the Decline of Great Britain', *Political Register*, 29 September 1804.]

*

After a revolution in his political views in the early 1800s, Cobbett opposed the War of 1812, which had been triggered by disputes about trade and the impressment of American sailors by the British navy. In the following extract from an open letter to the Prime Minister, Lord Liverpool, he lamented the persistence of colonial attitudes towards America.

It has always been the misfortune of England, that her rulers and her people have spoken and have thought *contemptuously* of the Americans. Your Lordship and I were boys, and, indeed, not born, or, at least, I was not, when our King first was involved in a quarrel with the Americans. But almost as long as I can remember any thing, I can remember, that this contempt was expressed in the songs and saying of the clod-hoppers, amongst whom I was born and bred; in doing which we conducted down to the earth that we delved the sentiments of the 'Squires and Lords. The result of the former war, while it enlightened nobody, added to the vindictiveness of hundreds of thousands; so that we have entered into this war with all our old stock of *contempt*, and a vastly increased stock of rancour. To think that the American Republic is to be a *great power* is insupportable. Some men, in order to keep her down in their language, and, at the same time, not use harsh expressions, observe, that she is only *another part of ourselves*. They wish her to be thought, if not dependent upon us, still to be a sort of younger child of our family, coming in after *Ireland, Jamaica*, &c. I met a very worthy Scots gentleman, a month or two ago, who wished that some man of ability would propose a scheme that he had, and without which, he said, *we never should have peace again*. "Well, Sir," said I, "and, pray, what is your scheme?"—"Why," said he, "it is very *simple*. It is to form an UNION with the American States." It was raining, and I wanted to get on; so that I had not time to ascertain what *sort* of Union he meant. This gentleman, however, was remarkably moderate in his views. The far greater part of the nation expect absolute Colonial submission; and, if our fleets and armies should not finally succeed in bringing a Property Tax from America into his Majesty's Exchequer, the far greater part of the people will be most grievously disappointed. [...]

Of the effects of this *contempt* I know nobody, however, who have so much reason to repent as the officers of his Majesty's navy. If they had triumphed, it would only have been over half a dozen of fir frigates, with *bits of bunting at their mastheads.* They were sure to *gain* no reputation in the contest; and, if they were defeated, what was their lot? The worst of it is, they themselves did, in some measure, contribute to their own ill-fate; for, of all men living, none spoke of "poor Jonathan" with so much contempt. To read their letters, or the letters which our newspaper people pretended to have received from them, at the out-set of the war, one would have thought, that they would hardly have condescended to *return a shot* from a *bunting* ship. And *now,* to see that bit of bunting flying so often over the British Flag! Oh! it is stinging beyond expression! The people in the country *cannot think how it is.* There are some people, who are for taking the American Commodores at their word, and ascribing their victories to the *immediate intervention of Providence.*

['To the Earl of Liverpool, On the American War', *Political Register*, 10 December 1814.]

*

Cobbett's memories of his time in Philadelphia changed as he attempted to reconcile his Tory pamphleteering with his later radicalism. In this extract, taken from the American edition of the *Political Register*, he gives a more light-hearted account of his experiences in the 1790s.

When the war of 1793 broke out between France and England, I was living at Wilmington in the state of Delaware, next door to a Mr. COMMONS, a carpenter, and upon a rising ground commanding a view of the Delaware. A French frigate, which had brought out the new ambassador from the republic, appeared in that river with the tricoloured flag at her masthead. Mr. Commons pointed to it, telling me, that that flag would soon drive the flag of England from the ocean. *England* was the object of attack, and I was an *Englishman.* From that time my neighbour and I became what are called *"natural enemies."* Hence, by degrees, I imbibed the strongest desire to see England triumph in the quarrel, without knowing, and without caring, any thing about its grounds. What trifles frequently give a bent to men's minds! To what important consequences do mere *nothings* lead! My great delight, at that time, was in a most beautiful flower garden, which I had made with my own hands out of a poor rough stony piece of ground that nobody thought worth tillage. It is probable that I never should have written for the press a single line in my life, had it not been for the discussions with my neighbour the carpenter. This set me to reading what people call politics;

reading led me to Philadelphia [...] The Philadelphians were dressed in tricoloured cockades, which were sold in the shops. Nothing was heard in the streets, but praises of the French, and abuse of the English. Never very patient, or given to yield to a torrent, I soon became a pretty busy partizan, and sought occasions to engage in disputes. [...]

Thus become *an author* I soon became known to the public, and then, I call to witness all those who lived in Philadelphia at that time, what torrents of abuse were poured forth upon me. All manner of falsehoods were published respecting me, every sort of crime was falsely laid to my charge; and, what I believe, was never done in any other case, the foulest assertions were made respecting even my wife. Young, strong, with good health, always buoyant spirits, careless of consequences, I was a match for my antagonists. I have laughed a thousand times, and I laugh at this moment, at the recollection of the wars that we used to carry on. My opponents contended that *nothing* was good that belonged to England. I contended that nothing was good that *did not* belong to her. I was quite sincere; and I solemnly declare, that I believed, that even the poultry and the apples were not half so good as those in England.

['Introductory Address', US edition of *Political Register*, 21 May 1816.]

*

Following the suspension of Habeas Corpus, and faced with the very real prospect of a second spell in Newgate, Cobbett sailed for the United States at the end of March 1817. After landing in New York he made the short journey to Long Island, where he remained for the next two and a half years.

On Wednesday evening, the 27th of March, we embarked on board the ship IMPORTER, D. OGDEN master, bound to New York, where we arrived on the 5th of May, with about 40 steerage passengers, farmers and tradesmen, who were fleeing from ruin and starvation. In all respects that can be named our passage was disagreeable; and, upon one occasion, very perilous from lightning, which struck the ship twice, shivered two of the masts, killed a man, struck several people slightly, between two of whom I was sitting without at all feeling the blow. Some of our fellow passengers have found great disappointment; and, it is stated in some of the public papers here, that many hundreds have, during the last year, accepted of the offer of our Consul at New York *to go and settle in Canada*. You know, that I have never *advised* any body to emigrate. I have always said, that it is no place for manufacturers; no place for men to live without work; no place for a farmer who does not work himself; no place, in short, for any one who is not able and *willing* to work at the *ordinary sorts of work*, but, for such men, there is every where a plentiful, happy, and easy life. [...]

All that I see around me here is well calculated to attract the attention and to please the sight of one like myself, brought up in the country, always greatly delighted with, and somewhat skilled in, its various and pleasing and healthful pursuits. The people are engaged busily in planting their Indian Corn. The Cherry Trees, of which there are multitudes, planted in long avenues, or rows, or round the fields, have dropped their blossom and begin to show their loads of fruit. The apple and pear orchards, in extent from one to twenty acres on each farm, are in full and beautiful bloom. [...] We lodge and board in this Inn, each have a bedroom and good bed, have a room to sit in to ourselves, we eat by ourselves; and it really *is eating*. We have smoaked fish, chops, butter, and eggs, for breakfast, with bread (the very finest I ever saw), crackers, sweet cakes; and, when I say, that we *have* such and such things, I do not mean, that we have them for *show*, or just enough to *smell to;* but in *loads*. Not *an egg*, but a dish full of eggs. Not a snip of meat or of fish; but a plate full. Lump Sugar for our tea and coffee; not broke into little bits the size of a hazle-nut; but in good thumping pieces. For dinner we have the finest of fish, bass, mackarel, lobsters; of meat, lamb, veal, ham, &c. Asparagus in plenty; apple pies (though in the middle of May). The supper is like the breakfast, with preserved peaches and other things. And for all this an excellent cider to drink, with the kindest and most obliging treatment, on the part of the Landlord and Landlady and their sons and daughters, we pay no more than *twenty-two shillings and sixpence a week each*. In England the same food and drink and lodging at an Inn would cost us nearly the same sum *every day*. [...]

All this is the effect of good government; of just and mild government, which takes so little from the people in taxes, that they have the means of happiness fully left in their hands.

[*Political Register*, 12 July 1817.]

*

In his account of living on Long Island, Cobbett compared the national characters of England and America. The juxtaposition shows his renewed admiration for the democratic culture of the United States, as well as an acute sense of exile.

There are very few really *ignorant* men in America of native growth. Every farmer is more less of *a reader*. There is no *brogue*, no *provincial dialect*. No class like that which the French call *peasantry*, and which degrading appellation the miscreant spawn of the funds have, of late years, applied to the whole mass of the most useful people in England, those who do the work and fight the battles. And, as to the men, who would naturally form *your* acquaintance, they, I know from experience, are as kind, frank, and sensible men as are on the general run, to be found in England, even with the power of selection. They are all well-informed; modest without shyness; always free to communicate what they know, and never ashamed to acknowledge that they have yet to learn. You never hear them *boast* of their possessions, and you never hear them *complaining* of their wants. They have all been *readers* from their youth up; and there are few subjects upon which they cannot converse with you, whether of a political or scientific nature. At any rate, they always *hear* with patience. I do not know that I ever heard a native American interrupt another man while he was speaking. Their *sedateness* and *coolness*, the *deliberate* manner in which they say and do every thing, and the *slowness* and *reserve* with which they express their assent; these are very wrongly estimated, when they are taken for marks of *a want* of feeling. It must be a tale of woe indeed, that will bring a tear from an American's eye; but any trumped up story will send his hand to his pocket, as the ambassadors from the beggars of France, Italy and Germany can fully testify.

However you will not, for a long while, know what to do for want of the *quick responses* of the English tongue, and the *decided* tone of the English expression. The *loud voice;* the *hard squeeze* by the hand; the *instant assent or dissent;* the *clamorous joy;* the *bitter wailing;* the *ardent friendship;* the *deadly enmity;* the *love that makes people kill themselves;* the *hatred that makes them kill others.* All these belong to the characters of Englishmen, in whose minds and hearts every feeling exists in the *extreme.*

[*A Year's Residence in the United States of America* (London, 1819), paras 360–1.]

*

Morris Birkbeck's *Letters from Illinois* (1818) was one of many emigration manuals published after the end of the war with France and the lifting of restrictions on emigration. Cobbett strenuously contested Birkbeck's account of new settlements in the West and advised potential emigrants to stay near the Atlantic coast.

You do indeed fairly describe the rugged roads, the dirty hovels, the fire in the woods to sleep by, the pathless ways through the wildernesses, the dangerous crossings of the rivers; but, there are the beautiful meadows and rich lands *at last;* there is the *fine freehold domain at the end!* There are the giants and the enchanters to encounter; the slashings and the rib-roastings to undergo; but, then, there is, *at last*, the lovely languishing damsel to repay the adventurer. [...]

Persons of advanced age, of settled habits, of deep rooted prejudices, of settled acquaintances, of contracted sphere of movement, do not, to use Mr. GEORGE FLOWER'S expression, "*transplant well*."[5] Of all such persons, Farmers transplant worst; and, of all Farmers, English Farmers are the worst to transplant. [...]

It is no "*every-day evil*" that they have to bear. For an English Farmer, and, more especially, an English Farmer's wife, after crossing the sea and travelling to the Illinois, with the consciousness of having expended a third of their substance, to purchase, as yet, nothing but sufferings; for such persons to boil their pot in the gipsy-fashion, to have a mere board to eat on, to drink whisky or pure water, to sit and sleep under a shed far inferior to their English cow-pens, to have a mill at twenty miles' distance, an apothecary's shop at a hundred, and a doctor no where: these, my dear Sir, are not, to *such people*, "*every-day* evils of life." [...] Why should an English Farmer and his family, who have always been jogging about a snug home-stead, eating regular meals and sleeping in warm rooms, push back to the Illinois, and encounter those hardships, which require all the habitual disregard to comfort of an American back-woods-man to overcome? The undertaking is hardly reconcileable to reason in an Atlantic *American* Farmer who has half a dozen sons, all brought up to use the axe, the saw, the chisel and the hammer from their infancy, and every one of whom is ploughman, carpenter, wheelwright and butcher, and can work from sun-rise to sun-set, and sleep, if need be, upon the bare boards. What, then, must it be in an English Farmer and his family of helpless mortals? Helpless, I mean, in this scene of such novelty and such difficulty? And what is his *wife* to do; she who has been torn from all her relations and neighbours, and from every thing that she liked in the world, and who, perhaps, has never, in all her life before, been *ten miles* from the cradle in which she was nursed? An American farmer mends his plough, his wagon, his tackle of all sorts, his household goods, his shoes; and, if need be, he *makes* them all. Can our people do all this, or any part of it? Can they live without bread for months? Can they live without beer?

[*A Year's Residence in the United States of America* (London, 1819), paras 971–80.]

*

---

5   George Flower (1780–1862), explorer, and Birkbeck's partner in the Illinois settlement.

Cobbett returned to England at the end of 1819, but the following letter to an American friend shows him wistfully looking back on his time in America.

> I never spent happier days than in Long Island, and, amongst those days, none happier than those passed at *Grasshopper-Hill*. That was real liberty, by God. Real *free-and-easy*. Whenever I think of those happy days I am melancholy, and think nothing of all the gains and all the glory. I hope that England will yet be free; and, if I did not, by God, I would not remain here any longer than necessary to obtain the means of easy life in America.
>
> In addition to what you will find in the copy of a letter to D^r. Taylor, I must tell you, that *tradesmen*, as well as farmers, have been *ruined by whole droves*, and are all ruining now. If it had not been for the *insolvent acts* there would have been fifty times as many as the jails could have held. The King's bench sends out every six weeks about 1,000 tradesmen and 500 farmers! You must have been reduced to labourers, if you had remained. So that you acted the prudent part.

[William Cobbett to George Woodward, Kensington, 4 July 1822, British Library Add. MSS. 31,127, ff. 25–6.]

Chapter 11
Scotland and Ireland

Cobbett inherited many of the prejudices which were common to almost everyone in eighteenth-century England. Opposition to the French or Spanish was a stock-in-trade reaction at a time when Britain was contesting with them for colonial and maritime supremacy and was also coloured with a vigorous dose of anti-Catholicism. Relations with the nations nearer to home were more problematic. When Cobbett was born in 1763, the Act of Union with Scotland was just over 50 years old and less than 20 years earlier, in 1745, Bonnie Prince Charlie's Jacobite army had marched as far south as Derby in an attempt to topple the Hanoverian dynasty and the government of George II. Although that threat was decisively ended with the defeat of the Jacobite forces at Culloden the following year, suspicion of the Scots remained. When the young King George III came to the throne in 1760 and promoted his old tutor, the Scottish Earl of Bute, to the post which effectively made him the equivalent of Prime Minister, Scotophobia reached new heights. Supporters of the politicians dislodged by Bute accused him and a host of carpet-bagging followers for exercising undue influence on the King – cartoons even suggested the King was being cuckolded by Bute – and accused the Scots of conniving with a resurgence of Crown power. Bute was eventually dismissed from office but the resentments remained. Moreover the theme of Scots 'on the make' which had its origins in stories surrounding 'greedy Scotch minions' who had travelled south with James I in 1603 received fresh impetus as the economy developed. Dr Johnson of dictionary fame was famously, if more genteely, to express the anti-Scottish theme well into the late eighteenth century. Cobbett grew up amidst these prejudices and clearly imbibed them. When in America during the 1790s he encountered the writing of a Scottish radical, he condemned him with all the vulgar stereotypes usually aimed at Scotsmen. Although he was later to show greater sympathy, such abuse was not confined to his early years as a journalist. As late as 1830, he vented his spleen against the Scots: 'Base and degraded are we if we suffer in silence those beggarly burgoo-eaters to swagger over us, while they are sucking our blood [...] These vagabonds have contributed largely towards the ruin of England: they have been sucking its blood since James I [...] but ever since George III mounted the throne. They have been eating up our flesh [...] They will *not work*; they depend on the taxes in all countries whither they go [...] Even those who employ them hate them.'[1] By then, Cobbett's fire was directed

---

[1]   See D. Green (ed.) *Cobbett's Tour in Scotland* (Aberdeen, 1984), Appendix B 'Cobbett's Scotophobia', p. 135.

largely at what he called 'Scotch feelosophers', the political economists whose prescriptions he blamed for the condition of the country rather than ordinary Scotsmen. His readiness to take a benign view of ordinary Scots was reinforced when he finally visited Scotland in late 1832. Now he saw the Scots, in the main, as common brethren in the cause of reform. Although the Great Reform Act had received the Royal Assent earlier in the year, it was now necessary to effect change. As ever, Cobbett was concerned with the plight of the Scottish farm workers, casting a baleful eye over the 'boothies', the dormitories in which some labourers lived. He was ambivalent too about what he saw of New Lanark, Robert Owen's 'model' factory and settlement, recognising the decent conditions provided, but suspicious of the regimentation it implied in its mode of education and living. Elsewhere, however, he was often impressed by what he saw of Scottish agriculture and even, despite himself, some aspects of textile manufacture. The quality of Scottish food and produce also found favour as did the warmth of the reception and recognition he received and felt, to an extent, he deserved.

Cobbett's first visit to Ireland came even later in his life, in 1834. As he confessed himself, he had grown up with prejudices against Catholics which he freely admitted. But he had lost them relatively early in his life in 1792 when he had gone to France and recorded 'I went to that country full of all those prejudices, that Englishmen suck in with their mother's milk, against the French and against their religion; a few weeks convinced me that I had been deceived with respect to both [...] I found the people, among whom I lived [...] honest, pious, and kind to excess'.[2] Moreover, Cobbett seemed not to have any inbuilt prejudice towards the Irish as a race in the same way as he had towards the Scots and they did not figure in his litanies of evil-doers in the same way as Scots, Quakers, Jews, Methodists, evangelical Parsons, amongst others. They were not protected, however, from his early strictures against democratic republicanism, so that Cobbett's first printed comments on Irish affairs were a vehement attack upon the radical association formed in Ireland in 1791 under the name the United Irishmen. Initially a reformist body, embracing both Protestants and Catholics, under the polarising impact of events in France they were eventually to become a militant republican movement, driven underground in 1795. For Cobbett, they were simply an off-shoot of evils he saw emanating from revolutionary France. Subsequent developments in Ireland were, however, to elicit more sympathy. The 1790s were to prove a tumultuous decade in which a major rebellion and attempted French landings, one of which actually occurred in 1798, led to the deaths of tens of thousands. It also provoked the British government into a radical measure, the abolition of the separate Irish Parliament in Dublin under the Act of Union in 1800. As a *quid pro quo* it was

---

[2]   *The Life and Adventures of Peter Porcupine*, p. 39, in G.D.H. Cole (ed.) *Life and Adventures*.

proposed to remove the current prohibition of Catholics from sitting as MPs which it was hoped would cement the loyalty of respectable Catholics to the United Kingdom. But this measure, known as Catholic Emancipation, was frustrated by political opposition at Westminster amongst those who feared that any undermining of the status quo might endanger the security and position of Protestant landowners in Ireland. The Act of Union failed to resolve Ireland's endemic problems of poverty, rural violence and the bitter sense of injustice amongst the majority of poor Irish Catholics. Catholic Emancipation became the symbolic issue for alleviating some of Ireland's grievances and Cobbett gave his wholehearted support. Moreover he protested against the coercive nature of British rule in Ireland and recognised that forcing a majority Catholic population to pay tithes to the minority Anglican Church of their largely English landlords was not only unjust but a recipe for bitterness and violence. He claimed that his motive for writing his *History of the Protestant "Reformation"* in 1824 was to show that the Catholic Church had provided for the poor in a way that the current clerical establishment did not and which actually impoverished them by the levying of tithes. Ireland in particular was doubly wronged as the majority of its population did not worship in Anglican churches. Alert to Ireland's sense of grievance, he welcomed the granting of Catholic Emancipation, but continued to believe that poverty remained the fundamental problem, resolving in 1834 to go and see for himself. By this time Cobbett had been preoccupied with the defence of the so-called 'Old Poor Law' – which had never applied to Ireland – against the reforms promoted in the Act of 1834 which reorganised the system of Poor Relief and aimed to provide relief only in a workhouse under such rigorous conditions as to deter all but the genuinely needy. Much of Cobbett's description of Ireland was cast in the form of letters addressed to Charles Marshall, one of the labourers on Normandy Farm, as a warning about what a world without the provisions of the older system of poor relief could be like. Cobbett undoubtedly had an axe to grind as he toured Ireland, but there was little doubt that he was genuinely shocked by what he saw, comparing the situation of both urban and rural poor in Ireland as even worse than that of the English labourers. Cobbett saw an Ireland which other commentators agreed was teetering on the edge of a precipice of overpopulation and dependency on the potato crop for survival, plagued by absentee landlords, and bitterly divided on religious lines. Into the last months of his life, deeply affected by his experiences in Ireland, he continued to bombard the Prime Minister Peel with vehement demands to alleviate Ireland's condition and a passionate denunciation of the wrongs visited upon that country by England.

*

Cobbett unleashed some of his coarsest attacks on things Scottish when the Edinburgh radical James Callender[3] fled to America to escape almost certain imprisonment during the Pitt government's repression of radical writings during the early 1790s. Callender, a former member of the Edinburgh Society of the Friends of the People, with English radicals such as Joseph Priestley and Thomas Paine, was the target for Cobbett's hostility for his promulgation of radical views in his *The Political Progress of Britain*. Callender found supporters amongst Americans such as Thomas Jefferson who also earned Cobbett's condemnation.

> Let me then ask; what could induce him to come a' the wa' from Edinborough to Philadelphia to make an attack upon poor old England? And, if this be satisfactorily accounted for, upon principles of domestic philosophy, which teaches us, that froth and scum stopped in at one place will burst out at another, still I must be permitted to ask; what, could induce him to imagine, that the citizens of the United States were, in any manner whatsoever, interested in the affair? What are his adventures in Scotland, and his "narrow escape," to us, who live on this side the Atlantic? What do we care whether his associates, *Ridgway* and *Symons*, are still in Newgate, or whether they have been translated to Surgeon's Hall?[4] Is it anything to us whether he prefers Charley to George, or George to Charley,[5] any more than whether he used to eat his burgoo[6] with his fingers or with a horn spoon? What are his debts and his misery to us? Just as if we cared whether his posteriors were covered with a pair of breeches, or a kelt, or whether he was literally sans culotte? In Great Britain, indeed, his barking might answer some purpose; there he was near the object of his fury; but here he is like a cur howling at the Moon.
>
> [*A Bone to Gnaw for the Democrats. By Peter Porcupine* (Philadelphia, 1795), p. 2.]

*

As his attitude towards government hardened Cobbett could be kinder to Scots. When in exile in America in 1819 he lamented the forced emigration of a

---

3   James Thomson Callender (1758–1803), Scottish radical forced into exile in 1793, first to Ireland and then to the United States. Author of *The Political Progress of Britain* (1792), he became actively engaged in political controversy in the United States.

4   James Ridgway, journalist and printer, and Henry Symons, printer and bookseller, were imprisoned in Newgate for distributing radical literature. Cobbett speculates on whether they will be executed and their bodies used for dissection by the surgeons as was permitted.

5   Cobbett refers to the conflict between the supporters of the Jacobite cause (Bonnie Prince Charlie) and the current Hanoverian dynasty (George III).

6   A kind of porridge; in America a spicy stew.

body of Scotsmen. Scots emigrants were, in fact, flooding into North America, many of them victims of the Highland Clearances when landlords were forcing subsistence crofters off the land in order to turn it over to sheep or cattle farming.

> The heart sickens at the sight of a great country perishing by piece-meal under the hands of a set of arrogant, ignorant, brutal Boroughmongers. Not less than thirty *Scotsmen*, from the neighbourhood of Paisley, lately arrived here, have visited me within this week. To see these decent, sober, thoughtful men; to hear their accounts of the motives that have induced them to quit their native land; to hear the recital of their sufferings and their sacrifices; to behold the tear ready to start when they say that nothing but a dread of starvation could have driven them from Scotland; is enough to drive one mad. One's tongue involuntarily exclaims: "Perdition light on the villains who have done this!"

> ['To the Middle Classes of England', *Political Register*, 13 November 1819.]

*

When he finally visited Scotland Cobbett was concerned near Dunfermline to investigate the state in which labourers lived in the collective dormitories known as 'boothies'. Framed as 'Advice' to the labourers of England, he urged them not to allow themselves to be reduced to a similar state.

> I went to the "*boothie*" between twelve and one o'clock, in order that I might find the men at home, and see what they had for their dinner. I found the "*boothie*" to be a shed, with a fire-place in it to burn coals in, with one doorway, and one little window. The floor was the ground. There were three wooden bedsteads, nailed together like the berths in a barrack-room, with boards for the bottom of them. The bedding seemed to be very coarse sheeting with coarse woollen things at the top; and all seemed to be such as similar things must be where there is nobody but men to look after them. There were six men, all at home; one sitting upon a stool, four upon the sides of the berths, and one standing talking to me. Though it was Monday, their beards, especially of two of them, appeared to be some days old. There were ten or twelve bushels of coals lying in a heap in one corner of the place, which was as nearly as I could guess, about sixteen or eighteen feet square. There was no back-door to the place, and no privy. There were some loose potatoes lying under one of the berths.
>
> Now, for the wages of these men. In the first place the average wages of these single farming men are about ten pounds a year, or not quite four shillings a week. Then they are found provisions in the following manner:

each has allowed him two pecks of coarse oatmeal a week, and three
"*choppins*" of milk a day, and a "*choppin*" is, I believe, equal to an English
quart. They have to use this meal, which weighs about seventeen pounds,
either by mixing it with cold water or with hot; they put some of it into
a bowl, pour some boiling water upon it, then stir it about and eat it; and
they call this BROSE; and you will be sure to remember that name. When
they use milk with the meal they use it in the same way that they do the
water. I saw some of the brose mixed up ready to eat; and this is by no
means bad stuff, only there ought to be half-a-pound of good meat to eat
along with it. The Americans make "brose" of the corn-meal; but then
they make their brose with milk instead of water, and they send it down
their throats in company with buttered beef-steaks. And if here was some
bacon along with the brose, I should think the brose very proper; because,
in this country, oats are more easily grown in some parts than wheat is.
These men were not troubled with cooking utensils. They had a large iron
saucepan and five or six brose-bowls; and they are never troubled with
those clattering things, knives, forks, plates, vinegar-cruets, salt-cellars,
pepper-boxes, mustard-pots, table-cloths, or tables.

[D. Green (ed.), *Cobbett's Tour in Scotland* (Aberdeen, 1984), pp. 42–3.]

*

Much of the agriculture of Scotland met with Cobbett's approval, casting an
appreciative eye over its cattle and thinking how he might use some himself.
Similarly, he praised the quality of the food in Scottish towns, though he
exercised his usual aversion to alcoholic drink.

When we got to GLASGOW [...] as I had not breakfasted, I therefore
set to that work at the inn, without loss of time, upon everything that
is good, but particularly upon some *tender* beef-steaks; a thing which
I have not met with before in more than one out of ten beef-steak jobs
in my life; and, I may as well stop here to observe, that which I have
omitted before, that all the beef that I have tasted in Scotland has been
excellent. It appears to come from the little oxen which the Highlands
send down in such droves; and a score of which, please God to give me
life, I will have next year in Surrey. I should suppose that these little oxen,
when well fatted, weigh about twenty score, which is about the weight
of a Hampshire hog eighteen months or two years old. The joints are, of
course, small compared with the general run of beef in London. A sirloin
appears to be no very great deal larger than a loin of large veal, rump and
all. The meat is exceedingly fine in the grain; and these little creatures
will fat where a Devonshire or Lincolnshire ox would halve starve. My

project is to get a score of them, let them run upon the common till the corn-tops and blades are fit to cut, then feed them with them; after that with mangel-wurzel or Swedish turnips, and have them fat as butter in the months of March, April, and May. [...]

So much for the meat of Scotland; and now I am talking about victuals, let me observe, first, that the wheaten bread, of which there is an abundance in all the towns, is just about as good as it is in London; that, besides this, there are oat-cakes made very thin, which are very nice things of the bread kind, it being understood that I am speaking of such as are made in the houses of gentlemen, merchants, and persons who do not very rigidly adhere to the saving of expense; for there are some of these cakes which rank with the "*brose*" mentioned in the former part of this article. Then the oatmeal, when ground and dressed in a nice manner, is made into porridge, just in the same manner as the Americans make the cornmeal into *mush*, and it is eaten with milk just in the same manner. Every morning but one, while I was in Edinburgh, it formed the principal part of my breakfast; and I greatly preferred it, and should always prefer it, to toasted bread and butter, to muffins, to crumpets, to bread and butter, or to hot rolls. This is the living in Scotland, along with plenty of eggs, very fine butter, and either Ayrshire or English cheese; and everywhere you see a sufficiency of good victuals (including poultry and game); you see it without ostentation; you see it without being compelled to sit whole hours over it; you see everything good, and everything sensibly done with regard to the victuals; and as to the drink, just as in England, you always see ten times too much of it; and I verily believe that I shall be the first human being that ever came into Scotland and went out of it again, without tasting wine, spirits, beer, or cider. Everyone drinks too much; and it is not just to reproach the working people with drunkenness, if you, whose bodily exertions do not tend to provoke thirst, set them the mischievous example, by indulging in drink, until habit renders it a sort of necessary of life.

[D. Green (ed.), *Cobbett's Tour*, pp. 52–4.]

*

Cobbett was flattered by the recognition accorded to him and delighted that the Scottish people gave him the recognition which he was denied by Whig leaders such as Lord Grey, the current Prime Minister.

Before I quit the CLYDE, to which the readers will say I cling, as Adam is said to have clung to Paradise, there is something which I have to mention, of which I am still more proud than of the things I have just treated of;

something that rouses the politician again, drives away the waterfalls and the trees and the orchards, and which would, were it not a shame, make me forget even the Scotch ladies amongst the rest! I mentioned before that Mr. HAMILTON took me and Mr. BELL to LANARK, on the 1. of November, and that I was to lecture in the town of LANARK in the evening of that day; to do which I had received an invitation from my readers in that town, to which invitation I had given my answer that I would do it. As we were going to LANARK from Mr. DOUGLAS's at MAULDSLIE CASTLE, we saw, out in the middle of a field, near a cottage, a blue flag flying at the top of a long pole. When we got near enough to see what was upon it, we saw that there was a GRIDIRON[7] *painted in colours of gold*, with these words over it: "COBBETT TRIUMPHANT;" and on the other side, "PERSEVERANCE, PUBLIC VIRTUE, JUSTICE TO THE WORKING PEOPLE." And, which added prodigiously to the interest of the thing, this flag had been made for the purpose of a reform jubilee at LANARK, and had been carried at that jubilee long before my coming to Scotland! Now, I will not bid the grovelling, the envious, the mercenary, the bribed, the base, the bloody villains of the London press to look at this; but I will bid *Lord Grey* to look at it, as something very well worthy of his attention.

[D. Green (ed.), *Cobbett's Tour*, pp. 109–10.]

*

Cobbett's first mention of Irish affairs came with his condemnation of the United Irishmen Society in Ireland. Formed in Belfast and Dublin including many Protestants, at this stage it was a reformist body, but Cobbett attacked it as an offshoot of the democratic republicanism which had its origin in France. Interestingly, compared with his denunciation of the Scottish radical, James Callender, he did not indulge in any ethnic abuse of the Irish. Later, the United Irishmen were to be radicalised, becoming a largely Catholic underground movement which lay behind the Irish rebellion in 1798.

The history of the *United Irishmen* will not detain us long. Soon after the ever-to-be-regretted epoch, when God, in his wrath, suffered the tinkers, butchers, harlequins, quacks, cut-throats, and other modern philosophers, to usurp the government of France, their brethren in Ireland, tempted by the successful example, began, with wonderful industry, to prepare

---

[7]   In 1819 Cobbett had declared that he would be prepared to be broiled alive on a Gridiron if his prophecies about the difficulties of withdrawing paper money from circulation proved false. Believing himself vindicated, he adopted the Gridiron as his symbol.

for taking the government of that country into their hands. With this laudable end in view, they formed what they called their *society*, in the city of Dublin. To say in what manner they proceeded to business would be superfluous, since we know they were democrats.—Their meetings, as among us, produced resolves in abundance, and good fortune seemed for a time, to smile upon them. The press was suffocated with their addresses and letters of fraternity, which were swallowed by the mob, for whom they were intended, with an appetite which generally characterizes that class of citizens. But, all of a sudden, when they were in the height of their work, mangling the carcase of the government, the magistracy soused down upon them, like an eagle among a flock of carrion crows. Here was fine helter skelter; fining, imprisoning, whipping and emigrating; some ran this way, others that; some came to America to brew whisky, some went to France to gather laurels, while others, of a more philosophical turn, set off to Botany Bay to cull simples. [...]

The ostensible object of the *United Irishmen,* like that of all other usurpers from the beginning of the world to the present day, was a *reformation* in the government of their country. To say much about a plan of reform proposed by a "band" of such obscure and illiterate persons as their proceedings prove them to be, would be paying ignorance too much attention, and would be, besides, in a great measure, superfluous, as we have already been favoured with the newest new constitution of a *sister* republic, of which that proposed by the *United Irishmen* was but a counterpart.

[*A Bone to Gnaw for the Democrats. By Peter Porcupine, Part II* (Philadelphia, 1795), pp. 2–7.]

*

As Cobbett's opposition to the government grew, he found himself increasingly sympathetic towards the plight of the Irish and outraged by the repressive policies of the British government. When in 1816 Robert Peel, then Chief Secretary for Ireland, refused to enquire into Irish poverty, blaming the Irish situation on the 'depravity' of the population, Cobbett reported the debate in a 'letter' to the people of the United States, ironically pointing to the difference in behaviour of the many Irishmen who had emigrated to America and their fellow-countrymen who had stayed in Ireland.

Do you ever hear of any of this depravity; any of this untameable ferocity; any of these "combinations against *all law*," on the part of these people? *You* want no army, no extraordinary police, no suspension of the ordinary laws, to keep them in order. [...] Considering the low class of life, of which the great mass of the Irish emigrants consist, my belief is, that they have surpassed in success the emigrants from any other nation. And, as to such of them as have gone to America with property or education to start with, they have certainly outstripped all others in the career of fame, as well as of prosperity. [...] Does the salt air change the nature of the people while they are crossing the seas? What is there in Pennsylvania, or New York, to subdue and keep down this ferocious disposition; this disposition to combine against "all *law?*" Not a single bayonet! Nothing but the constable's staff! [...] How will Mr. PEEL account for this?

[*Political Register*, 4 May 1816.]

*

Similarly, the murder of a magistrate in Ireland and the refusal, on his wife's pleading, of a condemned man to turn King's evidence to save his life was taken by Cobbett as evidence of the total misgovernment of Ireland and the depth of hatred the British government had engendered.

What in all the world can have placed a people in such a state, as to induce a woman, who dearly loved her husband, to beseech him to lose his life *on the gallows*, rather than incur the "*disgrace*" of giving evidence against an enemy of the government! [...] How came she to regard this as disgrace? Why, her neighbours so regarded it; and, what, then must be the state of mind of that neighbourhood? What must have been the *causes* of hatred so deep, of exasperation so terrible, as to induce a whole neighbourhood to mount upon houses, ricks, and trees, to behold *the murder of a magistrate*, and to give *three cheers* at the firing of the fatal shot!

Oh, no! it was not in the hearts of these people, it never was, and never can be, in the hearts of any district of people, to exult in what *they deem murder*. They did not deem this a murder any more than the poor woman deemed the hanging of her husband ignominious. That it *was* a murder is certain; that those people were under the influence of ungovernable fury is also certain; but, what was it which could have produced this furious state of mind?

[*Political Register*, 4 May 1816.]

*

Accordingly, Cobbett supported the demands of Catholics for their rights, including the right to sit in Parliament, so-called Catholic Emancipation, but urged them to go further to demand the end to other injustices, such as paying tithes to a church the majority of them did not attend.

The language of the Irish Catholics to the Parliament ought to have been this: You took away the tithes and the other property of our Church; you gave these to a Protestant Clergy, whom you sent hither with your Prayer-Book; you made no provision for the relief of our poor, who were formerly relieved by our Church; you took away from us all the means of preventing misery; your Clergy were to convert us to the new religion; but, at the end of three hundred years, here we are a Catholic people still, paying tithes and Church rates, to a Church which gives us neither religion, nor relief for the poor. [...] Let the Catholics of Ireland make these representations to the Parliament; let them thus openly and explicitly state the wishes of their hearts [...] Let them do this, and they will find themselves joined by the Protestants of England; and if so joined, they will soon look back to the days of the talk about Catholic Emancipation, with the sort of feeling with which the grown-up man looks back to the little fooleries of his childhood. [...]

This is my advice to the Catholics. I advise them by no means to give way to *lamentation*; and never again to think of obtaining redress by humility. [...] Their language ought to be full of resolution, not to say indignation. Their wrongs are without a parallel in duration as well as in magnitude. [...] Meekness never yet softened the asperity of the wrongdoer; and my surprise is that any thing like meekness should ever be apparent in the conduct of an Irish Catholic.

[*Political Register*, 21 May 1825.]

*

Amongst the measures he advocated was the disestablishment of the Anglican Church in Ireland. In a speech to the House of Commons in 1833, he proposed ending the privileged position of what many Irishmen saw as the church of their oppressors. Although Cobbett's proposal had no hope of success when he made it, it was an issue to which many reformers of the Irish situation would return in future decades. The Anglican Church in Ireland was eventually disestablished by Gladstone in 1868.

I am for totally and entirely abrogating, annulling, rendering frustrate, and of no effect, the Protestant hierarchy in Ireland. Nobody can misunderstand me, I trust. I do not say so because I shall gain anything by its abolition or by its continuance. I am no parson to receive tithes—and no Quaker to refuse for conscience sake to pay them; but I know that the putting down of that hierarchy is necessary to the happiness, peace, safety, and renown of this Kingdom. It can be endured no longer with security to the kingdom, or to the King's throne; therefore, as a loyal subject of the King, and a faithful representative of the people, I declare my opinion against it. Look at the history of the church, and in it you read all the great calamities of the country [...] to maintain it [...] one king was brought to the block and another driven from the throne. What it is destined next to effect, I leave you, gentlemen, to determine; but I cannot sit down without expressing my gratitude to the House for the great attention which I have received.

[*Political Register*, 16 February 1833.]

*

On his first visit to Ireland, Cobbett confronted the reality of Irish poverty, casting his impression in the form of letters to one of his labourers. This device allowed him to compare Irish conditions with those which his labourers and animals enjoyed in England. In Dublin, he found stark poverty both in its charitable institutions and on its streets.

I have this morning seen more than one thousand of working persons, men and women, boys and girls, all the clothes upon the bodies of all of whom were not worth so much as the smock-frock that you go to work in; and you have a wife and eight children, seven of whom are too young to go to work. I have seen the *food* and the *cooking* of the food, in a LARGE HOUSE, where food is prepared for a part of these wretched people. Cast-iron coppers, three or four times as big as our largest brewing copper, are employed to boil *oatmeal* (that is, *ground oats*) *in water*, or *butter-milk,* or *skim-milk;* and this is the food given to these poor creatures. The *white cabbages*, the *barley-meal*, the *pot-fat*, the *whey*, and the *butter-milk*, which George boils daily for our little pigs and their mothers, is a dish, to obtain a mouthful of which, thousands of these people would go on their knees. Marshall, you know how I scolded Tom Denman and little Barratt and your own son Dick, on the Saturday before I came away, for not sweeping the *sleeping-place* of the *yard-hogs* out clean, and what a strict charge I gave George to fling out the old bed, and to give them a bed of fresh straw every Saturday. Oh, how happy would thousands upon thousands in this city be, if they could be lodged in a place like that roughest hog bed! I this morning saw a *widow* woman and her four children, in the spot where they had slept; on *their bed*, in short. George remembers my looking over at the sows and their sucking pigs, and at the two youngest calves, just before I came away; and that I told him to keep them in that nice condition all the time that I should be away. Now, Marshall, this poor widow and her little children were lying upon a quantity of straw not a twentieth part so great as that allotted to one of the sows and her pigs;

and if I, on my return, were to see, as I am sure I shall not, the straw of the calves as dirty, and so broken, as that upon which this widow and her children were lying, I should drive George out of the house, as a slovenly and cruel fellow. And this, you will observe, is the case of thousands upon thousands of persons; it is the case of whole streets as long as the main streets of Guildford and Farnham. Your pig-sty and Turvill's pig-sty, and the sties of other labouring men, are made by yourselves, with posts and poles and rods, and heath, and your supply of straw is very scanty, and compels you to resort to *fern* and *dead grass* from the common: but, now mind what I say, I saw Turvill's pig-sty the day before I came off, and I solemnly declare, in the face of England and of Ireland, that Turvill's two hogs were better lodged, and far better fed; and far more clean in their skins, than are thousands upon thousands of the human beings in this city; which, as to streets, squares, and buildings, is as fine a city as almost any in the world!

[*Letters of William Cobbett to Charles Marshall, 1834* in M. Townsend (ed.), *Not by Bullets and Bayonets: Cobbett's Writings on the Irish Question* (London, 1983), Letter 1, pp. 62–3.]

*

Outside Dublin, in the rural Ireland, Cobbett found conditions he scarcely believed, taking the opportunity to lament the absence of any poor law to relieve destitution.

The places, which I *call* houses, were, in general from ten to twelve feet square; the walls made of rough stone and mud, whited over, and about nine feet high; no ceiling; rough rafters covered with old rotten black thatch; in some a glass window the size of your hat, in two or four little panes; in others no window at all; but a hole or two holes in the wall; about a foot long, and four or five inches wide; the floor nothing but the bare earth; no chimney, but a hole at one end of the roof to let out the smoke, arising from a fire made against the wall of that end of this miserable shed; this hole is sometimes surrounded by a few stones put on that part of the roof a foot or two high; generally it is not, and in cold weather, the poor, ragged, half-naked creatures *stop up the hole to keep in the smoke to keep them from perishing with cold!* The fuel is *peat*, just such as that dug out of our moors, and never a stick of wood; and the people get the big *dead weeds* to light their fires and to boil their potatoes. One of these places costs the landowner about *four pounds* to build it, and the poor creatures pay from *thirty shilling* to *two pounds* a year rent for them, without any garden, without an inch of land, without any place for even a *privy*, WOMEN as well as men must go to the *dung-heap before the door,* and the former are exposed to that which your wife, or any woman of Normandy, would die at the thought of! [...]

As to the *goods* in the hole, there are, an *iron pot*, a *rough table,* or a *board laid across two piles of stones,* seats of stones, or of boards laid from one stone to another; and that is all of the stock of goods, except a *dish,* of which I shall speak presently. Every hole has a pig; the pig eats with the family, and generally sleeps in the same place. The potatoes are taken up and turned out into a great *dish,* which dish is a shallow basket made of oziers with the bark on. The family squat round this basket and take out the potatoes with their hands; the pig stands and is helped by some one, and sometimes he eats out of the pot. He goes in and out and about the hole, like one of the family; the family sleep, huddled up together, on dead weeds or a little straw in one corner of the hole, and the pig, on a similar bed in another corner. The pig is the person of most consequence; he is sold to *pay the rent*: if he fail, the family are turned out into the naked air to perish, which has been the case in many thousands of instances, there being *no poor-law* here to save their lives.

[M. Townsend (ed.), *Not by Bullets and Bayonets*, Letter 3, pp. 72–3.]

*

Cobbett was not alone amongst many commentators on the Irish situation to blame absentee landlords for taking profits out of Ireland and only returning the fruits of Irish agriculture to the wealthy and the military establishment.

But, now, Marshall, I am coming *nearer home;* and I beg you all to pay great attention to what I am going to say. You will think it strange, that all this food should be sent out of the country, and that the people should *get nothing back* for it. You will think, that we must send them *clothes* and *household goods* and *tea* and *sugar* and *soap* in return for the hogs and other things. To the *rich* we do; and to the *barracks;* but, the millions of working people have only rags for parts of their bodies, and they have neither goods nor tea nor sugar nor plate nor knife nor fork nor tea-kettle nor cup nor saucer.

The case is this: the owners of all the great estates *live in England or in France or in Italy.* The *rents are sent to them;* and, as there are *no poor-rates,* they get all the produce of the land from the miserable farmer, except just enough to keep him alive. They *spend these rents out of Ireland;* so that the working people here, who might eat meat three times a day, are compelled to live upon *lumpers!* [...]

But, Marshall, mind me well. You know, that, at Pepperharrow (only about four miles from your cottage) there lives LORD MIDDLETON. You know that he was a long while Lord-Lieutenant of our county. Now, Marshall, HE is one of the GREAT LANDOWNERS OF IRELAND. His real name is BRODERICK. He is the owner of a *town* called *Middleton,* half as big as Guildford. He is the owner of the lands for many miles round, and, it is supposed, that he draws, *yearly, from twenty-five to thirty thousand pounds from this estate!*

[M. Townsend (ed.), *Not by Bullets and Bayonets*, Letter 5, pp. 79–80.]

*

Almost the last things that Cobbett wrote was an appeal to Sir Robert Peel, now Prime Minister, to address the Irish question in the round. Although Catholic Emancipation had been passed in 1829, he urged Peel to remove the symbols of Irish subjection and undertake wholesale reform.

If you cannot do anything material directly, you might avoid every thing calculated to augment the evil. The Catholic Emancipation Bill placed Catholics and Protestants upon a level, with regard to fitness for emolument and power; but this only adds to the irritation arising from exclusion, if the provisions of the law be rendered of *non-effect*. The Orange power is nearly as dominant as it ever was [...] This is great and just ground of complaint. One of my first acts should be battering down the statue of WILLIAM THE THIRD, which is painted up by the Orangemen once a year, in insolent triumph of impunity to injustice. My next act should be to compel the residence of landholders, or forfeiture of rents to a certain extent, according to the nature of the case. I would take care, I warrant you, that the people of Ireland should not toil to furnish money to enrich the wretches of PARIS, of MILAN, and of ROME. I would take care that effectual provision should be made for the relief of the destitute; and not suffer Ireland to be peopled with *farmers* who never taste meat from year's end to year's end, while twenty thousand oxen, sheep, and hogs, are shipped from her shores every week in the year. [...]

It is said that capital is wanted in Ireland. The capital *is in the land*; the land produces twenty times as much as the people consume; I mean those who work upon the land; but how is there to be capital in Ireland, if all the fruits are taken away? [...]

This talk about "*capital*" is like all the rest of the botheration stuff which we hear from the at once sly and brazen Irish landlords, who, after making the working people pay for the sea-weed that is drifted upon the shore, and who bring the money over, swallowing the price of a cart-load in one gulp of turtle soup, tell us, with a sort of wise simper, "*What we want*, in Ireland, Mr. Cobbett, is CAPITAL."

It is for you, sir, to make Ireland abound with a sufficiency of capital. It has been formed by nature to be as happy as any country beheld by the sun in his whole course. It has the mildest of climates, the richest of soils, mountains green to their tips [...] It is by nature agricultural, though the greedy beasts that rob it are crying out for manufactures. In short, God seems to have done everything to make its inhabitants happy, and man seems to have done everything to make them miserable; and it is your bounden duty, and the duty of every man who at all meddles with public affairs, to neglect nothing within his power, now to undo all the mischiefs which England has inflicted upon this valuable part of his Majesty's dominions.

[*Political Register*, 31 January 1835.]

Chapter 12
Agriculture, Commerce and Industry

Cobbett is perhaps most well-known as the champion of rural England. He was proud of his background as the son of a small farmer and publican in Farnham, Surrey, and had worked in the fields as a young boy. His years in the army and early journalistic career in Philadelphia and London took him away from rural pursuits, but in 1805 he moved to the small village of Botley, outside Southampton. Botley quickly became an important part of his political identity, and he self-consciously presented himself as a traditional gentleman farmer, although one who was also intensely interested in agricultural improvement. Cobbett's correspondence with his political ally William Windham suggest that his investment in a rural hinterland began partly as an attempt to imitate Windham – an independent landowner with a large Norfolk estate – but after his break with Windham it became an equally important part of Cobbett's radicalism.

While still establishing himself as a Hampshire farmer – or 'Hampshire Hog', in Gillray's caricature – Cobbett published a series of articles in 1807–8 under the title, 'Perish Commerce!' This series argued that agriculture was the only true source of national wealth and trade merely an unproductive system of circulation. He maintained this view for the rest of his life, and his belief in the corrupting effects of commerce was widely echoed in radical literature.

Cobbett's large-scale agricultural ambitions were short-lived, mainly as a result of the government's persistent campaign against his journalism. He continued to run the farm at Botley during his imprisonment in Newgate (1810–12), writing detailed letters of instruction to Nancy and the children, but when he returned from American exile at the end of 1819 he was declared bankrupt. His later agricultural projects were more limited in scope, including a seed farm at Kensington and small farm at Barn Elm in Surrey. However, his tours of the depressed post-war countryside in the 1820s, published first in the *Political Register* and then in *Rural Rides* (1830), present an unrivalled account of English agriculture in the early nineteenth century.

When farm labourers' grievances erupted into the Swing Riots of 1830–1, a widespread campaign of machine-breaking and rick-burning, Cobbett was justified in declaring that he had predicted the riots, having spent several years writing about the pauperisation of rural labourers and warning farmers of potential unrest. His later speaking tours extended to northern England, Scotland and Ireland. Having long taken a sceptical view of the industrial revolution, the factories he saw at first hand impressed him, and he was gratified by the support he received from factory workers. Cobbett's later career, including his election to parliament as an MP for the industrial constituency of Oldham, led him to imagine a political alliance between agricultural and industrial workers.

*

Cobbett's correspondence with his political patron William Windham includes several letters extolling the beauties of Botley. The following description of catching salmon at the foot of his new garden seems to have been provoked by Cobbett's embarrassment that the fish had been sent to the leading Whig politician Charles James Fox before Windham had sampled them.

Botley, Monday, 12. Augt. 1805.

Sir,

Before this reaches you, you will have seen, that I have published some reflections upon the subject of boxing. An article from you would come in well now; and, of course, it need not be sent to me; but, just given to Wright,[1] who will copy it for the printers; and he shall have my directions to leave out any part of my other matter in order to insure its insertion.—I am anxious to know *how long* you will be in town for this time; because we catch here some of the finest fish in the world; and M[rs]. Cobbett as well as myself are very desirous that you should taste them. We can send by the Southampton night coach, and you will have, for dinner, the fish caught *the evening before.*—The fish are called *Salmon Peel*; that is to say, *young salmon*, from 1 to 4 pounds in weight, and the most delicious fish, the eaters say, in the world.—So stupid am I in all these matters, that I never thought of sending any to you, till being, on Saturday, invited to dine at Eling, on the other side of Southampton, at the parsonage house, there to meet M[r]. O'Brien[2] and D[r]. *Parr*,[3] and taking some of the fish with us, in order to convince O'Brien that I caught salmon at the foot of my garden, I, to my utter astonishment, saw the fish packed up, and sent off to Southampton, hence to go to S[t]. Ann's Hill, as a present, from our host, worthy of the acceptance of M[r]. Fox!—With a net that Wright, amongst other marks of his attention, was so good as to send me, I catch the fish at the bottom of my (for I venture to call it mine, & trust it will be so next year at this time) garden, and at about 50 yards from my door, in a river just about as wide as your parlour! We seldom put in the net without success; and sometimes with very great success. I care very little about fish; but, I shall be very glad to send some that M[rs]. W. may think

---

[1]   John Wright (1770/71–1844), Cobbett's London agent and publisher.

[2]   Dennis O'Bryen (1755–1832), playwright, pamphleteer and adviser to Fox.

[3]   Samuel Parr (1747–1825), schoolmaster, writer and clergyman, nicknamed the 'Jacobinical Parson' because of his support for Fox.

worthy of her acceptance.—Shall I hope for a line from you by return of post? Just a line to say whether you will be in London for some days longer, or not? If you were at Beaconsfield they would reach you fresh, by my instructing Wright to send them from London.—I need not say how much I am obliged by, and how sensibly I feel the honour of, the letters you have had the goodness to write me; and, I can only add, that I shall ever regard, as amongst the most fortunate moments of my life, that in which commenced the attachment with which I remain, Sir, your most obedient and most humble servant,

W^m. Cobbett.

P.S. The Blackheath adventure caps the climax, I think! I should like well enough to know who were the *heroes* that attacked naked men with the sword.—Botley is the most delightful village in the world. It has every thing, in a village, that I love; and none of the things I hate. It is in a valley, the soil is rich, thick set with wood, the farms are small, the cottages neat: it has neither workhouse nor barber nor attorney nor justice of the peace, and, though last not least, it has no volunteers. There is no justice within six miles of us, and the barber comes three miles once a week to shave & cut hair! "Would I were poetical", I would write a poem in praise of Botley.

[Cobbett to William Windham, Botley, 12 August 1805, British Library Add. MSS. 37,853, f. 177.]

*

Cobbett's articles against a commercial economy extended to a critique of colonialism, made through a homely analogy between national and parish economies.

The idea of Goldsmith, as expressed in the verses, taken as a motto to my last sheet, that is to say, *that slaves are purchased at home by the wealth pillaged from savage nations*, is not fully enough explained.[4] To be sure those savage nations are pillaged and most cruelly treated by those, who, through the means of commerce, purchase slaves at home. But, it is we here in England (I use this word because I hate a long compound name for a nation) who, in fact, pay the amount of the pillage. We pay armies and fleets, and we make direct grants of millions, for the maintenance of colonies. The people there are oppressed and pillaged; but we pay the

---

4   'The wealth of climes, where savage nations roam,/ Pillaged from slaves to purchase slaves at home': lines from Oliver Goldsmith's *The Traveller, or A Prospect of Society* (1764), which Cobbett had taken as the motto for the previous week's *Political Register*.

amount of the pillage. Suppose a parish were wicked or foolish enough to raise within itself a thousand pounds, and give it to an expert and gallant gentleman to go and raise contributions upon the next parish; that the various expences which he should be at for the hiring of subaltern ruffians, for the obtaining of arms, and for food and lodgings, cost him a thousand pounds; and, that, finally, he comes back with a thousand pounds worth of pillage. *He* has gained a thousand pounds; but the individuals of each of the parishes have lost to that amount; and, the only difference between them, as to the consequences, is, that the parish which has sent him out to plunder, has the satisfaction to see him raised above the heads of his former fellows, and making some of them, in fact, his slaves. Thus, does this sort of commerce, at any rate, deal its curses double-handed.

['Perish Commerce', *Political Register*, 12 December 1807.]

*

As an improving farmer himself, Cobbett welcomed the increased productivity achieved through the enclosure of common land. However, by the 1820s he believed the enclosure system had been carried too far and was causing misery for the rural poor without adding to production. The following extract shows how Cobbett used changes in the rural landscape to bring together debates about enclosure, paper money, migration from countryside to city and the widening gulf between farmers and labourers.

You, indeed, hear of *no more new enclosures*, and, I hope, most anxiously, that we shall hear of many of the late new enclosures being thrown again to common. They were, for the most part, useless in point of quantity of *production*; and, to the labourers, they were malignantly mischievous. They drove them from the skirts of commons, downs and forests. They took away their cows, pigs, geese, fowls, bees, and gardens. They crowded them into miserable outskirts of towns and villages, for their children to become ricketty and diseased, confined amongst filth and vermin. They took from them their best inheritance: sweet air, health, and the little liberty they had left. Downs, most beautiful and valuable too, have been broken up by the paper-system; and, after three of four crops to beggar them, have been left to be planted with *docks* and *thistles*, and never again to present that perpetual verdure, which formerly covered their surface, and which, while it fed innumerable flocks, enriched the neighbouring fields. LORD LIVERPOOL, in a speech made last spring, observed, that some *persons* thought, that the enclosure-system had been *carried too far*. Who were they, my Lord? I never heard of any body but myself who, in a *public manner*, expressed any such opinion. I, indeed, when Old Rose[5] used to be boasting of the number of enclosure Bills, as a proof of "*prosperity*," used, now-and-then, to show how beastly the idea was; and I proved, over and over again, that (taking in a space of eight or ten years) it was *impossible* to augment the *quantity of produce* by new enclosures; to say nothing about the mischievous effects as to the labourers.

However, the breaking up of the Commons and Downs was a natural effect of the forced increase of money; and, in this way, amongst the rest, that increase worked detriment to the labourer. It was out of his bones that the means came. It was the *deduction made from him by the rise of prices* and by the *not-rise of his wages:* it was the means thus raised that enclosed the Commons and Downs; and that put pianos into the farmhouses, and set the farmer up upon a cavalry horse. And these, and such as these, have been the effects of that accursed paper-money, that seven vials of wrath, which you wish to be poured out upon us again!

['To Mr. Attwood', *Political Register*, 5 May 1821.]

*

Rural Rides documents the depression of the post-Waterloo years, following the end of an inflated wartime economy. Cobbett believed that the increasing pressures faced by labourers, farmers and even landlords pointed towards an imminent crash.

In all parts of the country, I hear of landlords that begin to *squeak*, which is a certain proof that they begin to feel the bottom of their tenant's pockets. No man can pay rent; I mean any rent at all, except out of capital; or, except under some peculiar circumstances, such as having a farm near a spot where the fundholders are building houses. When I was in Hampshire, I heard of terrible breakings up in the *Isle of Wight*. They say, that the *general rout* is very near at hand there. I heard of one farmer, who held a farm at seven hundred pounds a-year, who paid his rent annually, and punctually, who had, of course, seven hundred pounds to pay to his landlord last Michaelmas; but who, before Michaelmas came, thrashed out and sold (the harvest being so early) the whole of his corn; sold off his stock, bit by bit; got the very goods out of his house, leaving only a bed and some trifling things; *sailed with a fair wind over to France with his family;* put his mother-in-law into the house to keep possession of the house and farm, and to prevent the landlord from entering upon the land for a year

---

5   George Rose (1744–1818), politician, staunch ally of Pitt and, for Cobbett, symbol of corruption due to his many paid offices and government sinecures.

or better, *unless he would pay to his mother-in-law a certain sum of money!* Doubtless the landlord had already sucked away about three or four times seven hundred pounds from this farmer. He would not be able to enter upon this farm without a process that would cost him some money, and without the farm being pretty well stocked with thistles and docks, and perhaps laid half to common. Farmers *on the coast* opposite France are not so *firmly bounded* as those in the interior. Some hundreds of these will have carried their allegiance, their capital (what they have left), and their skill, to go and grease the fat sow, our old friends the Bourbons. I hear of a sharp, greedy, hungry shark of a landlord, who says that *'some law must be passed';* that *'Parliament must do something* to prevent this!' There is a pretty fool for you! There is a great jackass (I beg the real jackass's pardon) to imagine that the people at Westminster can do any thing to prevent the French from suffering people to come with their money to settle in France! This fool does not know, perhaps, that there are Members of Parliament that live in France more than they do in England. I have heard of one, who not only lives there, but carries on vineyards there, and is never absent from them, except when he comes over *'to attend to his duties in Parliament'.* He perhaps sells his wine at the same time, and that being *genuine*, doubtless brings him a good price; so that the occupations harmonize together very well. The Isle of Wight must be rather peculiarly distressed; for it was the scene of monstrous expenditure. When the *pure* Whigs were in power, in 1806, it was proved to them and to the Parliament, that in several instances, *a barn* in the Isle of Wight was rented by the 'envy of surrounding nations' *for more money than the rest of the whole farm!* These barns were wanted as *barracks;* and, indeed, such things were carried on in that Island as never could have been carried on under any thing that was not absolutely 'the admiration of the world'. These sweet pickings, caused, doubtless, a great rise in the rent of the farms; so that, in this Island, there is not only the depression of price, and a greater depression than any where else, but also the loss of the pickings, and these together leave the tenants but this simple choice: *beggary* or *flight;* and as most of them have had a pretty deal of capital, and will be likely to have some left as yet, they will, as they perceive the danger, naturally flee for succour to the Bourbons. This is, indeed, something new in the History of English Agriculture; and were not Mr Canning so positive to the contrary, one would almost imagine that the thing which has produced it does not *work so very well.*

[*Rural Rides*, ed. I. Dyck (London, 2001), pp. 61–2 (26–28 November 1822).]

*

For Cobbett, the farmhouse table where the farmer, his family and his labourers sat down together was the image of a more harmonious lost society. The affected gentility of farmers, and their estrangement from the labourers they employed, was evidence of everything that was wrong about England in the 1820s.

Having done my business at Hartswood to-day about eleven o'clock, I went to a *sale* at a farm, which the farmer is quitting. Here I had a view of what has long been going on all over the country. The farm, which belongs to *Christ's Hospital*, has been held by a man of the name of CHARINGTON, in whose family the lease has been, I hear, a great number of years. The house is hidden by trees. It stands in the Weald of Surrey, close by the *River Mole*, which is here a mere rivulet, though just below this house the rivulet supplies the very prettiest flour-mill I ever saw in my life.

Every thing about this farm-house was formerly the scene of *plain manners* and *plentiful living*. Oak clothes-chests, oak bedsteads, oak chest of drawers, and oak tables to eat on, long, strong, and well supplied with joint stools. Some of the things were many hundreds of years old. But all appeared to be in a state of decay and nearly of *disuse*, There appeared to have been hardly any *family* in that house, where formerly there were, in all probability, from ten to fifteen men, boys, and maids: and, which was the worst of all, there was a *parlour!* Aye, and a *carpet* and *bell-pull* too! One end of the front of this once plain and substantial house had been moulded into a '*parlour*'; and there was the mahogany table, and the fine chairs, and the fine glass, and all as bare-faced upstart as any stock-jobber in the kingdom can boast of. And, there were the decanters, the glasses, the 'dinner-set' of crockery ware, and all just in the true stock-jobber style. And I dare say it has been '*Squire* Charington and the *Miss* Charingtons; and not plain Master Charington, and his son Hodge, and his daughter Betty Charington, all of whom this accursed system has, in all likelihood, transmuted into a species of mock gentle-folks, while it has ground the labourers down into real slaves. Why do not farmers now *feed* and *lodge* their work-people, as they did formerly? Because they cannot keep them *upon so little* as they give them in wages. This is the real cause of the change. There needs no more to prove that the lot of the working classes has become worse than it formerly was. This fact alone is quite sufficient to settle this point. All the world knows, that a number of people, boarded in the same house, and at the same table, can, with as good food, be boarded much cheaper than those persons divided into twos, threes, or fours, can be boarded. This is a well-known truth: therefore, if the farmer now shuts his pantry against his labourers, and pays them wholly in money, is it not clear, that he does it because he thereby gives them a living *cheaper* to him; that is to say, a *worse* living than formerly? Mind he has *a house* for them;

a kitchen for them to sit in, bed rooms for them to sleep in, tables, and stools, and benches, of everlasting duration. All these he has: all these *cost him nothing;* and yet so much does he gain by pinching them in wages that he lets all these things remain as of no use, rather than feed labourers in the house. Judge, then, of the *change* that has taken place in the condition of these labourers! And, be astonished, if you can, at the *pauperism* and the *crimes* that now disgrace this once happy and moral England.

The land produces, on average, what it always produced; but, there is a new distribution of the produce. This 'Squire Charington's father used, I dare say, to sit at the head of the oak-table along with his men, say grace to them, and cut up the meat and the pudding. He might take a cup of *strong beer* to himself, when they had none; but, that was pretty nearly all the difference in their manner of living. So that *all* lived well. But, the 'Squire had many *wine-decanters* and *wine-glasses* and 'a *dinner set*', and a '*breakfast set*', and '*desert knives*'; and these evidently imply carryings on and a consumption that must of necessity have greatly robbed the long oak table if it had remained fully tenanted. That long table could not share in the work of the decanters and the dinner set. Therefore, it became almost untenanted; the labourers retreated to hovels, called cottages; and, instead of board and lodging, they got money; so little of it as to enable the employer to drink wine; but, then, that he might not reduce them to *quite starvation*, they were enabled to come to him, in the *king's name*, and demand food as *paupers*. And, now mind, that which a man receives in the *king's name*, he knows well he has *by force;* and it is not in nature that he should *thank* any body for it, and least of all the party *from whom it is forced.* Then, if this sort of force be insufficient to obtain him *enough* to eat and to keep him warm, is it surprising, if he think it *no great offence against God* (who created no man to starve) to use *another sort of force* more within his own controul? Is it, in short, surprising, if he resort to *theft* and *robbery?* [...]

I could not quit this farm house without reflecting on the thousands of scores of bacon and thousands of bushels of bread that had been eaten from the long oak-table which, I said to myself, is now perhaps, going, at last, to the bottom of a bridge that some stock-jobber will stick up over an artificial river in his cockney-garden. '*By — it shant*,' said I, almost in a real passion: and so I requested a friend to buy it for me; and if he do so, I will take it to Kensington, or to Fleet-street, and keep it for the good it has done in the world.

[*Rural Rides*, ed. I. Dyck (London, 2001), pp. 182–4 (20 October 1825).]

*

Throughout *Rural Rides*, Cobbett combines trenchant political critique with simple delight in the landscape and rural traditions. Here, he reflects on what constitutes rural perfection.

> Arthur Young[6] calls the vale between Farnham and Alton *the finest ten miles in* England. Here is a river with fine meadows on each side of it, and with rising grounds on each outside of the meadows, those grounds, having some hop-gardens and some pretty woods. But, though I was born in this vale, I must confess, that the ten miles between Maidstone and Tunbridge (which the Kentish folks call the *Garden of Eden*) is a great deal finer; for here, with a river three times as big and a vale three times as broad, there are, on rising grounds six times as broad, not only hop-gardens and beautiful woods, but immense orchards of apples, pears, plums, cherries and filberts, and these, in many cases, with gooseberries and currants and raspberries beneath; and, all taken together, the vale is really worthy of the appellation which it bears. But, even this spot, which I believe to be the very finest, as to fertility and diminutive beauty, in this whole world, I, for my part, do not like so well; nay, as a spot to *live on*, I think nothing at all of it, compared with a country where high downs prevail, with here and there a large wood on the top or the side of a hill, and where you see, in the deep dells, here and there a farm-house, and here and there a village, the buildings sheltered by a group of lofty trees.

> [*Rural Rides*, ed. I. Dyck (London, 2001), pp. 210–11 (31 October 1825).]

*

In spite of his distaste for manufacturing enterprises, Cobbett visited Robert Owen's model factory community of New Lanark during his 1832 Scottish tour. One of the most famous sites for visitors to Scotland in the early nineteenth century and much publicised in Owen's own writings, especially his *A New View of Society* (1813), Owen pioneered the idea of running a factory on co-operative and philanthropic principles. Cobbett gave grudging admiration to the good order of the workpeople, but visiting a schoolroom formally used as a communal canteen, he cast a sceptical eye over the education and dance classes he witnessed, suggesting those superintending might be better employed in other, more productive employment. Above all he revolted against the regimentation it involved.

> This NEW LANARK, of which we have heard so much as connected with the name of Mr. OWEN, stands upon a little flat, which nature has made on one bank of the river, on which the manufacturing buildings stand, and

---

6   Arthur Young (1741–1820), agricultural reformer and writer.

also dwelling-houses for the work-people. This village is about a mile and a half from the town of LANARK. At one end of it is a beautiful park, which, together with its mansion, are occupied by Messrs. WALKERS, who are managers of this manufacturing concern on account of a company called the "NEW LANARK Company." [...] In going from the town of LANARK, down to the new village, you come to a spot, as you descend the hill, where you have a full view of the great falls of the CLYDE, with the accompanying rocks and woods which form the banks of the river. At the same time you see the green hills, and the cattle and sheep feeding on them, at the summits of the banks on each side, and over the tops of the trees. The fine buildings of the factories are just under you; and *this*, all taken together, is by far the most beautiful sight that my eyes ever beheld. [...]

After having been to the falls we came back through the manufacturing village. All is here arranged with great skill; and everything that you behold, dwelling places of the people (about fourteen hundred in number); their dresses; their *skins*; all bespoke cleanliness and well being; all savoured of the Quaker. I have never been into any manufacturing place without reluctance, and I positively refused to go into any of them here, alleging, that I had no understanding of the matter, that the wondrous things that are performed in these places, only serve, when I behold them, to withdraw my mind from things which I do understand. Mr. BELL prevailed upon me, during my first visit to the CLYDE, to stop at a manufacturing village, belonging to Messrs. MONTEITH, at a place called BLANTYRE. Here the water-wheels were wonderful to behold; but they afforded nothing interesting to me, who thought a great deal more about the condition of the people, which appeared to be very good here also, than I did about the cause of the movement, or about the mechanical effects of the machines. Being at NEW LANARK, however, I was rather curious to know whether there was any reality in what we had heard about the effects of the Owen "*feelosofy*." [...] The building in NEW LANARK, which OWEN had erected for the "*feelosofers*" to carry on their community of eating and of drinking, is used as a *school-room*; and here I saw boys in one place, and girls in another place, under masters appointed for the purpose, carrying on what is called "education." There was one boy pointing with a stick to something stuck up upon the wall, and then all the rest of the boys began bawling out what it was. In one large room they were all *singing out something* at the word of command, just like the tribe of little things in *Bolt-court*,[7] who there stun the whole neighbourhood with singing "*God save the King*," "*the Apostles Creed*," and the "*Pence table*," and the fellow, who leads the

---

[7]　Bolt Court was the site of a Lancastrian-style school where rote-learning of the type Cobbett most detested was practised.

lazy life in the teaching of whom, ought to be sent to raking the kennel, or filling a dung-cart. In another great apartment of this house, there were eighteen boys and eighteen girls, the boys dressed in Highland dresses, without shoes on, naked from three inches above the knee, down to the foot, a tartan plaid close round the body, in their shirt sleeves, their shirt collars open, each having a girl by the arm, duly proportioned in point of size, the girls without caps, and without shoes and stockings; and there were these eighteen couples, marching, arm in arm, in regular files, with a lock-step, slow march, to the sound of a fiddle, which a fellow, big enough to carry a quarter of wheat or to dig ten rods of ground in a day, was playing in the corner of the room, with an immense music book lying open before him. There was another man who was commanding officer of the marching couples, who, after having given us a march in quick step as well as slow step, were disposed of in dancing order, a business that they seemed to perform with great regularity and elegance; and, it was quite impossible to see the half-naked lads of twelve or thirteen, putting their arms round the waists of the thinly-clad girls of the same age, without clearly perceiving the manifest tendency of this mode of education to prevent "*premature marriages*," and to "*check population*."

It is difficult to determine, whether, when people are huddled together in this unnatural state, this sort of soldiership discipline may or may not be necessary to effect the purposes of schooling; but I should think it a very strange thing, if a man, calculated to produce effect by his learning, could ever come to perfection from a beginning like this. It is altogether a thing that I abhor. I do not say that it may not be useful when people are thus unnaturally congregated; and, above all things, I am not disposed to bestow censure on the *motives* of the parties promoting this mode of education; for the sacrifices which they make, in order to give success to their schemes, clearly prove that their motives are benevolent; but I am not the less convinced that it is a melancholy thing to behold; that it is the reverse of *domestic life;* that it reverses the order of nature; that it makes minds a fiction; and, which is amongst the greatest of its evils, it fashions the rising generation to habits of *implicit submission*, which is only another term for civil and political slavery.

[D. Green (ed.), *Cobbett's Tour*, pp. 98–101.]

*

A few months before the transportation of the Tolpuddle Martyrs, convicted as members of a friendly society of agricultural labourers in the village of Tolpuddle, Dorset, Cobbett warned the government that they should not try to check the rise of trade unions.

It is very well known, that the whole country is in a stir with what are called "TRADES UNIONS." This has become so formidable a matter, that it demands the attention of every one who meddles at all with public affairs. I have just received from Lancashire, and under the frank of my honourable colleague, an account of a society, of which he himself is a member, and of which he himself is one of the managers. I have long been contending that labour had not its just reward; that those who do the work have long been unfairly treated; and that, at last, it must, in some way or another, end in their being better treated. The working people have long been combining in one way or another to obtain better treatment; and at last they seem to have combined for some practical purpose. The nation has been divided very nearly into two classes, the idlers living chiefly on the taxes, in one way or another, and the industrious, who have their earnings taken from them to maintain the idlers. Lord BACON said, and the history of the world has said, that no state can long stand in peace, and maintain its power, in a state of things like this. The people hoped that a reformed Parliament would make a complete change in this respect; and they have been completely disappointed. Therefore, casting aside all disquisitions relative to forms of government, and political and constitutional rights, they have betaken themselves to what they deem the best method of insuring them sufficiency of food and of raiment in return for their labour. Many of the employers enter into the views of the workmen; and we are now about to see whether a working people will continue to live upon potatoes and salt, while so large a part of their earnings is taken from them to be given to pensioners, sinecure people, men and women, half-pay people, retired-allowance people, military-academy people, and to bands of usurers who pretend to have a mortgage upon the labour of the child that is in the cradle. The Government newspapers have been recommending the Parliament to pass a *law* to put an end to these unions. Better call for a law to prevent those inconvenient things called *spring-tides*.

['Rights of Industry', *Political Register*, 7 December 1833.]

Chapter 13
Literature, Sensibility and the Romantics

Cobbett was required reading for all the great writers of his age, whether or not they agreed with him. His political trajectory from Tory to Radical was the reverse of writers such as Wordsworth and Coleridge, and the latter described Cobbett as, 'this political Rhinoceros, with his Coat-armour of dry and wet Mud and his one Horn of brutal strength on the Nose of Scorn and Hate – not to forget the fleaing Rasp of his Tongue!'[1] Cobbett was read more sympathetically by younger poets such as Percy Shelley, who had back numbers of the *Political Register* and *A Year's Residence in the United States* sent to him in Italy. During this period of increasing political unrest in Britain, Shelley's enjoyment of Cobbett was still tinged with anxiety: 'Cobbett still more and more delights me, with all my horror of the sanguinary commonplaces of his creed. His design to overthrow Bank notes by forgery is very comic.'[2] Of Shelley's companions, Claire Clairmont wrote in her diary, 'Read Cobbett, which is a strange book to read with one's head full of the ruins of Rome', and Mary Shelley went on to create a character based on Cobbett – Ryland, a popular leader who becomes Lord Protector of England – in her 1826 novel *The Last Man*.[3] The letters of John Keats contain enthusiastic responses to Cobbett's political progress (at the 1820 Coventry election, 'Cobbett is expected to come in. O that I had two double plumpers [votes] for him'), while Keats's friend William Hazlitt, who had published his 1807 attack on Malthus in the *Political Register*, included an astute 'Character of Cobbett' in *The Spirit of the Age* (1825).[4] This collection of pen portraits identifies Cobbett as one of 25 writers and thinkers who had defined the age, part of a list that also includes Bentham, Godwin, Coleridge, Scott and Byron.

However, the writers who most influenced Cobbett were not his contemporaries but the satirists and novelists of the early eighteenth century, including Defoe, Dryden, Pope and, above all, Swift. He described reading *A Tale of a Tub*, aged 11, as a defining experience of his early life, and Swift's style became an important influence on his prose. By contrast, Cobbett's disregard for the writers later canonised as the Romantics reflects his distance from a literary culture based on the *avant-garde* and his suspicion of literature that did

---

[1]   E. L. Griggs (ed.), *Collected Letters of Samuel Taylor Coleridge, Volume V: 1820–1825* (Oxford, 1971), p. 115.

[2]   R. Holmes, *Shelley: The Pursuit* (London, 2005; first pub. 1974), p. 522.

[3]   M. K. Stocking (ed.), *The Journals of Claire Clairmont* (Cambridge, Mass., 1968), p. 100, 13 March 1819.

[4]   J. Mee (ed.), *John Keats: Selected Letters* (Oxford, 2002), p. 340.

not carry an overt political purpose. However, he had more in common with his contemporaries than he was prepared to admit, from the autobiographical basis of much of his writing to the importance accorded to landscape, memory and place. Despite his bluff persona, Cobbett's writing also contains many of the effusive displays of emotion that characterised the age of Sensibility. This late eighteenth-century phenomenon had an important effect on Cobbett, and he often presented himself as the new cultural type of the 'Man of Feeling': not a dry rationalist or utilitarian, like the political economists he despised, but an all too human collection of sympathies, antipathies, memories and affections.

*

During his unsuccessful campaign for parliamentary election at Coventry in 1820, Cobbett wrote about his first experience of reading Jonathan Swift, almost half a century earlier. Swift became one of his political and literary heroes; here, the memory of reading Swift's *Tale of A Tub* becomes a way of proclaiming his self-education and continued independence, at a time when he was being viciously assailed by the ministerial press.

> At *eleven* years of age my employment was clipping of box-edgings and weeding beds of flowers in the garden of the Bishop of Winchester, at the Castle of Farnham, my native town. I had always been fond of beautiful gardens; and, a gardener, who had just come from the King's gardens at Kew, gave such a description of them as made me instantly resolve to work in these gardens. The next morning, without saying a word to any one, off I set, with no clothes, except those upon my back, and with thirteen half-pence in my pocket. I found that I must go to Richmond, and I, accordingly, went on, from place to place, inquiring my way thither. A long day (it was in June) brought me to Richmond in the afternoon. Twopenny worth of bread and cheese and a pennyworth of small beer, which I had on the road, and one half-penny that I had lost somehow or other, left three pence in my pocket. With this for my whole fortune, I was trudging through Richmond, in my blue smock-frock and my red garters tied under my knees, when, staring about me, my eye fell upon a little book, in a bookseller's window, on the outside of which was written: "TALE OF A TUB; PRICE 3d." The title was so odd, that my curiosity was excited. I had the 3d. but, then, I could have *no supper*. In I went, and got the little book, which I was so impatient to read, that I got over into a field, at the upper corner of Kew gardens, where there stood a *hay-stack*. On the shady side of this, I sat down to read. The book was so different from any thing that I had ever read before: it was something so *new* to my mind, that, though I could not at all understand some of it, it delighted me beyond description; and it produced what I have always considered

a sort of birth of intellect. I read on till it was dark, without any thought about supper or bed. When I could see no longer, I put my little book in my pocket, and tumbled down by the side of the stack, where I slept till the birds in Kew Gardens awaked me in the morning; when off I started to Kew, reading my little book. The singularity of my dress, the simplicity of my manner, my confident and lively air, and, doubtless, his own compassion besides, induced the gardener, who was a Scotsman, I remember, to give me victuals, find me lodging, and set me to work. And, it was during the period that I was at Kew, that the present king and two of his brothers laughed at the oddness of my dress, while I was sweeping the grass plat round the foot of the Pagoda. The gardener, seeing me fond of books, lent me some gardening books to read; but, these I could not relish after my *Tale of a Tub*, which I carried about with me wherever I went, and when I, at about twenty years old, lost it in a box that fell overboard in the Bay of Funday in North America, the loss gave me greater pain than I have ever felt at losing thousands of pounds.

['To the Reformers', *Political Register*, 19 February 1820.]

*

Cobbett identified strongly with the Augustan tradition of satire, invoking Alexander Pope during the 1809 scandal surrounding the Duke of York, who was implicated in the sale of army commissions by his former mistress, Mary Anne Clarke. The Duke was forced to resign as commander-in-chief of the army, but was reinstated two years later.

The writers of former times; times when not a thousandth part of the present corruptions prevailed; the writers (from some of those works I am forming a collection to be published hereafter) who, in those times of comparative purity, surpassed in boldness, the writers of the present day; the bare name of those writers would fill a volume. I will, however, content myself with some extracts from POPE, who was one of the greatest scholars, the most acute reasoners, the most independent and virtuous men, and, without exception, the brightest genius that England ever produced. When he wrote, in the last reign, and in the year 1738, the laws and constitution of England were as well understood as they now are, and loyalty was not less a virtue than it now is. *Corruption* (under the administration of sir Robert Walpole) was only in its infancy. Now, then, let us hear how this accomplished scholar, this great genius, whose works are read with such admiration, and which make a part of the library of every man of sense who has the means of procuring books; let us hear how this all-accomplished writer expressed himself upon the subject of the then prevailing vice and corruption.

> Lo; at the wheels of her triumphal car,
> Old England's Genius, rough with many a scar,
> Dragg'd in the dust! his arms hang idly round,
> His flag inverted trails along the ground!
> Our youth, all liv'ry'd o'er with foreign gold,
> Before her dance: behind her, crawl the old!
> See thronging millions to the pagod run,
> And offer country, parent, wife, or son!
> Hear her black trumpet thro' the land proclaim,
> THAT NOT TO BE CORRUPTED IS THE SHAME.
> In soldier, churchman, patriot, man in pow'r,
> 'Tis av'rice all, ambition is no more!
> See, all our nobles begging to be slaves!
> See, all our fools aspiring to be knaves!
> The wit of cheats, the courage of a whore,
> Are what ten thousand envy and adore:
> All, all look up, with reverential awe,
> At crimes that 'scape, *or triumph o'er the Law*;
> While truth, worth, wisdom, daily they decry—
> *Nothing is sacred now but villainy.*
> Yet may this verse (if such a verse remain)
> Shew there was one who held it in disdain.[5]

This is only one instance. In many others he *named* the corrupt persons. But, POPE was called a "libeller;" and, in his preface to that part of his inestimable works, from which the above extract is made, he observes, that "there is not in the world a greater error, than that which *fools* are so apt to fall into, and *knaves* with good reason to encourage, the mistaking a *satyrist* for a *libeller.*" He says, that the clamour raised on some of his former writings, induced him to bring before the public the writings of HORACE and Dr. DONNE. With a similar view I now appeal to him, who exceeded them both in genius, and yielded to neither in any estimable quality. [...] In another poem, and that, too, the most admirable of all his admirable works, he has these verses.

> A nymph of quality admires our Knight;
> He marries, bows at court, and grows polite;

---

5   Alexander Pope, *Epilogue to the Satires. Written in 1738. Dialogue I*, ll. 151–72.

Leaves the dull cits, and joins (to please the fair)
The well-bred cuckolds of St. James's air:
First for his son a gay commission buys,
Who drinks, *whores*, fights, and in a duel dies:
His daughter flaunts a *Viscount's* tawdry wife;
She bears a coronet and p—x for life.[6]

If any of us were to publish, from our pens, a story like this, it would be produced as a *certain proof* of our intention, of our settled design, or our deliberate scheme, for overturning the privileged orders, and with them the whole of the establishments of the kingdom. Yet, in the days of POPE, that man would have been laughed to scorn, who should have attempted to set up such a clamour; though despotism was much less prevalent in that day, throughout the whole of Europe, than in the day in which we live.

['Duke of York', *Political Register*, 4 February 1809.]

*

The idolatry shown towards Shakespeare and Milton made them a tempting target for Cobbett's iconoclasm. The following passage associates their writings with one of his other pet hates – the potato – draws attention to the apparent absurdities of *Paradise Lost* and takes great delight in the Ireland Shakespeare forgeries of the 1790s.

It has become, of late years, the *fashion* to extol the virtues of potatoes, as it has been to admire the writings of Milton and Shakespear. God, *almighty* and all *fore-seeing*, first permitting his chief angel to be disposed to rebel against him; his permitting him to enlist whole squadrons of angels under his banners; his permitting this host to come and dispute with him the throne of heaven; his permitting the contest to be long, and, at one time, doubtful; his permitting the devils to bring cannon into this battle in the clouds; his permitting one devil or angel, I forget which, to be split down the middle, from crown to crotch, as we split a pig; his permitting the two halves, intestines and all, to go slap, up together again, and become a perfect body; his, then, causing all the devil host to be tumbled head-long down into a place called Hell, of the local situation of which no man can have an idea; his causing gates (iron gates too) to be erected to keep the devil in; his permitting him to get out, nevertheless, and to come and destroy the peace and happiness of his new creation; his causing his

---

[6] Alexander Pope, 'Epistle III. To Allen Lord Bathurst' (1733), ll. 385–92.

son to take *a pair of compasses* out of *a drawer*, to trace the form of the earth: all this, and, indeed, the whole of Milton's poem, is such barbarous trash, so outrageously offensive to reason and to common sense, that one is naturally led to wonder how it can have been tolerated by a people, amongst whom astronomy, navigation, and chemistry are understood. But, it is the *fashion* to turn up the eyes, when Paradise Lost is mentioned; and, if you fail herein you want *taste;* you want *judgment* even, if you do admire this absurd and ridiculous stuff, when, if one of your relations were to write a letter in the same strain, you would send him to a mad-house and take his estate. It is the sacrificing of *reason* to *fashion*. And as to the other "Divine Bard," the case is still more provoking. After his ghosts, witches, sorcerers, fairies, and monsters; after his bombast and puns and smut, which appear to have been not much relished by his comparatively rude contemporaries, had had their full swing; after hundreds of thousands of pounds had been expended upon embellishing his works; after numerous commentators and engravers and painters and booksellers had got fat upon the trade; after *jubilees* had been held in honour of his memory; at a time when there were men, otherwise of apparently good sense, who were what was aptly enough termed *Shakespear-mad*. At this very moment an occurrence took place, which must have put an end, for ever, to this national folly, had it not been kept up by infatuation and obstinacy without parallel.[7] Young IRELAND, I think his name was WILLIAM, no matter from what *motive*, though I never could see any harm in his motive, and have always thought him a man most unjustly and brutally used. No matter, however, what were the inducing circumstances, or the motives, he did write, and bring forth, as being Shakespear's, some *plays*, *a prayer*, and *a love-letter*. The learned men of England, Ireland and Scotland met to examine these performances. Some *doubted*, a few *denied;* but, the far greater part, amongst whom were Dr. PARR, Dr. WHARTON, and Mr. GEORGE CHALMERS, declared, in the most positive terms, that *no man but Shakespear* could have written those things. There was a *division;* but this division arose more from a suspicion of some trick, than from any thing to be urged against the merit of the writings. The players went so far as to be ACTED. Long lists of subscribers appeared to the work. And, in short, it was decided, in the most unequivocal manner, that this young man of sixteen years of age had written so *nearly like Shakespear*, that a majority of the learned and critical classes of the nation most firmly believed the writings to be Shakespear's; and, there cannot be a doubt, that,

<hr />

7   In 1795, the printmaker and writer Samuel Ireland (?–1800) announced the discovery by his son, William Henry Ireland (1775–1835), of a lost cache of Shakespearean manuscripts, including two lost plays. The papers were put on display and, at first, widely believed to be genuine. However, they were later exposed as fakes and the younger Ireland confessed to the fraud.

if Mr. Ireland had been able to keep his secret, they would have passed for Shakespear's 'till the time shall come when the whole heap of trash will, by the natural good sense of the nation, be consigned to everlasting oblivion; and, indeed, as folly ever doats on a darling, it is very likely, that these last found productions of *"our immortal bard"* would have been regarded as his *best*. Yet, in spite of all this; in spite of what one would have thought was sufficient to make blind people see, the fashion has been kept up; and, what excites something *more* than ridicule and contempt, Mr. Ireland, whose writings had been taken for Shakespear's, was, when he *made the discovery*, treated as an impostor and a *cheat*, and hunted down with as much rancour as if he had written against the buying and selling of seats in Parliament. The *learned* men; the *sage critics*; the *Shakespear-mad folks*; were all so *ashamed*, that they endeavoured to draw the public attention from themselves to the young man. It was of *his impositions* that they now talked, and not of their *own folly*.

[*A Year's Residence in the United States of America* (London, 1819), para. 270.]

*

As he grew older, Cobbett also became increasingly intolerant of fiction, associating novels such as *Tom Jones* with frivolity, immorality and middle-class pretension.

I deprecate *romances* of every description. It is impossible that they can do any *good*, and they may do a great deal of harm. They excite passions that ought to lie dormant; they give the mind a taste for *highly-seasoned* matter; they make matters of real life insipid; every girl, addicted to them, sighs to be a Sophia Western, and every boy, a Tom Jones. What girl is not in love with the *wild* youth, and what boy does not find a justification for his wildness? What can be more pernicious than the teachings of this celebrated romance? Here are two young men put before us, both sons of the same mother; the one a *bastard* (and by a parson too), the other a *legitimate child*; the former wild, disobedient, and squandering; the latter steady, sober, obedient, and frugal; the former every thing that is frank and generous in his nature, the latter a greedy hypocrite; the former rewarded with the most beautiful and virtuous of women and a double estate, the latter punished by being made an outcast. How is it possible for young people to read such a book, and to look upon orderliness, sobriety, obedience, and frugality, as *virtues*? And this is the tenor of almost every romance, and of almost every play, in our language. In the "School for Scandal," for instance, we see two brothers; the one a prudent and frugal man, and, to all appearance, a moral man, the other a hair-brained squanderer, laughing at the morality of his brother; the former turns out to be a base hypocrite and seducer, and is brought to shame and disgrace; while the latter is found to be full of generous sentiment, and Heaven itself seems to interfere to give him fortune and fame. In short, the direct tendency of the far greater part of these books, is, to cause young people to despise all those virtues, without the practice of which they must be a curse to their parents, a burden to the community, and must, except by mere accident, lead wretched lives. I do not recollect one romance nor one play, in our language, which has not this tendency. How is it possible for young princes to read the historical plays of the punning and smutty Shakspeare, and not think, that to be drunkards, blackguards, the companions of debauchees and robbers, is the suitable beginning of a glorious reign?

There is, too, another most abominable principle that runs through them all, namely, that there is in *high birth*, something of *superior nature*, instinctive courage, honour, and talent. Who can look at the two *royal youths* in CYMBELINE, or at the *noble youth* in DOUGLAS, without detesting the base parasites who wrote those plays? Here are youths, brought up by *shepherds*, never told of their origin, believing themselves the sons of these humble parents, but discovering, when grown up, the highest notions of valour and honour, and thirsting for military renown, even while tending their reputed fathers' flocks and herds! And, why this species of falsehood? To cheat the mass of the people; to keep them in abject subjection; to make them quietly submit to despotic sway. And the infamous authors are guilty of the cheat, because they are, in one shape or another, paid by oppressors out of means squeezed from the people. A *true* picture would give us just the reverse; would show us that "*high birth*" is the enemy of virtue, of valour, and of talent; would show us, that with all their incalculable advantages, royal and noble families have, only by mere accident, produced a great man; that, in general, they have been amongst the most effeminate, unprincipled, cowardly, stupid, and, at the very least, amongst the most useless persons, considered as individuals, and not in connexion with the prerogatives and powers bestowed on them solely by the law.

[*Advice to Young Men* (London, 1829), paras 311–12.]

*

Cobbett's description of teaching his youngest son, Richard, echoes the pedagogical practice of Jean-Jacques Rousseau, who believed in the primacy of education by nature. Cobbett even echoes Rousseau's choice of reading matter:

in Rousseau's educational treatise *Émile*, *Robinson Crusoe* is the only book that the young Émile is given to read.

> He began to talk in anticipation of the sport he was going to have, and was very inquisitive as to the probability of our meeting with fox-hounds, which gave me occasion to address him thus: 'Fox-hunting is a very fine thing, and very proper for people to be engaged in, and it is very desirable to be able to ride well and to be in at the death; but that is not ALL; that is not every thing. Any fool can ride a horse, and draw a cover; any groom or any stable-fellow, who is as ignorant as the horse, can do these things; but, all gentlemen that go a fox-hunting (I hope God will forgive me for the lie) are scholars, Richard. It is not the riding, nor the scarlet coats, that make them gentlemen; it is their scholarship.' What he thought I do not know; for he sat as mute as a fish, and I could not see his countenance. 'So,' said I, 'you must now begin to learn something, and you must begin with arithmetic.' He had learned, from mere play, to read, being first set to work of his own accord, to find out what was said about THURTELL, when all the world was talking and reading about THURTELL.[8] That had induced us to give him Robinson Crusoe; and that had made him a passable reader. Then he had scrawled down letters and words upon paper, and had written letters to me, in the strangest way imaginable. His knowledge of figures he had acquired from the necessity of knowing the several numbers upon the barrels of seeds brought from America, and the numbers upon the doors of houses. So that I had pretty nearly a blank sheet of paper to begin upon; and I have always held it to be stupidity to put book-learning into children who are too young to reason with.

[*Rural Rides*, ed. I. Dyck (London, 2001), pp. 259–60 (20 November 1825).]

*

On his first visit to Selborne in Hampshire, Cobbett referred in passing to Gilbert White, naturalist and author of *The Natural History and Antiquities of Selborne* (1789). However, 'at that time, the THING was biting *so very sharply* that one had no attention to bestow on antiquarian researches'. In the extract below, he describes his return to the village the following year. Raymond Williams suggestively compares Cobbett, White and Jane Austen in 'Three Around Farnham', from *The Country and the City* (1973).

---

8   John Thurtell (1794–1824), son of the Mayor of Norwich, Royal Marine, failed manufacturer, prize-fighter, hanged for the murder of William Weare.

At Tisted I crossed the turnpike-road before mentioned, and entered a lane which, at the end of about four miles, brought me to this village of SELBORNE. My readers will recollect, that I mentioned this Selborne when I was giving an account of Hawkley Hanger, last fall. I was desirous of seeing this village, about which I have read in the book of Mr White, and which a reader has been so good as to send me. From Tisted I came generally up hill till I got within half a mile of this village, when, all of a sudden, I came to the edge of a hill, looked down over all the larger vale of which the little vale of this village makes a part. Here Hindhead and Black-down Hill came full in my view. When I was crossing the forest in Sussex, going from Worth to Horsham, these two great hills lay to my west and north-west. To-day I am got just on the opposite side of them, and see them, of course, towards the east and the south-east, while Leith Hill lies away towards the north-east. This hill, from which you descend down into Selborne, is very lofty; but, indeed, we are here amongst some of the highest hills in the island, and amongst the sources of rivers. The hill over which I have come this morning sends the Itchen river forth from one side of it, and the river Wey, which rises near Alton, from the opposite side of it. Hindhead which lies before me, sends, as I observed upon a former occasion, the Arun forth towards the south and a stream forth towards the north, which meets the river Wey, somewhere above Godalming. I am told that the springs of these two streams rise in the Hill of Hindhead, or, rather, on one side of the hill, at not many yards from each other. The village of Selborne is precisely what it is described by Mr White. A straggling irregular street, bearing all the marks of great antiquity, and shewing, from its lanes and its vicinage generally, that it was once a very considerable place. I went to look at the spot where Mr White supposes the convent formerly stood. It is very beautiful. Nothing can surpass in beauty these dells and hillocks and hangers, which last are so steep that it is impossible to ascend them, except by means of a serpentine path. I found here deep hollow ways, with beds and sides of solid white stone; but not quite so white and so solid, I think, as the stone which I found in the roads at Hawkley. The churchyard of Selborne is most beautifully situated. The land is good, all about it.

[*Rural Rides*, ed. I. Dyck (London, 2001), pp. 112–13 (7 August 1823).]

*

Having left Selborne, Cobbett's description of the surrounding landscape brings together folklore, childhood memory, topographical and geological detail with a vivid sense of wonder. Such passages suggest Cobbett's common ground with the Romantic writers he affected to despise. However, feelings of wonder are always carefully grounded in the empirical details of the landscape and the popular traditions associated with it.

> From Selborne, I had first to come to Headley, about five miles. I came to the identical public-house, where I took my blind guide last year, who took me such a dance to the southward, and led me up to the top of Hindhead at last. I had no business there. My route was through a sort of hamlet called Churt, which lies along on the side and towards the foot of the north of Hindhead, on which side, also, lies the village of Thursley. A line is hardly more straight than is the road from Headley to Thursley; and a prettier ride I never had in the course of my life. It was not the less interesting from the circumstances of its giving me all the way a full view of Crooksbury Hill, the grand scene of my exploits when I was a taker of the nests of crows and magpies. At Churt I had, upon my left, three hills out upon the common, called the *Devil's Jumps*. The Unitarians will not believe in the Trinity, because they cannot account for it. Will they come here to Churt, go and look at these 'Devil's Jumps', and account to me for the placing of these three hills, in the shape of three rather squat sugar-loaves, along in a line upon this heath, or the placing of a rock-stone upon the top of one of them as big as a Church tower? For my part, I cannot account for this placing of these hills. That they should have been formed by mere chance is hardly to be believed. How could waters rolling about have formed such hills? How could such hills have bubbled up from beneath? But, in short, it is all wonderful alike: the stripes of loam running down through the chalk-hills; the circular parcels of loam in the midst of chalk-hills; the lines of flint running parallel with each other horizontally along the chalk-hills; the flints placed in circles as true as a hair in the chalk-hills; the layers of stone at the bottom of hills of loam; the chalk first soft, then some miles farther on, becoming chalk-stone; then, after another distance, becoming burr-stone, as they call it; and at last, becoming hard, white stone, fit for any buildings; the sand-stone at Hindhead becoming harder and harder till it becomes very nearly iron in Herefordshire, and quite iron in Wales; but, indeed, they once dug iron out of this very Hindhead. The clouds, coming and settling upon the hills, sinking down and creeping along, at last coming out again in springs, and those becoming rivers. Why, it is all equally wonderful, and as to not believing in this or that, because the thing cannot be proved by logical deduction, why is any man to believe in the existence of a God any more than he is to believe in the doctrine of the Trinity? For my part, I think the 'Devil's jumps', as the people here call them, full as wonderful and no more wonderful than hundreds and hundreds of other wonderful things. It is a strange taste which our ancestors had, to ascribe no inconsiderable part

of these wonders of nature to the Devil. Not far from the Devil's jumps, is that singular place, which resembles a sugar-loaf inverted, hollowed out and an outside rim only left. This is called the '*Devil's Punch Bowl*'; and it is very well known in Wiltshire, that the forming, or, perhaps, it is the breaking up of Stonehenge is ascribed to the Devil, and that the mark of one of his feet is now said to be seen in one of the stones.

I got to Thursley about sunset, and without experiencing any inconvenience from the wet. I have mentioned the state of the corn as far as Selborne. On this side of that village I find it much forwarder than I found it between Selborne and Ropley Dean. I am here got into some of the very best barley-land in the kingdom; a fine, buttery, stoneless loam, upon a bottom of sand or sand-stone.

[*Rural Rides*, ed. I. Dyck (London, 2001), pp. 116–17 (7 August 1823).]

Chronology of Cobbett's Life

1763	Born (9 March) at the Jolly Farmer in Farnham, Surrey, the third of four children of George Cobbett, publican and farmer, and Anne, née Vincent.
1783	Runs away to London; works as a lawyer's clerk in Gray's Inn.
1784	Enlists as a private soldier in the West Norfolk 54th foot.
1785	Sails with regiment to New Brunswick. Remains there until 1791; promoted to Regimental Sergeant Major and meets his future wife, Anne 'Nancy' Reid (1774–1848).
1789	Fall of the Bastille (14 July).
1791	Regiment returns to England; obtains honourable discharge (19 December).
1792	Marries Anne in Woolwich (5 February). Publishes *The Soldiers Friend* and attempts to bring superior officers to court martial for corruption. Fearing retaliation, flees to France (March) and settles near St. Omer. However, following the massacre of the Swiss Guard and arrest of Louis XVI and Marie-Antoinette, sails for America (September).
1793	The French Republic declares war on Britain (1 February). First son born.
1794	Move from Wilmington to the capital, Philadelphia. Second son stillborn. First son dies. Publishes *Observations on the Emigration of Dr Priestley*.
1795	Daughter, Anne, born. Publishes *A Bone to Gnaw for the Democrats*.
1796	Opens a bookshop in Philadelphia (July). Publishes *The Life and Adventures of Peter Porcupine*. Makes an enemy of Thomas McKean, Chief Justice of Pennsylvania.
1797	Launches a daily newspaper, *Porcupine's Gazette* (March).
1798	Son, William, born.
1799	Moves to New York, days before losing a libel case brought by Dr Benjamin Rush for Cobbett's attacks on his treatment for yellow fever (December).
1800	Returns to England (July); launches a daily newspaper, *The Porcupine* (October). Son, John Morgan, born.
1801	Sells his interest in *The Porcupine* (November).
1802	*Cobbett's Weekly Political Register* launched (January) with financial support from William Windham. Peace of Amiens (until May 1803).
1803	*Important Considerations for the People of this Kingdom* published, without attribution, on the resumption of war with France, and

circulated by the government to every parish in England and Wales. Son, James Paul, born.

1804   Begins publishing *Cobbett's Parliamentary Debates* (sold to the printer Thomas Hansard in 1812).

1805   Moves to Botley, five miles from Southampton (July). Daughter, Eleanor, born.

1806   Agrees purchase of Fairthorn farm, 260 acres (May). Puts himself forward as a candidate for parliamentary election at Honiton, Devon, before standing aside for the naval hero Lord Cochrane (June).

1807   Daughter, Susan, born.

1809   Duke of York scandal over the sale of army commissions.

1810   Convicted of seditious libel for an article criticising the flogging of militiamen at Ely by German soldiers. Sentenced to two years in Newgate (July). Start of the Regency.

1812   Assassination of Spencer Perceval (11 May). War of 1812 between Britain and the United States.

1814   Son, Richard Baverstock Brown, born.

1815   Battle of Waterloo. *Paper Against Gold* published, having been serialised in the *Register* from Newgate.

1816   'The summer without sun' produces poor harvests and high food prices. Publishes a 2*d.* edition of the *Political Register* – the 'Twopenny Trash' – from November; circulation soars to 50,000 copies a week.

1817   Escapes to America after the suspension of Habeas Corpus (March), takes a lease on a Long Island farm.

1818   *A Grammar of the English Language* and *A Year's Residence in the United States of America* published.

1819   Peterloo Massacre (16 August). Returns to England with the bones of Thomas Paine. The Six Acts force Cobbett to increase the price of the *Register* to 6*d.*

1820   Death of George III. Stands as a parliamentary candidate at Coventry. Files a petition for bankruptcy. Supports Caroline of Brunswick against George IV.

1821   Moves to a small seed farm at Kensington. *Cottage Economy* and *Cobbett's Sermons* issued in monthly parts. Begins the tours of southern England that will be collected as *Rural Rides* (1830).

1824   *A History of the Protestant "Reformation" in England and Ireland* published in monthly parts.

1826   Publishes *Cobbett's Poor Man's Friend*. Stands for parliament at Preston.

1827   Takes a lease on an 80-acre farm at Barn Elms, Surrey.

1829   Roman Catholic Relief Act. *Advice to Young Men* published in monthly parts.

1830   Death of George IV; accession of William IV. July Revolution in France and Captain Swing riots and rick-burning in England. First Whig government since 1783.

1831   Tried for sedition, accused of inciting the Swing riots, and acquitted (July).

1832   Great Reform Act. Rents a 160-acre farm at Normandy, near Ash. Tours Scotland. Elected to parliament as MP for Oldham (December).

1834   Poor Law Amendment Act. *Cobbett's Legacy to Labourers* published. Tour of Ireland.

1835   Dies (18 June) and is buried in St Andrew's churchyard, Farnham (27 June). 8,000 people, including Daniel O'Connell, attend his funeral.

Bibliography

Many of Cobbett's writings are available in new or relatively recent editions. I. Dyck, *Rural Rides* (London, 2001) edits, with an excellent introduction, his most famous work. There has been a recent edition of *Cottage Economy* (Bath, 2008) and Oxford University Press has produced editions of *The English Gardener* (Oxford, 1980) and *Advice to Young Men* (Oxford, 1980), the latter with a Preface by George Spater (see below). M. Townsend, *This Happy Land: William Cobbett on America, 1794–1835* (London, 2007) provides an extensive selection of his writings on America, while D. A. Wilson (ed.), *Peter Porcupine in America: Pamphlets on Republicanism and Revolution* (Ithaca and London, 1994) reprints his journalism from the 1790s. D. Knight (ed.), *Cobbett in Ireland: A Warning to England* (London, 1984), M. Townsend (ed.), *Not by Bullets and Bayonets: Cobbett's Writings on the Irish Question, 1795–1835* (London, 1983), and D. Green (ed.), *Cobbett's Tour in Scotland: by William Cobbett (1763–1835)* (Aberdeen, 1984) collate his writings on Ireland and Scotland respectively. For a range of Cobbett's writings on gardening, farming and rural sports, see R. Ingrams (ed.), *Cobbett's Country Book: An Anthology of William Cobbett's Writings on Country Matters* (Newton Abbot, 1974). Many of Cobbett's autobiographical writings have been drawn together into a continuous narrative in W. Reitzel (ed.), *The Autobiography of William Cobbett: The Progress of a Plough-Boy to a Seat in Parliament* (London, 1967), while G.D.H. Cole brought together several of his writings about and from his early life in *Life and Adventures of Peter Porcupine with other Records of his early career in England and America* (London, 1927). There is an abridged, modern edition of Cobbett's unduly neglected work, with an introduction by M. Townsend, *A History of the Protestant Reformation* (abridged by H. Arnold, Sevenoaks, 1994). There is an extensive modern edition of many of Cobbett's most important political writings, with valuable and informative notes and apparatus, in L. Nattrass (ed.), *William Cobbett: selected writings* (6 vols, London, 1998), while N. Thompson and D. Eastwood have edited *The Collected Social and Political Writings of William Cobbett* (17 vols, London, 1998). Still of immense value for setting Cobbett's writings in chronological order is M. L. Pearl, *William Cobbett: A Bibliographical Account of his Life and Times* (Oxford, 1953). The first modern anthology of his writings was A.M.D. Hughes (ed.), *Cobbett: Selections with Hazlitt's Essay and other Critical Estimates* (Oxford, 1925), followed by G.D.H. and M.I. Cole, *The Opinions of William Cobbett* (London, 1944), and J. Derry (ed.), *Cobbett's England: A Selection from the Writings of William Cobbett with Engravings by James Gillray* (London, 1968). A group of Cobbett's letters during his early years in America was edited by G.D.H Cole, *Letters from*

William Cobbett to Edward Thornton written in the years 1797 to 1800 (Oxford, 1937), but there are many extracts from his correspondence with Windham and others in L. Melville, *The Life and Letters of William Cobbett in England and America based upon hitherto unpublished family papers* (2 vols, London, 1913).

Cobbett has attracted many biographers and interpreters. The most accessible modern biography is R. Ingrams, *The Life and Adventures of William Cobbett* (London, 2005), while G. Spater, *William Cobbett: the Poor Man's Friend* (2 vols, Cambridge, 1982) remains the fullest account of his life. G.D.H. Cole, *The Life of William Cobbett* (London, 1924, reprinted 1947, 1971) was the first modern biography, and one alive to the debates about economic and social change which informed many of Cobbett's writings. Other major lives are J. W. Osborne, *William Cobbett: His Thought and his Times* (Rutgers, 1966) and J. Sambrook, *William Cobbett* (London, 1973), both couched in terms of interpretations of his writings and thought. D. Green, *Great Cobbett, the Noblest Agitator* (Oxford, 1984), A. Burton, *William Cobbett: Englishman, a Biography* (London, 1997) and W. Baring Pemberton, *William Cobbett* (Harmondsworth, 1949) are more explicitly biographical.

I. Dyck, *William Cobbett and Rural Popular Culture* (Cambridge, 1992) is a particularly valuable and wide-ranging account of Cobbett's relationship with the rural world, while P. Spence, *The Birth of Romantic Radicalism: War, Popular Politics and English Reformism, 1800–1815* (London, 1996) locates Cobbett's views within the radicalism produced by war. Cobbett's role in America is considered in P.W. Gaines, *William Cobbett and the United States, 1792–1835* (New York, 1971), M. Durey, *Transatlantic Radicals and the Early American Republic* (Lawrence, Kansas, 1997) and M. Daniel *Scandal and Civility: Journalism and the Birth of American Democracy* (Oxford, 2008). His relationship with that other famous transatlantic radical, Thomas Paine, is considered in D.A. Wilson, *Paine and Cobbett: the Transatlantic Connection* (Kingston and Montreal, 1988), and his relationship with another contemporary radical, Henry Hunt, by P. Young, *Two Cocks on the Dunghill* (South Lopham, 2009). K.W. Schweizer and J.W. Osborne, *Cobbett in his Times* (Leicester, 1990) profiles critically a number of Cobbett's views. W. Stafford, *Socialism, Radicalism and Nostalgia: Social Criticism in Britain, 1775–1830* (Cambridge, 1987) places Cobbett in the context of other contemporary writers on social conditions, while G. Duff, *William Cobbett and the Politics of Earth* (Salzburg, 1972) deals with his agricultural views. L. Nattrass offers a detailed reappraisal of Cobbett's literary style in *William Cobbett: The Politics of Style* (Cambridge, 1996) and especially good accounts of Cobbett and political discourse are given by O. Smith, *The Politics of Language, 1791–1819* (Oxford, 1984), and K. Gilmartin, *Print Politics:The Press and Radical Opposition in Early Nineteenth-Century England* (Cambridge, 1996). Dyck has contributed an excellent entry on Cobbett in the *Oxford Dictionary of National Biography*.